# bluestem

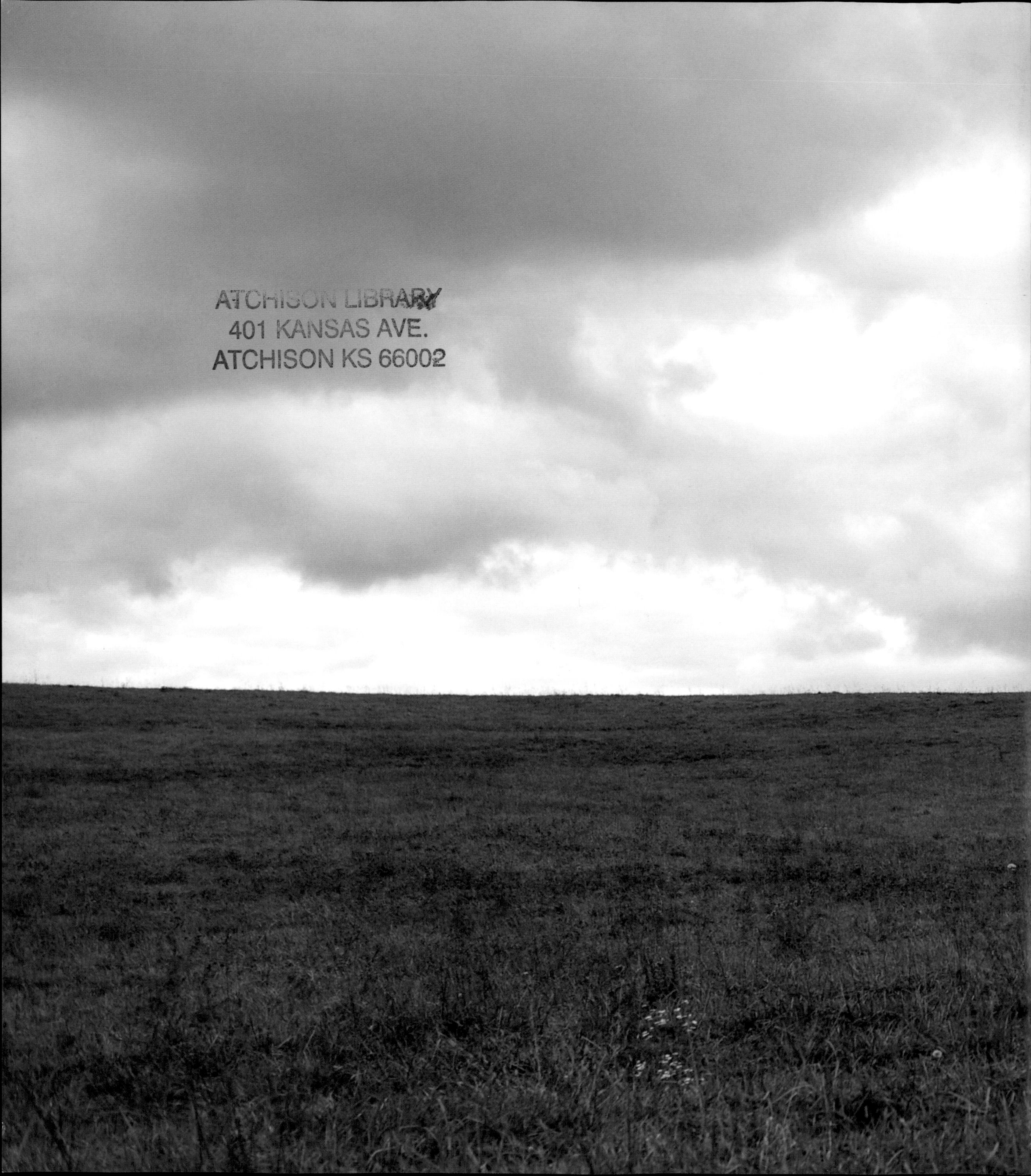

# bluestem

## the cookbook

Colby Garrelts and Megan Garrelts,
with Bonjwing Lee

Foreword by Graham Elliot

Photography by Bonjwing Lee

Andrews McMeel
Publishing, LLC
Kansas City • Sydney • London

Andrews McMeel Publishing, LLC
an Andrews McMeel Universal company
1130 Walnut Street, Kansas City, Missouri 64106

www.andrewsmcmeel.com

11 12 13 14 15 SDB 10 9 8 7 6 5 4 3 2 1

ISBN: 978-1-4494-0061-3

Library of Congress Control Number: 2011921497

Design: Tim Lynch and Holly Ogden

www.bluestemkc.com

**Attention: Schools and Businesses**

Andrews McMeel books are available at quantity discounts with
bulk purchase for educational, business, or sales promotional use. For
information, please e-mail the Andrews McMeel Publishing Special Sales
Department: specialsales@amuniversal.com

For our wonderful children, Madilyn and Colin

# contents

# preface

I was just a kid when I first walked into Bluestem, a bright-eyed law-school student home on summer break. Just beyond its infancy (it had been open for a little more than a year), the restaurant had accrued a fair amount of positive press, both outside of and throughout the food-obsessing subculture, where I tended to subsist.

A young couple, I heard, were the chefs and owners. And their food was changing the face of Kansas City dining.

Skeptical, I went. And skeptical, I left. Technically sound, the restaurant was still a little rough around the edges, flawed in ways that were neither unforgivable nor unexpected for a young restaurant. But overall, I was excited by Bluestem's daringly creative menu and impressed by its reach. I hoped to see it improve and succeed in a city where chain restaurants dominated the dim culinary landscape. Regrettably, an opinionated loudmouth by birth, I failed to pad my thoughts sufficiently in a brutally honest online post I wrote about my experiences, which managed to earn the young chef's attention.

Failing at the time to realize that we were both the choir and the preacher, Colby and I landed in a heated e-mail exchange. Thankfully, neither of us actually believed that the other was as idiotic as he sounded in print. A year later, after I finished my studies and returned to Kansas City to practice law, Colby and I shared a laugh over our well-meaning but misguided egos. Two native sons bound by a common desire to see good food planted and grown in the Midwest, we became fast friends.

As the co-author and photographer of *Bluestem* and friend to Colby and Megan Garrelts, I would like to share a few things that they are too modest to say.

The protagonist of this cookbook is not Colby, Megan, or the food they serve. It's Bluestem, a finely woven web of stories and souls.

Here, the nightly headline is man meets woman, worker meets colleague. Friends gather, expense accounts massage, and families celebrate. Here is where I dined upon passing two bar exams, toasted the closing of my first "deal," and celebrated my sister's marriage, among many other smaller triumphs. With every dish, local farmers and food producers showcase their best. And in the kitchen, two wunderkinds and their cooks spin a nightly playlist full of love in all different flavors.

When Bluestem expanded into an adjacent space in 2006, opening its lounge, the frequency of my visits increased. The lounge has since become my landing pad after a hard day at work, a place to unfold and, most important, a familiar corner where everyone knows my name. Indeed, the lounge has a life and story of its own that I hope gets its own telling in due time.

This cookbook focuses on the type of food served in the restaurant's more formal dining room. You won't find all of these dishes on the menu at Bluestem; quite a few were developed especially for this cookbook. But they are all offered in the spirit of Bluestem. Collectively, the 100 or so stories that follow are pieces of Colby and Megan's lives, their adventures, and their love of food and the Midwest.

Some, like the foie gras *au torchon* (page 82) and beef tartare (page 16), have become permanently affixed to the menu by popular demand, deservedly so in both cases. Some, like the crab, trofie (page 214), have earned the restaurant a roster of regulars, who now call to request their favorite dishes. And others, like the pea soup (page 20) and gazpacho (page 72), are perennial wonders, appearing for a few weeks every year as Mother Nature wills.

Many of these recipes were born out of a collaborative spirit, which Colby and Megan embrace and encourage in their kitchen.

Dave Crum, the restaurant's first chef de cuisine, who wrote many menus at Bluestem over the years, has contributed a couple of dishes, including the beautiful pork tenderloin, piquillo peppers, on page 165. Bill Espiricueta, the restaurant's second and current chef de cuisine, might just be more Asian than I am; the *chawanmushi* on page 202, for example, is his.

I insisted that a number of my favorite dishes be included, like the char on page 162, campo lindo hen, pistachio pistou (page 101), and poached braeburn apples (page 181). And there are even a few recipes that Colby and Megan allowed me to help create; the braised artichoke, potatoes confit (page 78), foraged mushrooms (page 140), and peanut cream fritters (page 182) are among them.

Regardless of their provenance, all of the dishes in this cookbook, like those served in the restaurant, demonstrate that fine dining can be playful and, with a bit of care and dedication, doable in the home kitchen (see the User Manual, or How to Use This Cookbook, by Someone Who Is Not a Chef, page xx). The most important thing I've learned from spending more than a year writing and testing recipes with Colby and Megan is to enjoy the process. As one very famous and jovial chef put it, be "happy in the kitchen." If you can accomplish this, then this cookbook will serve as a wonderful road map to enjoying life.

Though I underestimated Bluestem at first, over countless subsequent meals I've had the tremendous pleasure of watching it take root, mature, and grow. Dish by dish, menu by menu, season by season, like its namesake prairie grass, Bluestem has truly reshaped Kansas City's landscape. It has turned out to be the game changer that I initially expected to find.

In the seven years so far that the restaurant has been open, Colby and Megan have inspired other chefs in our area to work harder and diners to demand better.

Bluestem is not about linen and china, although you'll find both dressing the tables in its dining room, or about food that tastes as beautiful as it looks, which at Bluestem it does. It's not about knowledgeable servers who understand and practice excellent hospitality either, although you'll find that too.

Bluestem is about the everyday enjoyment of life. It's about a laugh, a handshake, and a pat on the back. Bluestem will charm your socks off effortlessly, and the fact that it also serves some of the best food in the area seems like the happiest coincidence ever.

I had dinner at Bluestem one night with Joe West, a former cook and pastry assistant there. Then working at Alex at the Wynn Las Vegas, he was back in Kansas City to cook at an event. He told me that on the last night he worked at Bluestem, after the restaurant had closed its doors for the night, he stood up on the bar, spread out his arms, and declared it "the best place in the world."

Bluestem can have that effect on you.

The restaurant is a little patch amidst a field of dreams, proving, indeed, that if you build it, they will come. And they have come. I hope you do too.

—*Bonjwing Lee*

# foreword

It's not every day that chefs have the opportunity to redefine the cuisine in their hometown. Colby and Megan Garrelts have done exactly that. Having worked together in some of the nation's finest kitchens, from the beaches of California to the windy, skyscraper tunnels of Chicago, these two packed up their valuable culinary experiences and moved back to Colby's hometown of Kansas City, where they opened one of the best fine-dining establishments that town had ever seen.

In many ways, Colby is my shorter, thinner, better-looking twin.

I was working at Charlie Trotter's in Chicago when Colby appeared in the kitchen, a *stagier* (or apprentice). Having been a skater in my younger days, I immediately homed in on the rat skull-and-bones Powell-Peralta skateboard sticker on his knife kit. We instantly hit it off. On top of being a talented cook, this guy was cool. After a few days, Colby was offered a permanent position with the Trotter team. But he declined. Although I was used to the revolving-door life of the restaurant kitchen, I was truly sad to see Colby go.

But the wonderful thing is that life itself is also a revolving door.

Serendipitously, Colby and I found each other in the same car on the El train one day. He told me that he had landed a job at Chicago's newest four-star restaurant, Tru. I mentioned that I was looking to move on to a new kitchen, and he offered to put in a good word for me with Tru's executive chef, Rick Tramonto. Shortly thereafter, I was hired.

After Colby trained me on the *saucier* station at Tru, we went on to work side by side as co–*sous chefs* of the restaurant. I shouldered the brunt of the cooking while he, the "numbers ninja," focused more on the business end, a skill set that would benefit both of us later.

A lot of life happened for Colby and me at Tru, not the least of which for Colby was Megan Schultz, who worked under Tru's executive pastry chef, Gale Gand. I watched them fall in love and move on to other kitchens, other cities.

While Colby and Megan headed west, I headed east, landing my first executive chef position at the Jackson House Inn in Vermont. On opposite ends of the country, we cut our teeth and kept in touch.

After two years away, the Midwest got all three of us back. Colby and Megan opened a restaurant, I opened a restaurant. They had a kid, I had a kid. I was named one of the Best New Chefs of 2004 by *Food & Wine* magazine, and Colby followed the next year. We were both nominated for James Beard Awards for the first time in 2007, repeating again in 2008 for another nomination each. And just as this cookbook goes to print, Megan and my wife, Allie, each gave birth to a second child.

With brimming plates of their own, Colby and Megan have always made time for me. Having already opened their own restaurant successfully, they were an invaluable resource when I decided to leave Avenues at The Peninsula hotel in Chicago to open my first restaurant, sending me their business plan and loads of encouragement. Colby even came up with my first restaurant's name, Graham Elliot.

In many ways, this cookbook is a mirror of my own journey as a cook and chef, a sounding board for my work and career. I hope you feel the passion come through in the recipes, stories, and photographs on the following pages. I hope you come to understand why Colby and Megan Garrelts are extraordinary cooks and people.

**—*Graham Elliot***
Executive Chef, Graham Elliot and Grahamwich

# introduction

When Megan and I opened Bluestem, we weren't sure we'd be in business a year later, let alone did we imagine writing a cookbook about our restaurant seven years later. But here we are, filling these pages with our stories and recipes from a journey and labor of love in the kitchen.

In many ways, the road to Bluestem ended right where it started. I grew up on the prairie plains of Kansas with long hair and a skateboard stitched to my feet. I was the nightmare of every prudent parent. There wasn't a lot of direction to my life until I found the kitchen. And even then, the kitchen was nothing more than a channel for my unguided energy, not a serious career path.

I worked my way up the line in the kitchens of commodity restaurants before landing a position as the *sous chef* at the Stolen Grill, a fifteen-table matchbox in Kansas City's neo-hippie Westport district. For the time—mid-1990s—and the place, it was producing fairly progressive food, some of the best in the city. I wasn't aware of it at the time, but I was working with some of Kansas City's most talented young chefs. That's where I first met Dave Crum, who would later become my first chef de cuisine and right hand at Bluestem. [Dave's parents, Jim and Debbie, have also become one of the restaurant's most important suppliers (see page 74).]

Then Chicago happened. And it changed my life forever. I was exposed to restaurants, like Charlie Trotter's, that were operating at a level I never imagined possible. An interview with chef Rick Tramonto at Brasserie T landed me with a paid position at Tru, then the crown jewel of Richard Melman's Lettuce Entertain You restaurant group and Chicago's

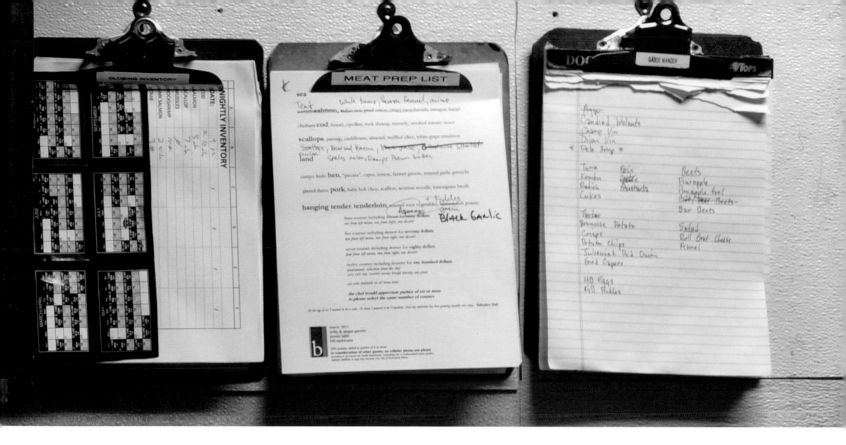

newest four-star restaurant. I started as a roundsman there, and, within the year, I was promoted to *sous chef*. That's when Graham Elliot joined the crew. The two of us saw a lot of traffic as co–executive *sous chefs*, but we stayed on to earn our stripes in the corporate outfit—Elliot would assist with writing the menu; I would help manage the kitchen costs.

It was in the kitchen at Tru that I met the blond bombshell who became the love of my life. Megan Schultz had grown up in Naperville, a suburb of Chicago. An avid baker from a young age, Megan had earned her associate's degree in baking and pastry at the Culinary Institute of America. After working under Richard Leach in New York's Park Avenue Café, she had returned home to work under Gale Gand, the executive pastry chef of Tru.

Megan and I started dating, which was against company policy. So I left, heading to Las Vegas. Megan followed soon after. I stopped in briefly to work at Jean Joho's Eiffel Tower, also a Lettuce Entertain You restaurant, before settling in at Charlie Palmer's Aureole at Mandalay Bay, where Megan had taken a job in the pastry station under pastry chef Megan Romano. Las Vegas was big and bright. The corporate hotel outfits were monstrosities—both physically and in the volume we handled. Running to the storage area for supplies was an expedition.

Having both steadily grown frustrated working for others, it was there in Las Vegas that Megan and I began to develop a business plan for our own restaurant. We even took a trip back to Kansas City to scout potential locations. But little came, little happened.

After a bit more than a year in Sin City, Megan and I decided to leave the desert for the coast. We packed up our car and drove to Los Angeles. Death Valley, Joshua Tree, Californication, Howard Stern, and Red Bull; we were young and poor, and the change of scenery was everything we wanted.

Megan and I did a lot of growing as cooks in Los Angeles. I landed at Hans Röckenwagner's eponymous restaurant as chef de cuisine. It was there that I started to hone our business plan and really get a sense of the type of restaurant we wanted to open. It was here that I learned how to write out composed dishes—I would create the menus, and Chef Röckenwagner would edit them. More important, it was there that I started to understand the size and feel of the restaurant we wanted. Megan was hired as the executive pastry chef at the restaurant atop the Getty Center in Los Angeles. There, for the first time, she was in charge of her own kitchen, her own menus, and her own crew. There she really learned how to run a pastry operation.

After a year and a half in Los Angeles, we headed back to the Midwest, with a plan and a prayer. That's when serendipity called. The restaurant next to the Stolen Grill, where I started my career, was for sale. It was the perfect place for our first restaurant. Like a set of dominoes, life started to cascade into place for us.

Megan and I got married in Chicago in October, moved to Kansas City in November, and opened Bluestem on March 15 of the following year, 2004. I don't think we slept a wink the week before we opened. Excited, scared, and anxious, we lay awake dreaming of the possibilities, naively confident. And I don't think we slept a wink for the first year the restaurant was open.

We were a lo-fi operation in those early days. Megan was the hostess, wine gal, and pastry chef. I was the cook and all-around handyman. Wine was kept in the storage closet in the men's room. If the restroom was occupied, the wine would take a little time to come out.

Our experiences at Tru and Röckenwagner were palpable on our first menus. We offered an à la carte menu in addition to a seven-course tasting menu. We took a few chances, made a lot of mistakes, and gradually earned the trust of our clients. Together with Dave Crum, we fumbled through our first few menus, learning what Kansas Citians would and wouldn't eat, and more important, what they would and wouldn't pay.

There were times we weren't sure we'd make it. But thanks to a fantastic crew and loyal customers, we've been able to grow Bluestem over the years—adding a bar and lounge, a separate wine closet, and a pastry kitchen for Megan and her assistant. Business now ebbs and flows with good rhythm, growing steadily. Bill Espiricueta joined our crew as the kid on *garde manger*. Today he's our chef de cuisine, a talented everyman who props the restaurant up. He can prep. He can cook. He can fix. He's every chef's dream. Jeremy Lamb is our longtime general manager and wine director. He oversees the front of the house and curates our "cellar." You'll find his wine notes in the pages to come.

As for the food, Megan and I have developed and honed our own voices and cooking styles at Bluestem. Over the years, we've gained enough confidence to know what we like, our strengths, and our weaknesses. I like things clean and bright, simple and satisfying. I love raw fish and acidic flavors. I love herbs, vegetables, smoke, and meat. I love beer. All of these things, and more, you'll find in the dishes throughout this cookbook, each with my thoughts and stories about them in the headnotes.

Megan's desserts reflect the Americana of her childhood. In the headnotes of her recipes, you'll be taken on romps through the candy store, the soda fountain, the ice cream parlor, the cookie jar, or around the campfire—a license for fun and giggles. At Bluestem, no meal is complete without a parting reminder that, when it comes to sweets, all of us are really just oversized kids.

About two years after we opened Bluestem, we shifted from an à la carte menu to a series of multicourse prix-fixe menus. We now offer three, five, and seven courses with choices from seven categories: cold appetizers, hot appetizers, pastas, fish, meat, cheese, and dessert. (On weekdays, we also offer a twelve-course "spontaneous" tasting menu, at the chef's choice.) This cookbook mirrors our menu—the recipes are arranged according to these seven categories, and within each category we've ordered the dishes, generally, from the lightest to heaviest, in terms of both size and flavor. Although you can assemble a meal with as many courses as you like, the portion sizes in this cookbook are ideal for a three-course dinner. We recommend starting with a cold, hot, or pasta dish as first course, a fish or meat for the main course, and either cheese or dessert to finish.

There's a bigger picture to this cookbook than just the individual recipes that populate the pages or the restaurant whose story it tells. This cookbook is about community and family. It tells the story of nostalgia. It spotlights environmental awareness and gives a nod to unrighteous social responsibility. We hope this cookbook makes you more thoughtful about what you eat and where your food is grown or produced. Above all, we hope it inspires you to enjoy the abundance of life around you. So whether you cook all or none of the recipes we present here, don't lose sight of three things.

**Stay seasonal.** It was important to us that this book be useful and timely. So the recipes are organized by season, when you'll find particular ingredients at their best. Depending on where you live, the growing season will vary. Since Bluestem is situated in the heart of the Midwest, that's the growing season you'll find tracked in these pages.

The menu at Bluestem is a living entity, at the mercy of our creativity and the whim of Mother Nature. We are constantly adapting and tweaking dishes according to what lands on our doorstep from farmers or what is available at the market. You should too.

With the exception of a few dishes that are consistently on our menu, like the beef tartare (page 16) and the crab, trofie (page 214), the recipes included here are merely still frames in a constantly shifting set. The techniques are fairly non-negotiable, but some of the ingredients, especially the seasonings and vegetables, aren't. Feel free to improvise and experiment. If you can't find snap peas, use snow peas; if there aren't any turnips, use another root vegetable, like celeriac or rutabaga. The only exceptions to these rules are for pastries, which are explained in the User Manual (see page xx).

The important thing is to use fresh ingredients. They are the foundation of good food. Start there and you'll already be halfway to success.

**Stay local (as much as possible).** With the recent revival of locavorism—the practice of eating food produced and grown in your immediate area—it'll hardly surprise you that two Midwestern chefs would be ardent supporters of their local farmers.

In this book, we feature six farmers and food producers in the Kansas City area with whom we have developed a close working relationship. They are amazing people who do amazing work. Without them and the many, many others who produce the food that arrives at the restaurant daily, Bluestem would not be what it is.

It may take you some time to locate the farmers in your area who are dedicated to organic, sustainable farming, but we encourage you to do so. Finding and building those relationships will be well worth the time you invest. Food from down the road will invariably be fresher than food that's shipped from elsewhere.

That being said, far be it from us to preach absolutism. While we delight in highlighting the abundance that surrounds us, we also borrow the best of what neighboring regions have to offer in order to give our diners a fuller seasonal experience. In the Midwest, we revel in our beefy and porky blessings but are ever mindful of being landlocked. Beyond catfish and trout, we have little to offer in the way of aquatic goods. So all of the seafood that we serve at Bluestem is shipped to us.

You'll find other imported luxuries on our menu as well. Truffles, caviar, olives and olive oil, wine, citrus fruits, spices, and many other ingredients that we use come to us by way of long journeys. Unless you live in a particularly plentiful land (California comes to mind), you will have to look beyond your area for some ingredients. But to the extent that you can, try to discover the best of what's around you.

**Have fun.** If you're not having fun, it's probably not worth doing. Cooking is no exception. Owning and running a restaurant is hard work. But we wouldn't be keeping the lights on if we didn't enjoy what we do.

No one wants to meet a cranky chef or restaurateur when going out to eat. Likewise, no one wants to be greeted by a frazzled host upon arriving for dinner. The kitchen shouldn't be a war zone, and cooking shouldn't be a chore. Whether you're using this book to entertain friends, to cook for yourself, or just to learn about cooking, don't lose sight of the table. Relax, pour yourself a glass of wine, sit down and enjoy your company, and the food will follow naturally.

# user manual

## or how to use this cookbook, by someone who is not a chef

*—Bonjwing Lee*

I am not a chef. And I'm assuming you're not one either. I'm an intrepid home cook at best.

Over the course of an entire year, I had the privilege of spending countless hours in the kitchen with Colby and Megan, testing recipes, talking about ingredients and techniques, and observing the restaurant at work and play. But I also spent a fair amount of time with the recipes in my comparatively ill-equipped kitchen. And I made them work. So who better to tell you how to use this book than me?

I read a lot of cookbooks. There's a rotating stack of them permanently parked next to my nightstand. Some are clearly destined to be more useful on your coffee table than on your kitchen counter: gorgeous photos, complex techniques, ingredients from far-flung places. Others are workhorses. At their best, they're grease-stained, with cracked bindings, full of easy, accessible formulas for the midweek meal.

This one falls somewhere in between. Colby and Megan wanted to share with you the food that they cook at the restaurant (and, presumably, you bought this cookbook to learn about and reproduce it). So, first and foremost, this is

a restaurant cookbook with restaurant-level recipes. Any one of the dishes in the following pages might alight on your table when you dine at Bluestem.

But don't be intimidated. A few of the recipes in this book might be challenging, but they are far from impossible. With a little patience and a bit of practice, you can master any of them.

We recognize that the home cook doesn't have access to the wide range of industrial equipment that one would find in a restaurant. So we've simplified these recipes as much as possible and adapted them for the home kitchen without losing the essential technique or compromising the end result.

As the food at Bluestem focuses on natural ingredients, much of what is required is probably already in your pantry. Though you might have to make a special trip to an ethnic market or place a special order for foie gras, for example, you'll find the rest of what you need in your modern-day market.

From one home cook to another, here are a few tips:

## 1. read the instructions.

When I was in the third grade, my teacher passed out a sheet of instructions and told us to read them carefully. The first instruction on the list was "Read all of the instructions before starting." By the time I had gotten to the last one—

"Disregard everything on this page. Sit quietly and raise your hand."—I had drawn no fewer than a dozen critters in various colors as instructed in the text between.

Even if you think you know where the recipe is headed, read the instructions before starting. It will give you a better sense of the overall arc of the dish, the end goal, and perhaps most important, the timing. Some items are better made a day ahead, while others must be consumed quickly. Read the instructions.

## 2. *mise en place.*

*Mise en place* is a fancy French restaurant term for getting your act together. The concept isn't hard or novel. Basically, it involves running through the list of ingredients in a recipe and pulling them out on the counter, preferably measured and prepped, before you begin. Restaurant cooks do this every day, and I see no reason a home cook can't benefit from doing it either. It will help you mentally and physically organize the parts to a dish, which will streamline the cooking process. It will also ensure that you have the six eggs you need at step 5.

## 3. hardware.

I'll bet that you have most, if not all, of the equipment you need for the recipes in this cookbook. But there are a few tools that I'd like to highlight. Some, like an ice cream maker, are indispensable. A few, though not necessary, will be well worth the investment. They will make the cooking process considerably easier and help you produce the level of food that you'll want from the recipes in this cookbook. In addition to rubber spatulas, whisks, rolling pins, pots and pans, baking sheets and tins, and wooden spoons, all of which I'm assuming you have, I highly recommend the tools that follow.

**A good knife:** You really need only one good one. Unless you're a master Chinese chef who miraculously does everything with a cleaver, a good chef's knife will do just about everything you need to do with a knife except filleting a fish and boning meat. For the fish and meat, ask your fishmonger or butcher to break them down for you as specified in the recipes.

**Baking liners:** Although they are one of the greatest inventions of our time, silicone liners for your baking sheets aren't necessary. Parchment paper works just as well. But when a recipe calls for a nonstick liner, use one or the other.

**Blender:** A food processor's job can be replicated by a good knife, a box grater, or a pastry cutter. But a good blender has no peer. You will need one to make sauces and soups.

**Dutch oven:** A cast-iron Dutch oven heats evenly and, with its super-heavy lid, retains heat and moisture well for braising meats. You don't need a big one. A four- or five-quart one will do.

**Fine-mesh sieve:** Have you ever noticed that restaurant sauces and soups are just that much finer, and therefore that much more refined, than anything you normally make at home? One of the reasons is that restaurants pass their stocks, purees, and soups through a fine-mesh sieve, straining out impurities, debris, and, well, anything that's not smaller than the tip of a pin. Whether you use cheesecloth (double, triple, or quadruple layered, depending on how fine you want the liquid), a chinois (a cone-shaped strainer), or a simple wire-mesh sieve (which I find most useful since it doubles as a sifter for baking), straining your stocks, sauces, and soups will make a noticeable difference.

**Ice cream maker:** Without one, you really can't make proper ice cream. You don't need a fancy one. You just need one that churns ice cream at a predictably low temperature. I have one of those mass-produced commercial ones at home that involves freezing the bucket for a few hours before churning. It's low-tech, and it wasn't terribly expensive. But it works just fine.

**Mandoline:** You don't *need* a mandoline. But it's awfully nice to have one around when you want to reduce vegetables to paper-thin slices. Most of the thin slicing required in this cookbook can be accomplished with careful knife work. But a mandoline will make the job easier and quicker. Be sure to use the guard, or be very careful, as the sharp blade seems to love fingers.

**Microplane zester:** This is one gizmo that doesn't multitask. But what it does do—finely grate anything from zest to cheese—can't be replicated by any other.

**Skillet:** Most home cooks will have an assortment of sauté pans. But if you have a well-seasoned cast-iron skillet, you really don't need any other pans. Cast iron heats evenly and retains heat incredibly well. It's ideal for searing meat.

**Stand mixer:** I don't know how Grandma creamed butter and sugar together without a handheld mixer or a stand mixer. But a stand mixer is more useful than a handheld mixer because, as the name suggests, it's completely hands-free. A standard stand mixer also multitasks: It whisks, it beats, and it even brings dough together with a hook. Some stand mixers now also have optional attachments that grind meat, roll pasta, and even churn ice cream.

**Y-peeler:** Really, any peeler will do. But a Y-shaped peeler is particularly useful because it allows you to pull instead of push, giving you a little more control on the length and shape of each peel. This is particularly useful when peeling zest off citrus, for example. Y-peelers can also be purchased with blades of varying thickness, so that you can create strips of varying thickness. We recommend using a Kuhn Rikon #2 Y-shaped peeler. This peeler will remove the rind from the orange without picking up any of the bitter white pith.

# 4. techniques.

We've scattered helpful hints and techniques throughout the book where they're appropriate. But a few techniques are so commonly employed that I've decided to include them here instead of repeating them needlessly later.

**Blanching:** Blanching, also called parboiling, is a method of precooking food by briefly shocking it in boiling water and then refreshing it in an ice bath to stop the cooking process.

Blanching has many purposes. It takes the hard, grassy edge off raw vegetables, making them more tender and in some cases more palatable. It preserves and often intensifies the brilliant colors of vegetables. Blanching thin-skinned fruits and vegetables helps loosen the skins, making them easier to peel. And blanching foods in heavily salted water helps season them as well.

Blanching is simple. Bring a large stockpot full of heavily salted water (it should almost be like seawater) to a rolling boil. While the water is heating, prepare a large ice bath (see page xxv). If you are blanching more than one type of vegetable or fruit, you'll want to blanch them separately, as each item will have a different cooking time depending on the shape, size, and texture. When the water has reached a boil, drop in the food and cook for the desired amount of time (we suggest cooking times in most of the recipes, though you are free to adjust them according to your taste). Using a spider skimmer (or a ladle with holes), fish out the food and plunge it immediately into the ice bath. Bring the water back to a rolling boil before repeating the process with other foods.

**Blending:** Not much skill is required to use a blender. But when blending hot items, do be careful, as they tend to explode in blenders (not literally—they just blow the lid off). When blending hot items, it's best to hold the lid firmly down with one hand wrapped in a damp kitchen towel.

**Blooming gelatin:** Professional kitchens use sheet gelatin (also known as leaf gelatin) instead of powdered gelatin, which is much more common in the home kitchen. Both forms of gelatin must be "bloomed," or softened in cold liquid, before they can be used. At some point, the bloomed gelatin is usually heated to fully dissolve it.

Powdered gelatin is bloomed by sprinkling it over cold liquid that is being incorporated into the final product. Sheet gelatin, however, can be bloomed in water, drained and squeezed dry, and incorporated into another medium, making it advantageous in recipes where there is very little liquid. Although there is a sheet-to-powder conversion (depending on the manufacturer and the size of the gelatin sheets, ten sheets usually equals one ounce of powdered gelatin), to be consistent, this cookbook uses powdered gelatin, since it is much easier for the home cook to find.

**Bouquet garni:** A bouquet garni is a bundle of herbs and spices that's often added when making stocks and sauces to lend flavor; it is removed before they are served. The traditional bouquet garni includes parsley, thyme, and bay leaves, but the contents can vary. Some recipes in this cookbook will provide a short list of herbs and instruct you to make a bouquet garni out of them. To do so, simply gather the herbs together and secure them tightly with kitchen twine. Alternatively, you can put the herbs in a sachet, or a little homemade satchel made of cheesecloth. This is necessary when you have crushed herbs or spices that are too small to bundle together with twine (peppercorns, for example). To make a sachet, cut a large rectangle of cheesecloth and fold it over at the length to make a double-layered square. Put the herbs in the center of the square and gather the edges up to make a sack. Secure the sack closed with kitchen twine.

**Ice bath:** An ice bath is exactly what it sounds like—a mix of water and ice used to rapidly cool down hot food. Throughout the book, you will be required to make an ice bath. Sometimes the hot food is put directly into the bath, such as vegetables, which are plunged into the icy water to stop the cooking process after they've been blanched in boiling water. Sometimes the hot substance—usually liquids, such as stocks and ice cream bases—is put into a bowl and then placed over the ice bath and stirred until cool. Either way, the method is simple: Fill a large bowl or tub with equal parts ice and water. If you are setting a bowl or other vessel over the ice bath, make sure the container that you use to hold your ice bath is larger than the bowl.

**Seasoning:** Everyone has a different tolerance for salt and other seasonings. The recipes in this cookbook allow you to adjust the seasonings to your own taste.

- Season from up high, not down low, so that you get a wider, more even distribution over the food.

- At the restaurant and in this cookbook, we use kosher salt for cooking and baking. Table salt has added iodine, which gives it an especially harsh flavor.

- As a general rule, Colby likes to season vegetables and fish with white pepper, reserving black pepper, which has a slightly more aggressive flavor, for red meat. Depending on the flavors of the dish, he might season chicken and pork with either pepper. Of course, there are always exceptions to the rule, and ultimately, your personal preferences should guide you despite what is recommended in this cookbook.

- Unless otherwise specified, try to use fresh herbs instead of dried herbs.

**Zest:** The thin layer of skin on citrus rind—the zest—contains oils that make it incredibly fragrant. Zest is used frequently in this cookbook to brighten a dish. You can remove the zest by peeling it off with a Y-peeler (see page xxiii). Or you can use a finely toothed grater, like a Microplane zester, to shave off tiny flecks of zest to be used as a garnish or incorporated into baked goods or ice creams. The important thing to know is that the loamy, white pith that separates the zest from the flesh of the fruit is extremely bitter. So whether you're peeling or grating zest, leave the pith behind or trim it off before using the zest.

## 5. know thy monger and thy butcher.

Be it for fish, cheese, or meat, get to know your purveyors. They will be your best everyday guide to the products they sell. Building a relationship with them will ensure that you get the best and freshest of what they have.

Home cooks often don't have access to the specialty sources that industry professionals do. If the butcher, fishmonger, or meat or fish department at your local supermarket can't give you what you need, turn to the Sources section in the back of this book (page 272), where Colby and Megan have provided a list of reliable sources from whom you can order specialty ingredients.

## 6. cooking is an art; baking is a science.

That's an over-rigid generalization, more accurate about baking than cooking. Both can be artful, but pastry making, baking included, is a stricter discipline.

We've given you tested recipes that are designed to be followed. We know they work. But Colby and Megan will be the first to encourage you to adjust them to suit your taste. As a home cook, I'll be the second. Feel free to experiment, play, and discover the joy of cooking for yourself.

When it comes to desserts, however, I'll throw up a speed bump. Pastry making relies on a set of complex chemical reactions that are triggered by a meeting of precise measurements, timing, and temperature. If you adhere to the tested formulas, your cakes will rise, your panna cottas will set, and your meringues will become crisp. Deviate and the results will be unpredictable. That's not to say you'll meet with unmitigated failure. Who knows what you'll create? Some of the most famous desserts have been born from accidents.

## 7. a note on *sous vide*.

*Sous vide* is a cooking method whereby food is vacuum-sealed in plastic bags and poached in a water bath that is maintained at a constant temperature. Since the food is hermetically sealed, it does not spoil or get wet. And because it's held at a constant and relatively low temperature, the food can be kept for an extended period of time without overcooking.

Although it sounds like space-age technology, the concept was first visited in the eighteenth century. It became a practical reality in the 1960s and has been employed since in restaurants, high and low, all over the world, including Bluestem.

If you've ever had a chicken breast cooked by this method, you'll know why it is so popular among chefs today. Not only can food be prepared ahead of time and suspended in its perfectly cooked state, but the results are also unusually superior. Meat emerges at a level of tenderness that's otherwise unattainable. Fish is supremely silky. And fruits and vegetables, when cooked with a little bit of their own puree, intensify in flavor.

So why not try this at home? If you can afford the equipment, by all means, do it. At the risk of overselling *sous vide*, it's easy, it's simple, and there's relatively little cleanup required. But for most home cooks, the cost of a vacuum sealer and an immersion circulator is prohibitively high.

Therefore, after much debate over whether or not to include instructions for *sous vide*, we decided to focus on the traditional methods of cooking that are familiar to all home cooks. There's nothing wrong with using a stovetop or an oven, both of which are used in restaurant kitchens, like Bluestem's, every day. Cooking in a skillet or Dutch oven is not an inferior method. In many ways, it's superior, since you get to touch and smell your way to doneness. It's a skill set that, once learned, you can take with you just about anywhere.

You don't need a vacuum sealer and immersion circulator. With a bit of attention, you can and will produce fabulous food with the directions we've given you. I have, and I'm not a chef.

If you do have access to a *sous vide* machine and want to try the *sous vide* method with the recipes in this cookbook, we highly recommend that you get a reliable *sous vide* cookbook, like Thomas Keller's authoritative *Under Pressure: Cooking Sous Vide*, which provides detailed instructions and cooking temperatures and times for just about everything you can imagine. Most of the meats and fish that are cooked by *sous vide* at Bluestem are finished on the stovetop or in the oven, just to give them a crust. Otherwise, fruits and vegetables are usually taken straight out of the bag and only slightly warmed on the stove, as appropriate, before serving.

# wine

Every guest is different. As a wine director, I must remind myself of this every day.

My goal is to help our clients achieve the best wine experience for their taste and budget. And sometimes I provide them with ideas outside of the box—creative combinations that they might not have experienced before. Sometimes—most often with desserts—wine isn't the best option; it might be a cocktail or an aperitif.

There are no hard and fast rules. As a wine director, I must also remind myself of this every day.

When designing the wine program at Bluestem, I wanted to create an approachable experience for everyone. To that end, I've broken the restaurant's wine list into three parts: "seasonal" wines that are changed throughout the year to pair specifically with Colby and Megan's seasonal menus; a reasonably priced "cocktail" list of bottles that might be enjoyed with a variety of food; and a "reserve" list, offering the more discerning and wine-wise customers some all-stars of the wine world.

When pairing wine at Bluestem, I take three things into consideration. First is the food. I pair wines to complement Colby and Megan's food. Theirs is the main character; mine, the supporting cast. In this cookbook, I offer a few wine notes and suggested pairings for some of the recipes in each season. In those notes, you'll find my thoughts and read my mind's method for pairing wines.

Second, I consider the approachability of the wine. This requires an evaluation of the occasion—is this a special event or just another night out? It also requires an evaluation of the drinker and his or her preferences. Simplicity sometimes pleases more than sophistication.

Last, I must be mindful of the cost. Wine is a luxury and it has to be treated accordingly.

Regardless of what I have written here and in the pages that follow, I encourage you to experiment with wine. You will be your own best guide. You know what you like and what you don't like. And you know what you can and can't afford. Even within the narrowest field of taste and the strictest budget, the world of wine offers a staggering number of possibilities. The best way to discover your own sensibilities is to grab a glass and start tasting.

—*Jeremy Lamb*

spring

Spring is a time of great potential for chefs.
Farmers start appearing with fuller, greener crates.

Diners start coming out of the wintry woodwork. And the pace of life, both inside and outside the restaurant, accelerates.

Spring is fleeting, but every day offers a new show. Baby lettuces, spinach, and nettles appear in quick succession. They're followed by a rainbow of radishes. Asparagus sends up its creamy green stalks, fennel sprouts its furry fronds, and rhubarb arrives with a dazzling volley of hot pink. Morels sneak onto the scene just about as suddenly as they disappear, fresh herbs become more readily available, and garlic is green once again.

But we don't want to over-romanticize the vernal and the verdant. Spring in the Midwest isn't always pea shoots and cherry blossoms. The weather can be harsh. Torrential downpours and breathtaking winds whipping across the prairie can wreak havoc on the land and delay seeding. Late-season frosts, tornadoes, and hailstorms are always potential threats as well. When they occur, the effects are devastating. Farmers lose their crops, restaurateurs are forced to find alternative food sources, and consumers pay more.

Despite this volatility, spring remains exciting because it throws back the heavy curtain of winter and hits the reset button. It ushers in a breath of fresh air. And so should the food. At Bluestem, we try our best to convey this sense of renewal on every plate.

# spring

# menu

wine

After a harsh and heavy winter, the brighter, grassier flavors of spring call for lighter and more refreshing wines, such as Rieslings, or white wines from the Loire Valley—a Sancerre (made from the Sauvignon Blanc grape) or Savennières (made from the chenin blanc grape), for example.

I especially like Rieslings for their balanced sweetness and lively acidity. Rieslings are also particularly expressive of *terroir*—the soil and environment in which the grapes were grown. Those from the Alsace region of France are known for being particularly flinty, in addition to being drier than German Rieslings, which are usually sweeter, more acidic, and lower in alcohol. For example, the minerality in an Alsatian Riesling would pair nicely with the brininess of the shellfish in the bucatini pasta dish on page 25, whereas the residual sugar in a German Riesling would help bring out the herbaceous sweetness of the pea soup, which is garnished with fragrant pink peppercorns (page 20).

Always consider sauces and accompanying items on the plate when choosing a wine. For example, asparagus, one of the joys of spring, is a particularly cranky ingredient to pair with wine, so be sure to look to the other ingredients in the recipe for guidance. A Vouvray, for example, or an Oregon Pinot Gris or Californian Chenin Blanc will pair well with the tanginess and creamy texture of the goat cheese in the fava bean

notes

and asparagus salad (page 12). In like manner, the same wines would do well with the whipped lemon ricotta in the nettle soup amuse-bouche (page 6).

If there is one wine I'd pour with Colby's beef tartare (page 16), it'd be Vin Santo, a late harvest Italian wine with a creamy texture and low alcohol content. The darker characteristics of the wine pair especially well with the black olive caramel in that recipe.

But Vin Santo can be very expensive—even more expensive than Champagne, which would be my second choice for a wine pairing with the tartare. The effervescence helps to cut through the richness of the meat and the dressing.

The scallop dish on this spring menu (page 30), which includes miso-braised bacon, will hold up well with any good Sonoma Valley Pinot Noir, which tends to exhibit soft, cherry-cola and fruit flavors with a subtle streak of acidity. These wines draw a nice balance between the bacon and the soy caramel without overpowering the scallops.

For dessert, you'd be surprised by how well a chilled shot of Galliano—shaken with ice and then strained—goes with mint ice cream. The hint of anise flavor in the liqueur overlaps with the menthol flavor in the mint and the bitterness in the chocolate.

# nettle soup, whipped lemon ricotta

**Serves 4**

### whipped lemon ricotta

½ cup ricotta cheese

2 tablespoons olive oil

1 tablespoon freshly grated lemon zest

2 tablespoons freshly squeezed
    lemon juice

Salt and freshly ground white pepper

Finely grated lemon zest, for garnish

### nettle soup

3 tablespoons vegetable oil

1 large shallot, chopped

5 cloves garlic, smashed and chopped

4 cups packed nettle leaves

2 cups packed spinach leaves, stemmed

1½ cups heavy cream

Salt and freshly ground white pepper

1 bunch fresh flat-leaf parsley, stemmed

Dismissing them as a pesky weed, Thane Palmberg (see page 148) was hysterical when we asked for stinging nettles at the Stolen Grill, the restaurant where I got my start as a young chef.

As the name suggests, stinging nettles are covered, both leaf and stem, with bristly hairs that can cause topical discomfort when you handle them raw. We suggest that you put on latex or rubber gloves when working with them. You need only the leaves, so strip them off and discard the stem. Wash the leaves thoroughly before using them.

Although nettles grow throughout the warm months, they become tough and bitter as the plants mature. Use them at the start of spring, while they're still young and tender. Nettles have a slightly sour, grassy flavor that is rounded out in this soup with spinach, parsley, and heavy cream. A light, lemony ricotta cloud gives it a bright smile. If you can't find stinging nettles, substitute baby spinach leaves.

---

**Whip the ricotta:** Combine the ricotta and olive oil in the bowl of a stand mixer fitted with the paddle attachment. Whip at medium speed for 2 minutes. Scrape down the bowl and add the lemon zest and juice. Season with salt and pepper to taste and whip the cheese for a minute more to combine. Adjust the seasonings as necessary.

**Make the soup:** Heat 2 tablespoons of the oil in a large sauté pan over medium-low heat. Add the shallots and garlic and sweat for about 1 minute. Add the nettles and sauté for a minute more. Stir in the spinach and the remaining 1 tablespoon of oil and cook until the greens are just wilted, about 2 minutes. Add the cream and bring it to a simmer. Remove from the heat. Let it cool slightly, but it is important to blend the soup while it is still hot to preserve the color.

Transfer the contents to a blender. Add the parsley and season the soup with salt and pepper to taste. Puree the mixture on high speed until smooth. Adjust the seasonings as necessary. Strain the soup through a fine-mesh sieve, and discard the strained-out debris.

**To serve:** Divide the soup among 4 small bowls or cups. Float a spoonful of whipped ricotta in each bowl. Garnish with lemon zest and serve immediately.

# sunchoke panna cotta, prosciutto

**Serves 24 as an amuse-bouche,
8 as a first course**

4 ounces sunchokes, peeled

¾ cup Vegetable Stock, chilled (page 255)

2½ teaspoons powdered gelatin

¾ cup heavy cream

2 tablespoons freshly squeezed lemon juice

Salt and freshly ground black pepper

2 teaspoons extra-virgin olive oil

2 ounces prosciutto, sliced tissue-thin

Fresh flat-leaf parsley leaves, for garnish

I love sunchokes (which are also called Jerusalem artichokes) and will look for any excuse to use them. Here sunchokes are incorporated into a creamy, cool panna cotta that showcases their sweet, earthy flavor. At the restaurant, we serve this amuse-bouche with La Quercia's "prosciutto piccante"; a spicy ham that lends a nice contrast. The sunchoke is only one of many vegetables that you could use to make an amuse-bouche panna cotta. You can substitute an equivalent amount (by weight) of cauliflower, carrot, broccoli, parsnip, turnip, or beet, just to name a few options. To get the proper consistency for savory panna cotta, we generally use 4 to 5 teaspoons of powdered gelatin per 4 cups liquid.

---

Coat the inside of an 8-inch square (2-quart) pan with nonstick cooking spray.

Bring a large pot of water to a boil and blanch the sunchokes for 2 minutes, or until fork-tender (see the User Manual, page xxiv). Drain.

Pour the vegetable stock into a medium saucepan. Sprinkle the powdered gelatin evenly over the stock and let it sit for 5 minutes to bloom.

Bring the stock to a simmer over medium heat to dissolve the gelatin. Add the sunchokes and cream and bring the mixture back to a simmer. Cook for 1 minute. Remove from the heat and carefully transfer the contents to a blender. Puree the ingredients until smooth.

Add the lemon juice and season the panna cotta base with salt and pepper. Continue blending the panna cotta base, while adjusting the seasoning, until it suits your taste. Strain the base through a fine-mesh sieve, and discard the solids.

Pour the strained base into the prepared pan. Set the pan on a level shelf in the refrigerator and chill the panna cotta for at least 4 hours. Once the panna cotta has set, cover it tightly with plastic wrap if not using right away. The panna cotta can be made 1 day ahead.

At the restaurant, we punch out little cylinders of panna cotta with a thimble-size cutter and serve them on spoons with a drizzle of extra-virgin olive oil and a sliver of prosciutto and a parsley leaf as a garnish. If you don't have a mini-cutter, you can simply cut the panna cotta into tiny cubes with a thin-bladed knife.

## the sunchoke

Sunchokes are the knobby tubers of the sunflower plant, whose showerhead blossoms have been adopted as the state flower of my home state of Kansas. Available in either the fall or early spring, sunchokes (also known as Jerusalem artichokes) are especially sweet after they've wintered over.

While the panna cotta doesn't have to be served straight from the fridge, it will soften as it warms, making it harder to handle. For the best results, cut the panna cotta and arrange it on plates while it's cold and then let it come to room temperature slightly before serving.

# fiddleheads, burrata, arrope, olive oil

**Serves 4**

4 ounces fiddlehead ferns

2 ounces fennel bulb, trimmed and thinly shaved

1 pound *burrata* cheese, preferably 4 (4-ounce) rounds

4 teaspoons arrope, saba, or aged balsamic vinegar

¼ cup extra-virgin olive oil

Salt

1 tablespoon Sherry Vinaigrette (page 254)

Freshly ground black pepper

Shea Gallante, chef of Ciano in New York City, introduced me to *burrata* at a dinner shortly after we were both named Best New Chefs by *Food & Wine* magazine. I was immediately seduced by the milky freshness of its delicate curd, which is softer than mozzarella and only slightly firmer than softened butter.

There's not much technique to this dish. If you can blanch vegetables, you can make this simple but exquisite spring salad. If you can't find arrope, which is a Spanish sweet grape must syrup, use the finest saba or aged balsamic vinegar you can find. Fiddlehead ferns won't be easy to track down either. If they're unavailable in your area, you can substitute any fleshy green vegetable, like fava beans or asparagus (see page 12 for how to cook favas).

*Burrata*, which is a "purse" of mozzarella cheese stuffed with curds and cream, is highly perishable. Try to get *burrata* in individual, 4-ounce balls. If you can find only 1-pound or 8-ounce purses, make sure you divide them evenly so that each diner gets a bit of the precious insides. If you can't find *burrata*, fresh mozzarella is a good substitute.

---

Bring a large pot of heavily salted water to a rolling boil. While the water is heating, prepare an ice bath (see the User Manual, page xxv). Blanch the fiddlehead ferns and shaved fennel for 45 seconds (for blanching instructions, see the User Manual, page xxiv). Transfer the blanched fiddleheads to the ice bath and let them cool for a couple of minutes. Drain.

Divide the cheese among 4 plates or bowls. Drizzle a teaspoon of arrope and 1 tablespoon of the olive oil over each portion of cheese and season the cheese with salt.

Toss the fiddlehead ferns and fennel with the vinaigrette. Season them with salt and pepper to taste. You may either top the cheese with this salad or serve it on the side. Serve immediately.

# fava bean, asparagus, whipped chèvre, blis elixir

**Serves 4**

2 cups fava beans

8 asparagus stalks, trimmed, peeled, sliced into ¼-inch pieces (about the same size as the fava beans)

¼ cup plus 1 tablespoon Champagne Vinaigrette (page 253)

Salt and freshly ground black pepper

4 ounces cream cheese, softened

4 ounces chèvre

1 teaspoon Blis Elixir (you can also use saba or reduced balsamic vinegar; see box)

4 teaspoons extra-virgin olive oil

Coarsely ground black pepper, for serving

One of the most memorable dishes I've had was a bowl of freshly hulled and lightly dressed fava beans. As a chef, I appreciated how much work went into making that dish. As simple as it was, it was extravagant, and it inspired me to make my own version for Bluestem.

During the spring, my staff and I are constantly hulling favas. It's a mindless task that is made much more enjoyable by a round of beer.

Hulling fava beans for the first time will require a bit of patience. If you've ever encountered freshly hulled favas, then you know that the silky, almost custard-like treasure within is well worth the trouble. As with all things, practice makes perfect.

---

Bring a large pot of heavily salted water to a rolling boil. While the water is heating, prepare an ice bath (see the User Manual, page xxv). Blanch the fava beans in the boiling water for 3 minutes. Drain. Blanch the asparagus in the boiling water for 1 minute (see the User Manual, page xxiv). Drain. Hull the fava beans by popping the "cap" off the bean by either pinching or pushing it back with your thumbnail (you will see a dark mark on one end of the bean). Gently, with the tips of your forefinger and thumb, squeeze the bean from the other end. The silky halves of the bean should slip out of the hull. If the bean does not come out separated, gently split it with your fingers.

In a small bowl, toss together the fava beans, asparagus, and vinaigrette. Season with salt and pepper to taste. The mixture can be made 1 day ahead and refrigerated. Bring to room temperature before serving.

In the bowl of a stand mixer fitted with a paddle attachment, beat the cream cheese and chèvre on medium speed, scraping down the bowl once, until the cheeses become light and fluffy. Scrape the bowl once more and season with salt and pepper to taste. Mix for an additional 30 seconds to incorporate the seasoning. Transfer the cheese to a bowl, cover, and keep chilled until you are ready to use. The cheese mixture can be made 1 day ahead and refrigerated. Bring to room temperature before serving.

To serve, divide the whipped chèvre equally among 4 plates by spooning it into a neat, circular mound in the center of each plate. Using the back of the spoon, dent the middle of the mound to form a crater deep enough to hold at least 1½ teaspoons of liquid. Pour ¼ teaspoon of the Blis Elixir into the crater, followed by 1 teaspoon of olive oil. Divide and arrange the dressed favas and asparagus around the cheese mixture, banking them against the cheese in a ring. Season the plate with coarsely ground black pepper. Serve immediately.

At Bluestem, we use Blis Elixir (see Sources, page 272) because of its complex flavor. This sherry vinegar is aged in bourbon casks that have also been used for aging maple syrup. But it is expensive. If you can't use Blis, I recommend using a high-quality saba instead. Saba, also known as *mosto cotto* ("cooked grape juice"), is a syrup made from the must of trebbiano grapes. It has a rich, caramelized, raisin-like sweetness to it. You can create something similar by reducing ¼ cup balsamic vinegar by one-third in a small saucepan over medium-low heat. Cool the reduced balsamic vinegar before using it in the recipe.

# oysters, **spring onion** mignonette

**Serves 4**

**spring onion mignonette**

2 scallions, white parts finely minced and green parts shredded into chiffonade

⅔ cup red wine vinegar, preferably made from Garnacha wine

Salt and freshly ground black pepper

Crushed ice or coarse sea salt, for serving

24 oysters, shucked and picked over for shell fragments

Chef Patrick Webber introduced me to the beauty and simplicity of oysters and mignonette when I worked at the Stolen Grill. For the mignonette, he used cider vinegar, giving the French sauce, traditionally made with wine vinegar, a distinctly Midwestern twist.

At Bluestem, I use Spanish red wine vinegar made from Garnacha wine for the base of the sauce. A beautiful blush color with a hint of copper, this vinegar has a slightly smoother, fruitier flavor than other red wine vinegars. Minced stalks of first-harvest scallions give the mignonette a fresh, springtime flavor.

Although oysters are available year-round, it is best to consume them out of spawning season, when the ocean water is cooler (early spring). Serve them on a bed of crushed ice or coarse sea salt slightly dampened with water.

**Make the mignonette:** Stir together the minced scallion white stalks and the red wine vinegar. Season the mignonette with salt and pepper to taste.

**To serve:** Mound the crushed ice (or coarse salt dampened with a few drops of water) onto individual plates or a large platter. Arrange the oysters on the half shell on the ice. Serve the mignonette on the side with the green scallion chiffonade as garnish, and serve immediately.

# hamachi, black radish, celery

**Serves 4**

**hamachi**

2 tablespoons coriander seeds, crushed

1 teaspoon togarashi (Japanese seven-spice blend)

2 teaspoons paprika

1 teaspoon mustard seeds, crushed

¼ teaspoon ground dried chile

1 teaspoon sea salt

¼ teaspoon freshly ground black pepper

8 ounces sushi-grade hamachi, cut into 4 (2-ounce) pieces

2 tablespoons peanut oil

**salad**

Juice of ½ lime

1 tablespoon olive oil

Sea salt and freshly ground white pepper

4 black radishes, thinly shaved

2 celery hearts, thinly sliced

I love raw fish and all of the clean, refreshing, and bright flavors that go well with it. I especially like it paired with the flavors and ingredients of Asia, which I incorporate in this dish.

This recipe showcases a variety of heat levels—chile-spiked togarashi, the warmth of ginger, and the bite of spicy radish—all of which is countered with a cool splash of lime. You can also substitute red radishes.

You'll likely have to work with your fishmonger to get hamachi, also known as Japanese amberjack or yellowtail. Insist on the best-quality raw fish that he or she can find. If you can't find hamachi, any light-colored fish will work, such as fluke.

---

**Make the hamachi:** Combine the coriander, togarashi, paprika, mustard seeds, ground chile, salt, and pepper in a small bowl. Rub the spices all over the pieces of fish to coat well.

Heat the oil in a small skillet over high heat. When the oil begins to shimmer, sear the fish for 5 seconds on each side.

Using a very sharp knife, slice the fish against the grain into ⅛-inch-thick slices.

**Make the salad:** Whisk together the lime juice, olive oil, and salt and pepper to taste in a small bowl. Toss the shaved radishes and celery in the dressing to coat.

**To serve:** Divide the slices of fish among 4 plates. Garnish the plates with the salad. Serve immediately.

# beef tartare, giardiniera, black olive caramel

**Serves 4**

12 ounces boneless beef, preferably top round

3 tablespoons Dijon Vinaigrette (recipe follows)

Black Olive Caramel (recipe follows)

Giardiniera (recipe follows)

This dish is so popular that it has become a permanent fixture on the Bluestem menu.

Because you are serving this beef raw, you will want to make sure to use the freshest beef you can find. Using high-quality beef, such as meat from an American Wagyu or Piedmontese breed, both of which we have used in our restaurant, is also essential. For the ideal texture, I recommend using top round. You can also use the rib eye or strip sirloin for this tartare, but stay away from the tenderloin, which is too soft.

It is important not to grind the meat. Chopping the meat by hand will give the tartare the ideal meaty yet tender texture.

Slice the beef into 1/16-inch-thick (or as thin as possible) pieces. Slice the pieces into 1/16-inch-wide strips and the strips into uniformly sized cubes. Toss the diced beef with the vinaigrette.

Using a 2-inch ring mold, form the tartare into individual cylinder-shaped cakes by filling the ring mold with the beef directly on each plate.

Drizzle some black olive caramel across each plate and garnish each dish with some giardiniera.

## dijon vinaigrette  Makes ¾ cup

I've probably made this vinaigrette more often than any other recipe. When I worked at the Stolen Grill in Kansas City, chef Patrick Webber wouldn't allow us to make this dressing ahead of time. We had to whisk it to order. At Bluestem, we make it in large batches because we use so much of it. Sorry, Chef Pat; we're cheating.

½ cup Dijon mustard

2 tablespoons honey

½ teaspoon Tabasco sauce

1 tablespoon plus 1 teaspoon truffle oil

1 tablespoon Worcestershire sauce

1 tablespoon sherry vinegar

Whisk all the ingredients together in a small bowl. This vinaigrette will keep in an airtight container in the refrigerator for up to 1 month.

## black olive caramel  Makes 1½ cups

This thick sauce, a unique contrast of sweet and savory, is an especially wonderful condiment for cured meat and cheeses. At the restaurant, as here, we serve it with our steak tartare. It's pretty strong, so you won't need much.

1 cup sugar

¼ cup plus 1 tablespoon red wine

2 cups pitted kalamata olives

Heat the sugar in a small saucepan over medium heat until it dissolves. Continue to cook the sugar until it begins to caramelize and turn amber. Watch it carefully at this stage. When it becomes light brown, carefully whisk in the red wine. The mixture will spatter and bubble vigorously. Once the red wine is thoroughly incorporated, remove the caramel from the heat and let it cool slightly.

While the caramel mixture is still hot and fluid, pour it into a blender and add the olives. With one hand, hold a kitchen towel firmly over the lid of the blender to protect yourself in case the hot mixture comes out of the blender. This shouldn't happen if you hold the lid down firmly. Blend on high speed until the mixture becomes smooth.

Pour the caramel through a fine-mesh sieve to strain out the olive pulp. Transfer the caramel to an airtight container. Let the mixture cool before covering it and storing it in the refrigerator, where it will keep for up to 1 month. Let the caramel come to room temperature before using it.

# *giardiniera*  Makes about 1 quart

This isn't a true giardiniera, as the vegetables are dressed with vinaigrette rather than pickled. While you could blanch and store all of these vegetables together, at the restaurant we blanch and store them separately.

---

1 cup small cauliflower florets

1 cup small broccoli florets

1 small carrot, peeled and finely diced

6 pearl onions

¼ cup Sherry Vinaigrette (page 254)

Bring a large pot of heavily salted water to a rolling boil. While the water is heating, prepare an ice bath (see the User Manual, page xxv).

Blanch the cauliflower and broccoli in the boiling water for 1½ minutes and the carrot and onions for 2 minutes (see the User Manual, page xxiv).

Cool the vegetables in the ice bath. Drain and pat dry. Dress the vegetables with the vinaigrette and serve.

If you are not using the vegetables immediately, store them separately in airtight containers in the refrigerator for up to 2 days. When you are ready to use them, toss the vegetables together with the vinaigrette and let them come to room temperature before serving.

# asparagus soup, white beans, bottarga, marjoram

**Serves 4**

1 pound asparagus stalks, trimmed, tips cut off and separated

4 cups Vegetable Stock, chilled (page 255)

1 bunch fresh flat-leaf parsley

Salt and freshly ground white pepper

1 tablespoon unsalted butter (optional)

1 batch White Beans (page 261)

Fresh marjoram leaves, for garnish

4 teaspoons shaved *bottarga*, for garnish

Asparagus is abundant in the spring. The tender shoots are so wonderful by themselves—lightly cooked, steamed, or grilled—that it's hard to justify doing anything else with them. But this velvety soup is a simple and comforting alternative. On a warm spring day, you can serve it chilled with nothing more than a few croutons and a dollop of crème fraîche (for homemade, see page 251). At the restaurant, we serve it warm with white beans and a blanket of freshly shaved *bottarga*, the cured roe of tuna (or sometimes mullet), which releases a savory, briny scent as it melts into the soup. If you can't find bottarga, a couple of thinly shaved slices of prosciutto to top each serving will give the soup a similarly salty kick.

Bring a large pot of heavily salted water to a rolling boil. While the water is heating, prepare a large ice bath (see the User Manual, page xxv). Blanch the asparagus stalks and tips for 2 minutes and cool them in the ice bath. Drain well.

Combine the asparagus stalks, stock, and parsley in a blender and puree until smooth. Strain the soup through a fine-mesh sieve to remove the solids. If you aren't serving the soup right away, cover and chill for up to 1 day.

If you've chilled the soup, reheat it in a saucepan over medium heat. Season it with salt and pepper to taste. To get a richer texture, whisk in the butter, beating vigorously until it has completely been absorbed into the soup.

Divide the white beans and asparagus tips among 4 soup bowls and garnish them with the marjoram. Pour the soup over each portion of the beans. Grate the *bottarga* over the soup with a Microplane zester and serve immediately.

# pea soup, preserved lemon, crème fraîche

**Serves 4**

4½ cups fresh English peas, shelled, blanched for 1 minute (see the User Manual, page xxiv), and chilled

4 cups Vegetable Stock, chilled (page 255)

1 bunch fresh flat-leaf parsley

Salt and freshly ground white pepper

1 tablespoon unsalted butter (optional)

Crème Fraîche, whipped (page 251)

1 tablespoon preserved lemon, finely chopped (page 263)

1 tablespoon freshly crushed pink peppercorns

Orange powder (page 263)

You'll know that spring has officially arrived when this velvety soup appears at Bluestem. I put it on the menu as soon as fresh English peas become available. The soup bursts with the grassy, sweet flavors of the season. It gets a hit of tanginess from whipped crème fraîche and tart preserved lemons, and orange powder adds a bright, fragrant note. Although it's served warm at the restaurant, on a warm spring day I'll make this soup at home and serve it chilled, with a glass of white wine. If you do this, remember to taste and season it just before serving.

Diners at the restaurant often ask how the soup maintains its vibrant, green color. The trick: All of the ingredients are blended together while they are cold, and the soup is kept chilled until it is ready to be served. It is not seasoned or warmed until the very last minute.

At Bluestem, all soups and sauces are poured tableside to give our guests an interactive experience. This allows the diner to see the other ingredients before the liquid is added. It also ensures that the soup makes it to the table without sloshing around and staining the sides of the bowl.

Although fresh peas are preferable, frozen peas are an alternative. You do not need to blanch the frozen peas, but you will want to let them thaw and drain off any extra water.

Crush the pink peppercorns between two kitchen towels or in a tightly sealed plastic bag with a rolling pin. Or you can crush the peppercorns between your fingers or the palm of your hands.

In a blender, combine 4 cups of the peas, the vegetable stock, and the parsley. Blend on high speed until the ingredients become a smooth puree. Transfer the soup to an airtight container and refrigerate for up to 3 days.

When you are ready to serve, heat the soup over medium heat until it has warmed through (do not boil the soup, which will hasten its discoloration). Season with salt and pepper to taste. At the restaurant, we finish the soup by whisking in a touch of butter to give it a richer texture and flavor.

Place a dollop of whipped crème fraîche in the center of each of 4 soup bowls. Divide the remaining ½ cup peas and the preserved lemon among the bowls, arranging them around the crème fraîche. Sprinkle the crushed pink peppercorns and a pinch of orange powder over the top. Pour the warmed soup around the crème fraîche and over the other ingredients at the table.

# walu, wild arugula, black garlic

**Serves 4**

**black garlic aïoli**

1 head black garlic, cloves separated and peeled

1 egg yolk

¼ teaspoon salt

Pinch of freshly ground white pepper

Juice of 1 lemon

½ cup extra-virgin olive oil

**fish**

4 cups extra-virgin olive oil

4 (4-ounce) walu (also known as escolar),
   halibut, or cod fillets

**vinaigrette and salad**

2 tablespoons rice wine vinegar

⅛ teaspoon sugar

Juice of ½ lemon

½ cup extra-virgin olive oil

Salt and freshly ground white pepper

2 cups loosely packed arugula

2 tablespoons radish sprouts (optional)

Black garlic is garlic that has been fermented, rendering the cloves soft and sweet, tasting like a cross between burnt caramel and garlic. You can use black garlic as a condiment, as we do in this recipe to add a rich, earthy flavor to oil-poached walu, an especially fatty fish also known as escolar. Or you can use black garlic in any way that you would use oven-roasted garlic (see page 141), which is a good substitute if you can't find black garlic at your local market. (See the Sources section on page 272 for online purchasing information.)

---

**Make the aïoli:** Combine the black garlic, egg yolk, salt, pepper, and lemon juice in the bowl of a food processor. With the food processor running, slowly drizzle in the olive oil in a thin stream until the mixture emulsifies. It should have the consistency of mayonnaise.

**Cook the fish:** Heat the oil in a medium saucepan over low heat until it registers 128°F on an instant-read thermometer (the oil should be very warm to the touch, but you should be able to keep your finger in it without burning yourself). Lower the fish fillets into the oil.

Holding the temperature as steady as possible, let the fish poach for 10 to 15 minutes. The fish should turn slightly opaque and be just warmed through. Carefully, transfer the fish to a plate with a slotted spoon.

**Make the vinaigrette and salad:** Whisk together the vinegar, sugar, lemon juice, and oil. Season with salt and white pepper to taste.

Toss the arugula and sprouts with ¼ cup of the vinaigrette.

**To serve:** Smear a spoonful of the aïoli across each of 4 plates. Divide the fish among the plates and garnish with the dressed greens. Serve immediately.

# gnocchi, brown butter, nettles

**Serves 4**

2 pounds starchy potatoes, such as russet

2 large eggs

2 cups "00" flour, plus 1½ cups for dusting

1 tablespoon extra-virgin olive oil

6 tablespoons (¾ stick) unsalted butter

4 ounces nettle leaves (see the headnote on page 6)

Salt and freshly ground white pepper

I love the simplicity of gnocchi. They can be served year-round—with barely blistered tomatoes and fresh basil in the summer; with caramelized, meaty squashes in the fall; and with a hearty meat ragu in the wintertime. This version calls for little more than browning the gnocchi in a bit of brown butter. A fistful of nettles gives it a springtime feel.

Type "00" flour is a finely milled flour used primarily in Italian baking and pasta making. Look for it at an Italian market or check the Sources on page 272. Alternatively, you can substitute all-purpose flour.

---

Bring a large stockpot of heavily salted water to a rolling boil. Drop the potatoes in and let them boil for 35 to 40 minutes, until they are fork tender. Drain the potatoes and let them cool. Peel and discard the skins. Process the potatoes through a ricer or a food mill.

Mound the riced potatoes onto a floured work surface. Make a well in the center of the potatoes and drop in the eggs. Gently knead the potatoes and eggs together while incorporating the 2 cups of flour. Knead until just combined.

Lightly flour the work surface again. Divide the dough in half. Cover one piece of dough with plastic wrap or a damp towel. Roll the other piece of dough into a rope about ½ inch in diameter. Cut the rope into ¾-inch-long pieces. Toss the gnocchi with some flour to lightly dust them. Make a second batch of gnocchi by repeating this process with the remaining half of the dough.

Line a baking pan or large plate with a kitchen towel.

Bring a large stockpot of salted water to a rolling boil. Drop the gnocchi in a few at a time, making sure you don't crowd the pot so the gnocchi don't stick to each other. Let the gnocchi cook until they float to the top, about 3 minutes. Using a slotted spoon or spider skimmer, transfer them to the lined pan and gently pat dry with a towel.

In a large sauté pan, heat the oil over medium-high heat. Carefully add the gnocchi to the hot pan (if they are too wet, the water from the gnocchi will cause the oil to splatter). Shaking the pan to keep the gnocchi rolling, toast the gnocchi for about 1 minute. Add the butter, swirling it around until it melts. Add the nettles and continue to swirl the pan until the butter becomes toasty and brown and the gnocchi have developed a golden crust. Season with salt and pepper to taste.

Divide the gnocchi among 4 bowls and serve immediately.

# bucatini, "oysters and mussels"

**Serves 4**

10 ounces bucatini or spaghetti

1 tablespoon unsalted butter

4 ounces oyster mushrooms, trimmed

Salt and freshly cracked white pepper

2 shallots, chopped

4 cloves garlic, minced

1 teaspoon saffron

1½ cups white wine

1 pound mussels, cleaned and debearded

Chopped fresh chives or chervil, for garnish

I love the flavors of shellfish, saffron, and white wine, and this simple pasta dish showcases them together. The "oysters" in this dish are actually oyster mushrooms, whose round, lobed shape vaguely resembles their bivalve counterpart.

Make sure that your mussels are fresh. They should smell like a clean beach. Toss out any mussels that are chipped, cracked, or don't close when you gently tap them against the counter. To keep your mussels fresh, take them out of the bag and put them into a bowl. Cover with a damp kitchen towel and ice cubes and put them in the refrigerator. Stored this way, they should keep for up to 3 days.

---

Bring a large stockpot of heavily salted water to a rolling boil. While the water is heating, prepare a large ice bath (see the User Manual, page xxv).

Cook the pasta in the stockpot according to the package directions. Drain the pasta and drop it into the ice bath. Let the pasta cool in the bath for 2 minutes, then drain well and set aside.

Heat the butter in a large sauté pan. When the butter is melted and frothy, add the mushrooms. Season with salt and pepper. Sauté the mushrooms until they have softened, about 2 minutes. Transfer the mushrooms to a plate lined with paper towels to drain.

In a large bowl, combine the shallots, garlic, saffron, wine, and mussels.

Heat a large sauté pan with a tight-fitting lid over high heat. When the pan is extremely hot, carefully dump the contents of the bowl into the pan and cover immediately. Steam the mussels until they just start to open, about 2 minutes. As soon as they have opened, remove the pan from the heat and add the cooked pasta and mushrooms. Toss everything together, allowing the pasta to heat through and absorb some of the cooking liquid. Pick out any of the mussels that have not opened and discard them. Season with salt and pepper to taste.

Divide the pasta, mussels, and mushrooms among 4 large pasta bowls. Garnish with chives and serve immediately.

# walleye, snow peas, white asparagus, kumquat

**Serves 4**

**kumquat sauce**

1 tablespoon vegetable oil

½ cup chopped fennel bulb

1 clove garlic, chopped

¾ cup kumquats, stemmed and sliced

2 tablespoons dry white wine

1 tablespoon mirin

1¼ cups Fish Stock (page 255)

Salt and freshly ground white pepper

1 teaspoon unsalted butter

**vegetables**

20 white asparagus stalks, trimmed and peeled

2 cups snow peas, strings removed

1 cup kumquats, stemmed and halved lengthwise

1 tablespoon unsalted butter

**fish**

4 (6-ounce) walleye fillets

Salt and freshly ground white pepper

2 tablespoons vegetable oil

Freshwater fish has gotten a bad reputation in the Midwest because of poor-quality fish and farmed fish, which can have a muddy flavor. Diners in this part of the country tend to avoid freshwater fish, and therefore, so do chefs.

But good-quality, clean-tasting freshwater fish can be found. When I'm able to get good ones, I put trout and walleye on the menu. These two Midwestern fish are not only delicate and light, but also have skin that's perfect for crisping in a hot frying pan.

Here, unlikely accompaniments—snow peas, white asparagus, and kumquats—all come together to form a light and refreshing supporting cast. Kumquats look like miniature oranges. The interior is very tart, but the skin is strangely sweet—eat or use whole.

---

**Make the sauce:** Heat the oil in a medium-size pot over medium-high heat. Add the fennel and garlic and sauté for 2 minutes. Add the kumquats, wine, and mirin and bring the mixture to a simmer. Cook the sauce until reduced by half, about 6 minutes. Add the stock and return the sauce to a simmer. Reduce the heat to medium and cook for another 3 minutes.

Transfer the sauce to a blender, season with salt and pepper to taste, and blend until smooth. Strain the sauce through a fine-mesh sieve to remove the solids.

Clean the blender and return the sauce to it. Add the butter and puree until smooth.

**Make the vegetables:** Bring a large pot of heavily salted water to a rolling boil. While the water is heating, prepare an ice bath (see the User Manual, page xxv). Blanch the asparagus and snow peas in the boiling water for 2 minutes (see the User Manual, page xxiv).

Transfer the vegetables to the ice bath to cool. Drain.

Slice the snow peas on the bias, discarding the fibrous ends. Slice the asparagus stalks on the bias to about the same size as the snow peas.

Halve the kumquats and, as best as you can, remove the seeds.

Heat the butter in a large sauté pan over medium-low heat. When the butter has melted, add the snow peas, asparagus, and kumquats and toss until they are coated with butter and warmed through. Remove from the heat.

**Cook the fish:** Preheat the oven to 400°F.

Season the fish fillets with salt and pepper. Heat the oil in an ovenproof sauté pan over high heat. Add the fish, skin side down, and cook for 1 minute. Transfer the fish to the oven and roast for 1 more minute.

**To serve:** Spoon some sauce onto the center of each of 4 plates. Top the sauce with the fish and divide the vegetables among the plates, arranging them around the fish. Serve immediately.

# tuna, artichokes, white beans, lemon broth, bottarga

**Serves 4**

2 cups White Beans (page 261)

4 artichoke hearts, cut into ½-inch slices

Sweet and Sour Pearl Onions (recipe follows)

¼ cup Whipped Butter (page 251)

Salt and freshly ground white pepper

2 cups Lemon Broth (recipe follows)

4 (6-ounce) tuna fillets

2 tablespoons canola oil

4 teaspoons *bottarga*, for garnish

Here, lemon and artichokes bring a sunny smile to meaty tuna and the briny punch of *bottarga*, which is cured fish roe from tuna or mullet. This dish is particularly great for dinner parties, as almost everything can be made a day or two ahead. Only the whipped butter and fish need to be made right before serving, so if you have all of the other accompaniments already prepared, the finished dish will come together very quickly.

Heat the beans, artichokes, pearl onions, and whipped butter together in a shallow saucepan over medium heat until the vegetables are warmed through. Season with salt and pepper to taste.

Reheat the lemon broth in a saucepan over medium-high heat. Transfer the broth to a heat-resistant container, such as a small pitcher. Keep warm. Season the fish with salt and pepper.

Heat the oil over high heat in a large sauté pan. Sear the fish for 30 seconds per side, or until golden brown. Transfer to a plate lined with paper towels.

Evenly divide the vegetable mixture among 4 shallow bowls. Slice each fish fillet in half—to show off the rosy interior of the fish—and divide the pieces among the plates, arranging the fish atop the vegetables. Grate the *bottarga* over each dish with a Microplane zester. Pour ¼ cup of lemon broth around the vegetables in each bowl either just before serving or at the table.

## sweet and sour pearl onions   Makes 16 pearl onions

1½ cups sherry vinegar

¾ cup sugar

16 pearl onions, peeled

Bring the vinegar, sugar, and onions to a simmer in a small saucepan over medium heat. Cook until the liquid has turned into a thick glaze and the onions have softened, about 5 minutes.

## lemon broth   Makes about 4 cups

2 tablespoons vegetable oil

4 shallots, thinly sliced

3 cloves garlic, chopped

2 cups white wine

2 teaspoons sugar

¼ cup packed lemon verbena leaves

4 sprigs fresh lemon thyme

4 lemons

4 cups Vegetable Stock (page 255)

Salt and freshly ground white pepper

Heat the oil in a sauté pan over medium-high heat. Add the shallots and garlic and cook until softened, about 1 minute. Add the white wine, sugar, lemon verbena, and lemon thyme and cook for 1 minute more.

Peel the lemons (removing the white pith as well) and add the flesh to the wine and sugar. Simmer until the mixture is reduced by half. Add the stock and simmer for 20 minutes. Strain the broth and discard the solids. Season with salt and pepper to taste. Transfer the broth to an airtight container and keep refrigerated until ready to use.

# scallop, red miso–braised berkshire bacon, bok choy, soy caramel

**Serves 4**

16 dry-pack sea scallops, preferably U-10s

Salt and freshly ground white pepper

¼ cup extra-virgin olive oil

8 tablespoons (1 stick) unsalted butter

12 sprigs fresh thyme

¼ cup Soy Caramel (recipe follows)

4 (2-ounce) slices Braised Berkshire Bacon
(recipe follows)

This dish is a teeter-totter between sweet and salty flavors: The natural sweetness of the scallops is countered by the savory smokiness of the bacon; sugar and soy sauce combine to make the soy caramel; and the alluringly sweet yet meaty flavor of red miso echoes the rest. The back-and-forth tug of flavors is addictive.

Assuming you can't get fresh scallops in their shells, it is best to use "dry-pack" scallops, which, unlike "wet-pack" scallops, have not been soaked in phosphates, a preservative that causes the scallops to bloat with water. Not only will you be paying more by weight for waterlogged scallops, but the liquid in wet-pack scallops also leaches when you cook them, causing them to steam or boil and preventing them from developing a nice crust. The water loss during cooking also causes them to shrink dismayingly.

Pat the scallops dry with a paper towel and season them with salt and pepper.

Heat the oil in a large sauté pan over high heat.

Working in two or more batches, place the scallops in the hot oil. Do not crowd the pan, as they will steam and not develop a good crust.

Let the scallops cook, untouched, for 2 minutes, or until a golden brown crust has formed. Using a fish spatula or large spoon, turn the scallops over. Turn off the heat and add the butter and thyme. Tipping the pan slightly so the butter collects on one end, carefully spoon the hot butter over the scallops, basting them for 1 minute. Transfer the scallops to paper towels to drain and rest. Repeat until all the scallops are cooked.

To serve, drizzle (or paint with a pastry brush) the soy caramel across the middle of each of 4 plates. Divide the scallops and sliced bacon evenly among the plates, placing them on top of and around the caramel. Serve immediately.

### *soy caramel*  Makes about ½ cup

½ cup sugar

½ cup soy sauce

Bring the sugar and soy sauce to a simmer in a small saucepan over medium heat. Continue to cook until the mixture thickens into a dark syrup, about 10 minutes. Remove from the heat and set aside to cool for 10 minutes before transferring it to a nonreactive container with a tight-fitting lid.

Extra caramel can be kept for up to 1 month. Bring the caramel to room temperature before using.

## "u" is for "under"

In this recipe, we recommend using U-10 scallops. "U" is an industry weight standard that stands for "under" per pound with regard to scallops and shrimp. Thus, "U-10" means that there should be 10 or fewer scallops or shrimp to the pound, or the individual scallops or shrimp should weigh about 1.6 ounces.

## *braised berkshire bacon*  Makes 8 ounces

Miso is a salty paste made from fermented grains or soybeans that is used primarily as a seasoning in Japanese and Chinese food. Miso ranges in color from light to dark. Generally, the saltiness and the flavor intensify as the color of the miso gets darker. The amount of miso used in this recipe may seem like a lot, but it is diluted by stock, tempered by the sugar and vegetables.

For this recipe, you'll want to ask your butcher for a block of smoked pork belly or slab bacon. Regular sliced bacon will not work.

---

8 ounces smoked pork belly or slab bacon

1 tablespoon olive oil

½ cup peeled and chopped fresh ginger

2 shallots, chopped

3 cloves garlic, chopped

¼ cup packed light brown sugar

½ cup red miso

3 cups Chicken Stock (page 256)

½ cup soy sauce

1 bay leaf

Preheat the oven to 250°F.

Score the skin side of the bacon with crosshatch marks.

Heat a large skillet over medium-high heat. When the pan is hot, brown the bacon on all sides, about 2 minutes per side.

Heat the oil in a 5-quart Dutch oven over high heat. When the oil is hot, add the ginger and shallots and cook until they soften and the shallots begin to turn translucent, 2 to 3 minutes. Add the garlic and continue to cook for 1 minute. Stir in the brown sugar and red miso and cook until it has fully dissolved.

Add the stock, soy sauce, and bay leaf and bring the mixture to a simmer. Add the bacon and cover the baking dish with a tight-fitting lid or heavy-duty aluminum foil.

Braise the bacon in the Dutch oven for 2½ hours. Remove the pot from the oven and let cool for 15 minutes.

Remove the bacon and discard the rest. Cut the bacon into 4 equal portions.

# lamb, fava puree, olives, broccoli rabe

**Serves 4**

### fava puree

1 cup fava beans

1½ cups packed fresh flat-leaf parsley leaves

1¾ cups Vegetable Stock (page 255)

Salt and freshly ground white pepper

### vegetables

1 cup fava beans

2 cups assorted pitted olives

4 ounces broccoli rabe florets, blanched for 45 seconds

2 tablespoons Garlic Butter (page 253), melted

Leaves from 2 sprigs fresh oregano

Salt and freshly ground white pepper

### lamb

2 racks lamb rib chops, frenched and chine bone removed

Salt and freshly ground black pepper

2 tablespoons vegetable oil

Shortly before we finished this book, Megan and I cooked a dinner at Green Dirt Farm in Weston, Missouri (see page 42). We were given two lambs to feed thirty people. I naturally went for the rack, the row of ribs with an attached chop or cutlet of meat. The rack of lamb is an elegant cut when you french the rib bones, and the attached meat is incredibly tender. From that dinner sprang this simple recipe, which has the bold, rustic flavors of the Italian countryside and showcases two wonderful spring greens—favas and broccoli rabe (you may also see it sold as rapini).

Although modern animal husbandry makes it possible to have lamb year-round, traditionally (and naturally), lambs were born and slaughtered in the springtime. Following this seasonal rhythm, I like to serve lamb at the beginning of the warm months, when so many other young and tender foods are also at their best.

**Make the fava puree:** Bring a large pot of heavily salted water to a rolling boil. While the water is heating, prepare an ice bath (see the User Manual, page xxv). Blanch the fava beans for 1 minute (see the User Manual, page xxiv). Transfer the beans to the ice bath to cool. Drain, then remove the hulls (see the recipe on page 12). Blend the fava beans, parsley, and stock together in a blender until thick and smooth. Transfer the puree to a small pot and warm it over medium-low heat. Season the puree with salt and pepper to taste.

**Cook the vegetables:** Preheat the oven to 400°F. Blanch and hull the fava beans as directed for the puree. Toss the olives and broccoli rabe with the garlic butter and spread them out on a roasting pan. Scatter the fava beans and oregano over the olives and broccoli rabe and season everything with salt and pepper to taste. Roast the vegetables in the oven for 10 to 12 minutes, or until the broccoli rabe is tender.

**Cook the lamb:** Season the lamb racks with salt and pepper.

Heat the oil in a large skillet over high heat. When the oil begins to shimmer, turn the heat down to medium-high and sear one rack of lamb, fat side down first, for

1 minute on each side to brown. Remove the rack of lamb from the heat and set it on the roasting pan, on top of the vegetables. Repeat with the second rack of lamb. Roast the lamb in the oven for 16 minutes for a medium-rare interior. Remove the pan from the oven and let the meat rest for 5 minutes.

Slice the rack between the ribs to create individual rib chops.

**To serve:** Spoon some of the fava bean puree onto the center of each of 4 plates. Top each pool of bean puree with 4 rib chops. Divide the vegetables evenly among the plates, arranging them around the puree and meat. Serve immediately.

# veal rib cap, ramps, morels

**Serves 4**

### morel sauce

1 tablespoon grapeseed oil

1 clove garlic, chopped

1 shallot, chopped

2 cups morel mushrooms, trimmed and sliced

½ cup bourbon

¼ cup Southern Comfort

¾ cup Veal Jus (page 257)

¼ cup heavy cream

### ramps and morels

2 cups morel mushrooms, trimmed and sliced

About 16 ramps or scallions

1 large shallot, sliced into ½-inch rings

2 tablespoons Garlic Butter (page 253)

Salt and freshly ground white pepper

### veal

1½ pounds veal rib cap, rolled and trussed

Salt and freshly ground black pepper

2 tablespoons vegetable oil

Padded by layers of fat, the tender flap of meat that wraps around the outside of the rib eye is one of the most flavorful and tender pieces of real estate on the calf. Since you'll probably have to special-order this cut from your butcher, ask him or her to roll and truss it for you. If you can't get your hands on a rib cap, you may substitute a 1½-pound strip of pork tenderloin. Follow the instructions for preparing, searing, and roasting the rib cap, except extend the roasting time for the pork tenderloin to 10 to 12 minutes.

Like spring, everything about this dish is young and fleeting: the calf, the ramps, and especially the morels, which disappear just as quickly as they pop up. While morels can be found all over the United States, ramps grow almost exclusively along the Appalachian Mountains, from Canada down to the Carolinas. We order them from foragers. If you can't find ramps in your area, substitute scallions. At the restaurant, we usually clean mushrooms with a brush or a damp towel, but you'll want to thoroughly wash morels, as their pocketed caps harbor a lot of dirt and sand.

---

**Make the morel sauce:** Heat the oil in a large sauté pan over medium-high heat. Add the garlic and shallot and sweat them for about 1 minute. Turn the heat to medium and add the morels, tossing them with the garlic and shallot to sauté for about 30 seconds. Turn the heat to low. Standing back from the stove, carefully pour the bourbon and Southern Comfort over the mushrooms. Reduce the sauce over low heat to ¼ cup, which should take 7 to 8 minutes. Add the veal jus and cream and bring the sauce back to a simmer. Cook for another 2 minutes.

Carefully pour the sauce into a blender. With one towel-wrapped hand firmly held over the lid, puree the sauce until smooth. Strain the sauce through a fine-mesh sieve to remove any solids.

**Roast the ramps and shallot:** Preheat the oven to 400°F.

Toss the mushrooms, ramps, and shallot with the garlic butter. Spread the mixture out on a roasting pan, season with salt and pepper, and roast in the oven for 4 minutes.

**Cook the veal:** Keep the oven at 400°F. Season the veal rib cap with salt and pepper.

In a large sauté pan, heat the oil over high heat. When the oil begins to shimmer, turn the heat down to medium and add the rib cap. Brown the meat on all sides, including the ends, about 30 seconds per side. Transfer the meat to the oven and roast for 2 to 3 minutes for a medium-rare interior. Let the meat rest for 5 minutes.

**To serve:** Slice the veal rib cap. Divide the meat, mushrooms, shallots, and ramps among 4 plates. Spoon the morel sauce around the meat and serve immediately.

# hanger steak, chimichurri, smoked shallot marmalade, potato-parsnip rösti

**Serves 4**

### smoked shallot marmalade

4 cups sliced shallots (about 8 large shallots)

¼ cup balsamic vinegar

¼ cup red wine

Pinch of ground dried chile

1 tablespoon honey

¼ cup olive oil

### chimichurri

8 cloves garlic, peeled

1 shallot

2 tablespoons capers

¼ cup sherry vinegar

1 teaspoon salt

½ cup water

Leaves from 4 bunches fresh flat-leaf parsley

½ cup olive oil

### potato-parsnip rösti

1 tablespoon salt, plus more for seasoning

2 large russet potatoes, peeled and grated

1 large parsnip, peeled and grated

1 shallot, thinly sliced

2 tablespoons grainy mustard

1 tablespoon honey

Leaves from 2 sprigs fresh oregano

6 scallions, thinly sliced

¼ cup fresh bread crumbs

6 tablespoons Garlic Butter (page 253), or more as needed

### steak

3 whole hanger steaks (2 pounds), trimmed and cut in half

Salt and freshly ground black pepper

2 tablespoons vegetable oil

This is a slightly more refined version of a popular steak *frites* dish that we serve in our lounge. The bright, herby chimichurri sauce, a popular condiment for steak in South America, is the same, but here I add a smoked shallot marmalade and replace the fries with crunchy, golden rösti. You will need wood chips, preferably cherry or pecan, to make the marmalade.

Although it has been popular among Europeans for centuries (in France, it's known as *onglet*), the hanger steak has only recently become popular in the United States. So named because it "hangs" from the underside of the steer when split open, this loose-grained muscle, when cooked properly, is one of my favorite cuts of beef. A tougher cut of meat, it is best cooked quickly over high heat and served medium-rare.

**Make the shallot marmalade:** Preheat a grill or stovetop smoker. Soak the wood chips in water according to the directions on their package. Add them to the grill or smoker. Put the shallots in a grill pan and set the grill pan over the grill. Close the lid of the smoker and smoke the shallots for 5 minutes.

Put the smoked shallots, vinegar, wine, chile, honey, and oil in a saucepan and bring to a simmer over medium-high heat. Turn the heat down to low and reduce the mixture until almost dry (you should have about 2 tablespoons), 25 to 30 minutes.

**Make the chimichurri:** Put the garlic, shallot, capers, vinegar, salt, water, and parsley in a blender and pulse until coarsely chopped. With the blender running, drizzle in the olive oil and puree until a thick emulsion forms.

**Make the rösti:** Preheat the oven to 375°F.

Using your hands, rub the salt into the grated potatoes, parsnip, and shallot. Let the mixture sit for 10 minutes, stirring occasionally, to let the salt draw out the liquid from the vegetables. Drain the liquid and discard. Pat the rösti mixture with paper towels, drying the mixture as much as possible. Add the mustard, honey, oregano, scallions, and bread crumbs. Mix to combine.

Heat 4 tablespoons of the garlic butter in a 10-inch ovenproof skillet over medium-high heat, swirling the pan to coat the bottom of the skillet evenly with the butter. Spread the rösti mixture in the hot skillet, patting

it down to make a flat patty covering the bottom of the skillet evenly. The rösti will begin to give off steam as it cooks. Using a spatula, lift up a corner of the rösti to check the underside every few minutes. Cook until the bottom starts to turn golden, 10 to 12 minutes. The bottom of the rösti shouldn't stick to the skillet. If it does, add another tablespoon of garlic butter around the rim of the skillet and carefully loosen it from the sides with your spatula. Carefully flip the rösti over onto a plate. Return the skillet to the heat and add the remaining 2 tablespoons of garlic butter to the skillet, swirling to coat the pan as before. Carefully slide the rösti off the plate and back into the skillet so that the uncooked side is down. Transfer the skillet to the oven and roast until the bottom has crisped and turned golden brown, about 12 minutes. Flip the rösti back onto a plate or a cutting board and cut it into wedges or squares.

**Cook the steak:** Keep the oven at 375°F. Season the steaks with salt and pepper.

Heat the oil in a large ovenproof skillet over high heat. Sear the steaks on all sides until they are nicely browned, about 2 minutes per side. Transfer the steaks to the oven and roast them for 15 minutes for a medium-rare interior. Remove from the oven and let the meat rest for 5 minutes.

**To serve:** Cut the steaks across the grain into ¼- to ½-inch-thick slices. Divide the meat and rösti wedges among 4 plates. Serve with the chimichurri and smoked shallot marmalade.

# green dirt farm's "dirt lover" sheep's milk cheese, **sweet onion** marmalade

**Makes 2 cups marmalade**

2 tablespoons unsalted butter

1 pound spring onion bulbs, sliced ¼ inch thick (cippolini onions or shallots will also work)

2 cloves garlic, smashed

½ cup sugar

2 tablespoons honey

¼ cup sherry vinegar

1 teaspoon chopped fresh thyme

Pinch of dried red pepper flakes (optional)

Salt and freshly ground black pepper

Green Dirt Farm "Dirt Lover" cheese, or an ash-covered sheep's or goat's milk cheese, for serving

Lavosh, for serving (page 264)

The sweetness of this onion marmalade, punctuated with a dash of chile and freshly cracked pepper, makes it an especially delicious accompaniment to lighter-flavored goat's and sheep's milk cheeses. At Bluestem, I like to serve it with the "Dirt Lover," an ash-coated, bloomy-rind sheep's milk cheese made locally by Green Dirt Farm (see page 42). In the spring, this cheese is a bit firm and nutty, pairing beautifully with the savory aspect of the silky marmalade. Later in the year, the cheese starts to soften and turn creamy just under the ashen layer, which seems to bring out the sweetness in the onions. Typically at Bluestem, we serve 1 to 2 ounces of cheese per person with a spoonful of marmalade on the side.

Young spring onions often come with the green stems and shoots attached. For this recipe, you'll want to use only the white part of the onion (the bulb). In other seasons, you can substitute sliced white or yellow onions by weight. You may substitute toasted bread for the lavosh if you wish.

Heat the butter in a large sauté pan over medium heat. Add the onions and garlic and cook, stirring occasionally, until sweated, about 4 minutes. Lower the heat to medium-low and stir in the sugar, honey, and vinegar. Cook for 10 to 15 minutes, until the onions have softened and the liquid is reduced by two-thirds (there should be about ¼ cup liquid left). Stir in the thyme and red pepper flakes. Remove the pan from the heat and season the marmalade with salt and pepper to taste.

Allow the marmalade to cool completely. Remove and discard the 2 smashed garlic cloves. Serve the marmalade with the cheese and lavosh. Store any leftover marmalade in an airtight container for up to 2 weeks.

# green dirt farm

Some 30 miles northwest of Kansas City lies an idyllic stretch of rolling, green hills dotted with wool. It echoes with the gentle bleating of a furry flock of ewes tended by Sarah Hoffman and Jacqueline Smith. This is Green Dirt Farm, a small farm that raises all-natural, grass-fed sheep and produces artisanal, farmstead sheep's milk cheeses the same way that sheep farmers have for centuries.

If California has happy cows, Weston, Missouri, is home to happy sheep (especially the six rams, who "tag" all 60 ewes with amazing zeal and speed each spring). Free to range and graze as they please, the farm's lambs have a slightly richer, muskier flavor than you'll find in most commercially produced lambs. Sweet and lean, yet tender, this is how lamb should taste.

Each year during the lambing season, the farm's ewes double the size of the flock. Sarah and Jacqueline prune the flock over the course of the year, saving ewes with desirable traits for milking and mating and sending the rams and the rest of the young ewes to slaughter.

We've had the pleasure of cooking and eating Green Dirt's lamb on their farm at special dinner events, and we've offered it in our dining room. We use and offer their sheep's milk cheeses on our menu.

Having trained with cheese makers in France and having then developed and refined their craft over a ten-year trial period, the two women now produce amazing, artisanal sheep's milk cheeses, including a bloomy-rind, Camembert-style cheese called "Wooly Rind" and the ash-coated "Dirt Lover," which we pair with a spring onion marmalade (page 40) on our cheese plate. Perhaps our favorite, however, is their "Fresh" cheese, a milky, ricotta-like product that is extremely versatile, suitable as a mild, creamy accompaniment for salty (see the snap bean salad on page 70) and sweet dishes alike.

Sheep's milk cheese is not easy to produce. The margin for both error and yield is low. Unlike cows, who produce an average of 20 to 30 quarts of milk per day, ewes give only 1 quart a day. In addition, Sarah and Jacqueline don't milk their sheep year-round like many larger, more commercial sheep farms. Sticking to more natural animal husbandry techniques, they rotate the ewes according to their lambing schedule to obtain the best milk possible. This dedication to quality is evident in their cheeses, which brim with *terroir* from the sheeps' steady diet of legume-fortified clover and grass. We proudly serve them in our restaurant.

# carrot cake, walnut streusel, carrot-ginger ice

**Makes one 9-inch round or 8-inch square cake**

### walnut streusel

⅓ cup all-purpose flour

¼ cup granulated sugar

¼ cup packed light brown sugar

⅛ teaspoon salt

¼ teaspoon ground cinnamon

¼ teaspoon ground nutmeg

¾ cup walnuts, coarsely chopped (optional)

6 tablespoons (¾ stick) unsalted butter, chilled and cut into small cubes

### cake

1½ cups all-purpose flour

1 teaspoon baking powder

1½ teaspoons salt

¾ teaspoon ground cinnamon

¼ teaspoon ground allspice

¾ teaspoon ground ginger

¼ cup plus 2 tablespoons vegetable oil

3 large eggs

1½ cups granulated sugar

Finely grated zest of 1 orange

3 cups peeled and coarsely grated carrots

½ cup walnuts, finely chopped (optional)

¼ cup golden raisins (optional)

Whipped cream, for serving (optional)

Carrot-Ginger Ice, for serving (recipe follows)

I've never really cared for carrot cake because either the carrot flavor is not intense enough or it's all about the cream cheese frosting. But this version, which I got from Megan Romano, for whom I worked at Aureole at Mandalay Bay in Las Vegas, was a game-changer; it was the first carrot cake I really liked.

If you like carrot cake and coffee cake, you'll love this cake. The orange zest in it brings a bright dash of unexpected sunshine, so don't leave it out. Together with the grated carrot, the zest stains the cake with an intense shade of orange. At Bluestem, I add nuts to the streusel but not to the cake. Nut lovers might want to add them to both. And, although I think that adding raisins makes for a more well-rounded carrot cake experience, the raisins are optional as well.

At the restaurant, we bake these cakes in individual 3-inch molds. However, this recipe fits nicely in a 9-inch round or an 8-inch square baking pan. For a more professional presentation, trim the crusts off of a square cake and cut the cake into bars. You can also cut out individual rounds with a cookie cutter and save the trimmings to use as a topping for ice cream or yogurt.

**Make the walnut streusel:** In a large bowl or a food processor, combine the flour, sugars, salt, cinnamon, nutmeg, and walnuts. Pulse in the processor or use a pastry cutter to work the cubed butter into the dry ingredients until the mixture forms pea-size crumbles. Cover and refrigerate the streusel while you make the cake.

**Make the cake:** Preheat the oven to 350°F. Butter a 9-inch round or 8-inch square baking pan or spray with nonstick cooking spray.

In a small bowl, sift together the flour, baking powder, salt, cinnamon, allspice, and ginger.

In the bowl of a stand mixer fitted with a paddle attachment, mix the oil, eggs, sugar, and orange zest on medium speed until incorporated, about 2 minutes. Scrape the bowl and continue to mix on low speed. Add the dry ingredients in thirds, making sure that they are well incorporated after each addition. Fold in the grated carrots, walnuts, and raisins with a spatula, scraping the sides of the bowl as you go.

Transfer the batter to the prepared pan. Bake for 30 to 35 minutes. The cake should rise to form a dome on top and take on a slightly golden orange color. Remove from the oven, spread the top generously with the cold streusel, and return it to the oven to bake for 10 to 15 minutes more. Test the doneness by inserting a toothpick into the middle of the cake. The toothpick should come out moist but clean. Let the cake cool on a wire rack for 10 minutes. Remove the cake from the pan while it is still slightly warm, as it will be harder to get out once it cools completely.

Serve the cake with whipped cream and a glass of the carrot-ginger ice on the side (in either a large shot glass or a small parfait glass).

## *carrot-ginger ice* Makes 3 cups

At Bluestem, we serve this light and refreshing carrot-ginger granita in large shot glasses alongside the carrot cake as an alternative to ice cream or sorbet. However, if you want a simple, cool dessert on a warm spring day, serve this in a larger portion with nothing more than a sprig of mint.

¼ cup plus 2 tablespoons water

3 tablespoons sugar

1 cinnamon stick

1 star anise

Pinch of freshly grated nutmeg

1 teaspoon peeled and grated fresh ginger

½ cup carrot juice (see Note)

Combine the water, sugar, cinnamon stick, star anise, nutmeg, and ginger in a small saucepan. Bring the mixture to a boil to dissolve the sugar. Remove from the heat and let cool completely, allowing the spices to infuse the syrup.

Strain the syrup through a fine-mesh sieve and discard the spices. Add the carrot juice and mix well. Pour the mixture into a shallow pan (preferably a metal one) and freeze overnight.

Place the serving glasses in the freezer.

When the mixture has fully frozen, take the pan out of the freezer. Working quickly, scrape the frozen mixture with the tines of a fork to produce icy flakes. If the ice begins to melt, stick the pan back in the freezer for 5 minutes. You may have to refreeze the carrot ice a few times before you get the entire batch scraped.

Spoon the shaved ice into the chilled glasses and serve immediately.

Scraped, the ice will keep in the freezer, tightly covered, for up to 1 week. Depending on how far in advance you scrape the ice, you may have to refluff the ice with a fork, as it tends to condense and solidify with time.

**NOTE:** If you are juicing your own carrots, be sure to peel the carrots. Doing so yields a sweeter and cleaner-tasting juice.

# chocolate **pudding cake**, fresh mint ice cream, chocolate sauce

**Makes 4 individual 4-ounce cakes**

3 tablespoons unsalted butter, softened and cut into ½-inch cubes, plus more for greasing the ramekins

½ cup sugar, plus about ½ cup for coating the ramekins

8 ounces bittersweet chocolate, finely chopped

4 ounces unsweetened chocolate, finely chopped

¾ cup plus 2 tablespoons water

1½ teaspoons vanilla extract

5 large eggs, lightly beaten

Chocolate Sauce (page 268), warm

Fresh Mint Ice Cream (recipe follows)

Fresh mint leaves, for garnish

This is a chocolate-lover's chocolate dessert. It is simple to make, and the result is stunning. Chocolate and mint, one of my favorite couples, complement a fresh, breezy spring day well. This cake has the texture of a warm baked pudding and is best served as soon as it has cooled enough to unmold. This recipe contains no flour, so it is a great option for our restaurant's guests (and yours) who are on a gluten-restricted diet.

**Prepare the ramekins:** Preheat the oven to 350°F. Butter four 4-ounce ovenproof ramekins. Pour some sugar into one ramekin and roll it around, making sure that the buttered surface is coated with sugar. Tap the sugar out into another ramekin. Repeat the process until all of the ramekins are coated with butter and sugar.

**Make the pudding cake:** Combine the chocolates and the 3 tablespoons butter in a large bowl.

In a medium saucepan, bring the ½ cup sugar, water, and vanilla to a rapid boil over high heat. It should bubble vigorously and achieve a clear, thick, and syrup-like consistency. Carefully pour the hot sugar syrup over the chocolate and butter and stir slowly, in a circular motion, until smooth. Whisk in the eggs.

Divide the batter among the prepared ramekins, filling them three-quarters full. Arrange the filled ramekins spaced evenly in a roasting pan or deep cake pan. Pour hot water into the pan around the ramekins, making sure that no water splashes into the cake batter, until the water reaches halfway up the side of the ramekins.

Transfer the pan to the oven and bake the cakes for 20 minutes, or until they have domed slightly and taken on a matte finish.

Carefully transfer the ramekins from the water bath to a wire rack. Let them cool to room temperature before unmolding. If the cakes are unmolded while they are still warm, they might collapse. To unmold, cover the opening of a ramekin with one hand and invert it. Gently tap the ramekin with the other hand. The cake should drop into the hand holding the ramekin. Alternatively, this can be done over a plate.

**To serve:** Drizzle 1 tablespoon of warmed chocolate sauce across each plate. Place one cake on each plate and top each cake with a scoop of mint ice cream. Garnish with fresh mint and serve immediately.

The cake batter can be made up to 3 days in advance and chilled in a tightly covered container. When ready to bake, scoop the cold batter into the prepared ramekins (as shown above) and bake in the preheated oven immediately. Unmold the cakes regardless of whether you are using them immediately or storing them. Do not store them in the molds; they will be difficult to unmold when cooled. The baked cakes will keep for up to 1 day at room temperature. For the best results, though, they should be served as soon as they are cool.

# *fresh mint ice cream*  Makes about 1 quart

Diners look forward to this refreshing ice cream every spring. If you have mint in your garden, you know how abundantly it grows. This is a great way to use up that extra mint.

---

6 large egg yolks

1½ cups fresh mint leaves and stems

2 cups heavy cream

1 cup whole milk

1 cup sugar

Fresh mint leaves, sliced into chiffonade, for garnish

In a nonreactive bowl, whisk the egg yolks together.

Bruise the mint by pressing on it with the back of a spoon. This will release its oils and maximize the mint flavor.

Bring the cream, milk, sugar, and bruised mint to a low simmer in a large saucepan over medium heat and simmer for just long enough to dissolve the sugar. Remove the pan from the heat and let steep for 30 minutes.

Temper the egg yolks by whisking in 1 cup of the hot cream mixture into the egg yolks in a slow, steady stream. This prevents the yolks from scrambling, which happens when the hot cream is added too quickly. If this occurs, you will have to start from the beginning.

Stir the tempered egg mixture into the remaining hot cream in the saucepan. Strain the ice cream base through a fine-mesh sieve and discard the solids.

Chill the strained base by setting the bowl over ice, whisking occasionally until cool.

Churn the chilled ice cream base in an ice cream machine according to the manufacturer's instructions. (This may require chilling your base before churning.) Transfer the ice cream to a freezer-proof container. For the best results, freeze the ice cream for at least 2 hours before serving. When you serve, garnish with the mint chiffonade.

# vanilla-**saffron** panna cotta, rhubarb consommé, strawberry sherbet

**Serves 6**

2½ teaspoons powdered gelatin

2 tablespoons cold water

2½ cups heavy cream

1½ cups whole milk

½ cup sugar

1 teaspoon saffron

1½ cups Rhubarb Consommé (recipe follows)

Strawberry Sherbet (recipe follows)

I first combined saffron and rhubarb in a dessert that I made for a dinner at the James Beard House in New York City. I loved the way the saffron's mellow warmth wrapped itself around the acidity of the fruit. I retooled the combination for this lighter, more refreshing spring dessert to serve at the restaurant.

This dessert has gorgeous coloring: The saffron-stained panna cotta is topped with a bright pink layer of rhubarb consommé and a neon-red scoop of strawberry sherbet. You'll do well to show it off in clear goblets.

---

In a medium-size heatproof bowl, sprinkle the powdered gelatin over the cold water. Set aside for 10 minutes to let the gelatin bloom.

Combine the cream, milk, sugar, and saffron in a medium saucepot. Heat the mixture over medium heat to scald. Watch it carefully to make sure that the pot does not boil over. When the mixture is hot, remove it from the heat and whisk vigorously for 1 minute. Set aside for a few minutes to let the saffron infuse into the panna cotta base.

While the base is infusing, set the bowl of bloomed gelatin over a double boiler and heat gently until the gelatin has melted. It should be smooth and viscous. Stir the melted gelatin into the warm cream mixture.

Strain the panna cotta base through a fine-mesh sieve or a cheesecloth-lined colander into a heat-resistant bowl. Divide the panna cotta base evenly among six 4-ounce ramekins or, preferably, parfait glasses. Cover and chill the panna cottas in the refrigerator until they have fully set, at least 6 hours.

To serve, spoon ¼ cup of Rhubarb Consommé onto the top of each panna cotta and nestle a scoop of Strawberry Sherbet on top of that. Serve immediately.

# *rhubarb consommé* Makes about 1½ cups

1¼ pounds rhubarb stalks, coarsely chopped into
    1-inch pieces

½ cup strawberries, stemmed and quartered

½ cup plus 2 tablespoons sugar

1 tablespoon plus 2 teaspoons freshly squeezed lemon
    juice

½ cup water

¼ cup semisweet wine (such as Riesling)

1 teaspoon vanilla extract

Line a heat-resistant colander with a double layer of cheesecloth large enough so that it overhangs the edges by at least 6 inches on all sides. Set the lined colander over a deep container (at least 4 quarts) that is wide enough to collect all of the strained liquid from the colander. Alternatively, drape a sheet of double-layered cheesecloth over the mouth of a lipped container large enough to hold at least 4 quarts of liquid. Secure the cheesecloth to the container by tying kitchen twine under the outside ledge of the lip, making sure that the cheesecloth sags slightly in the middle to accommodate the strained pulp from the stewed fruit.

Bring all of the ingredients to a boil in a large saucepan. Lower the heat and let simmer for 1 hour, or until the fruit has broken down to a pulp. Remove the fruit stew from the heat and let it cool slightly.

Ladle the pulpy stew into the strainer in batches, allowing liquid to drain off before adding more. Once all of the pulp is in the cheesecloth, cover the pulp with the overhanging cheesecloth and let it strain while cooling. When the pulp has cooled, refrigerate the entire setup, letting it strain further overnight.

Carefully remove the cheesecloth from the colander or pot and discard the pulp. Transfer the strained consommé to an airtight container and refrigerate until ready to serve. Covered and chilled, it will keep for up to 2 weeks. Stored in the freezer, it will keep for up to 1 month (although the color will fade).

# strawberry sherbet  Makes 1 quart

Sherbet means different things to different people around the world. Here in the Midwest (and in the United States in general), it's simply sorbet "with hips." The small amount of added milk fat gives it just enough body so that it lingers a bit on your tongue. Using the sweetest, ripest strawberries will give you the best flavor and an especially brilliant color.

2 pints strawberries, stemmed and quartered

1½ cups Simple Syrup (page 265)

¼ cup light corn syrup

½ cup water

Juice of 1 lemon

¾ cup heavy cream

Combine the strawberries, simple syrup, corn syrup, water, and lemon juice in a blender and blend on high speed until it is a smooth puree. Strain the puree through a fine-mesh sieve. Whisk in the cream.

Churn the chilled sherbet base in an ice cream maker according to the manufacturer's instructions. (This may require chilling the base before churning.)

Transfer the churned sherbet to a freezer-safe container, cover, and freeze for at least 1 hour before serving. Although sherbet can be stored in the freezer indefinitely, for the best results, consume it within 1 week. Sherbet tends to get icy if it is left in the freezer for too long. If this happens, thaw and melt the sherbet and rechurn it according to the instructions above. Any excess base you have can also be stored, frozen, for up to 1 month.

# chocolate truffle cookies

**Makes about 50 truffle cookies**

2 ounces unsweetened chocolate, chopped

3 tablespoons unsalted butter

½ cup all-purpose flour

½ cup granulated sugar

1 tablespoon unsweetened cocoa powder (preferably Dutch-processed)

⅛ teaspoon baking powder

¼ teaspoon kosher salt

2 large eggs

1 teaspoon vanilla extract

5 ounces miniature bittersweet chocolate chips

⅛ cup confectioners' sugar

1 lime, for zesting

## Chocolate is truly perennial.

As the name suggests, these cookies are extremely rich—you really don't need too many to be satisfied. Still, we have a hard time keeping these from disappearing in the kitchen.

While these little bites are great with nothing more than a tall glass of milk, I dress them up with a dusting of confectioners' sugar to make them more elegant. The addition of fresh lime zest also gives these cookies a bright spring fragrance. I've included other seasonal variations so that you can make these year-round (see the box).

---

In a double boiler (or a bowl set over a saucepan containing 1 inch of simmering water), melt the unsweetened chocolate and butter together over medium-low heat. Stir the chocolate and butter in the double boiler until it is melted and smooth. Remove the mixture from the heat and set aside.

Combine the flour, granulated sugar, cocoa powder, baking powder, and salt in a medium bowl.

In the bowl of a stand mixer fitted with a paddle attachment, beat together the eggs and vanilla on medium speed until combined, about 2 minutes. Add the dry ingredients and resume mixing on medium speed until incorporated, scraping the bowl as needed, about 2 minutes. At this point, the mixture should resemble cake batter.

Add the melted chocolate mixture to the batter and continue to mix, scraping the bowl as needed, until the batter thickens. Using a rubber spatula, fold in the chocolate chips by hand.

Cover the batter with plastic wrap and refrigerate for 1 hour.

Preheat the oven to 350°F. Line a baking sheet with parchment paper or a nonstick baking liner. You can bake 2 sheets at a time, rotating halfway through baking.

Using a small melon baller or a sturdy rounded teaspoon, scoop the chilled batter into balls and arrange them on the prepared baking sheet, leaving at least 1 inch between them. For a softer, chewier cookie, bake for 5 minutes. For a harder, cookie-like texture, bake them for 7 minutes.

Transfer the baking sheet to a wire rack and let the cookies cool slightly. Cooled cookies can be stored in an airtight container for up to 3 days. When ready to serve, dust them with confectioners' sugar. Using a Microplane zester, grate fresh lime zest over the top. Serve immediately.

## seasonal truffle variations

Here are some suggestions for tailoring these cookies to each season. Sift ⅛ cup confectioners' sugar with one of the following ingredients instead of the lime zest and use it as the dusting sugar before serving.

*summer:* 2 teaspoons malt powder

*autumn:* 1 teaspoon ground cinnamon

*winter:* 1 teaspoon ground cardamom

# raspberry–lemon thyme lollipops

**Makes twenty ¾-inch-diameter lollipops**

Leaves from a few sprigs fresh lemon thyme

½ cup sugar

2 tablespoons water

1 tablespoon light corn syrup

½ teaspoon natural raspberry extract

3 drops red food coloring

I love seeing the eyes of our guests light up at the end of the meal when we bring them these colorful candies. For that one moment, you get a glimpse into their childhood.

These lollipops are a tribute to two of my mentors, Gale Gand, who taught me the power of nostalgia with her lollipop petits fours, and Richard Leach, who introduced me to using herbs in desserts. We present the lollipops standing up, the stick end stuck into a bowl or large glass filled with coarse sanding sugar (or sugar in the raw). You can purchase the lollipop molds and sticks at a kitchenware store.

---

Place the molds on a Silpat mat on a baking sheet. Line the molds with lollipop sticks, making sure that at least ¼ inch of each stick is in the mold.

Place a few fresh thyme leaves in each mold.

In a clean, 4-cup saucepan free of any debris or grease, bring the sugar, water, and corn syrup to a gentle boil. Do not touch the pan or swirl the sugar—movement, along with dirt or grease, will cause the sugar to crystallize (see the box, opposite). To prevent crystallization, brush down the sides of the pan occasionally with a pastry brush dipped in water.

Heat the sugar mixture until it registers 305°F (hard crack stage) on a candy thermometer. Remove the pan from the heat and let cool for 1 minute. Add the raspberry extract and food coloring, swirling the pan to incorporate them evenly.

Carefully pour the hot syrup into the molds, filling them about two-thirds full and making sure that the syrup surrounds the end of the lollipop stick that sits in the mold. Let the lollipops cool completely. Unmold and store in an airtight container for up to 1 week. Make sure your container is well sealed, as the lollipops may stick to each other or get tacky if exposed to moisture.

As a woman, I can confidently say that sugar is definitely female: It can be cranky and temperamental. If I'm cursing in the kitchen, it's usually because I'm working with sugar. But don't be intimidated. Just keep these things in mind:

1.  Hell hath no fury like hot sugar. Hot sugar is extremely hot. Be careful.

2.  The slightest bit of grease or debris will prevent sugar from crystallizing properly. Make sure the pot in which you boil your sugar is squeaky clean. To be safe, scrub it out with some salt and vinegar and rinse it well before using.

3.  Once sugar syrup has reached the hard-crack stage (the temperature that sugar must reach before it will harden when cooled), try not to disturb it. If you are adding ingredients at this stage—such as food coloring—gently swirl in the ingredients by swirling the pot. Don't stir the sugar with a utensil.

# pink peppercorn shortbread

**Makes about 3½ dozen**

1 tablespoon plus 2 teaspoons pink peppercorns

½ cup (1 stick) unsalted butter

¼ cup sugar

1 teaspoon vanilla extract

½ teaspoon Saint-Germain elderflower liqueur (optional)

Scant ¾ cup all-purpose flour

⅛ teaspoon salt

These thin, flaky, and incredibly buttery shortbread cookies appear on our petit four tray throughout the year. Since the pink peppercorns have a refreshingly floral and herby spiciness, I'm including them with the spring recipes. The dough needs to freeze thoroughly to make it easier to slice, so it's best to make the dough the day before you plan to bake the cookies. To ensure these cookies have a nice shape, make sure that the bars of dough are as smooth and straight-edged as possible. When you're cutting the cookies, don't hesitate to refreeze the dough as necessary to preserve its form.

Grind the peppercorns in a spice grinder until they become small, rough flakes. Do not pulverize the peppercorns into a powder. If you do not have a spice grinder, you can achieve the same result by putting the peppercorns in a plastic freezer bag, pressing out the air and sealing it tightly, and bashing them with a rolling pin.

In the bowl of a stand mixer fitted with a paddle attachment, cream together the butter, sugar, vanilla, and liqueur on medium-high speed until light and fluffy, scraping the bowl at least a couple of times, about 3 minutes.

Combine the flour and salt in a medium bowl. With the mixer on low speed, add the dry ingredients to the creamed butter and mix until well incorporated. Scrape

down the sides of the bowl. Add the flaked peppercorns and mix briefly, just until the dough is speckled with the peppercorn flakes.

Line a 5 by 2½-inch mini loaf pan (preferably one with straight edges) with parchment paper. Press the dough into the bottom of the pan. Using a small offset spatula, smooth the surface of the dough as much as possible; otherwise your cookies will have a rough edge. Cover the pan with plastic wrap and push the plastic wrap down so that it is in contact with the dough. At this point, you can smooth the dough out more with your hands. Try not to make too many indentations.

Freeze the dough for at least 2 hours, or preferably overnight.

Preheat the oven to 350°F. Line a baking sheet with parchment paper or a nonstick baking liner. You can bake 2 sheets at a time, rotating them halfway through baking.

Using a paring knife dipped in hot water, slip the knife between the dough and the side of the pan to loosen the dough.

Turn the pan over on a lightly floured surface and give it a hard tap. The brick of dough should come out easily. Peel off the parchment paper. If the loaf pan you used has sloped edges, square the edges of the brick with the paring knife so that you have 90-degree-angle edges.

Starting from one end of the brick, cut the dough into ⅛-inch-thick slices. If the dough begins to soften slightly, carefully wrap it and freeze it for 10 minutes to help it reharden; this will make it easier to slice.

Arrange the cookies on the baking sheet, leaving 1 inch between them. Refreeze any dough that remains uncut between batches; the dough will get soft if left out, making it difficult to cut. Bake the cookies for 8 minutes, or until they are blond with golden edges. Transfer to a wire rack and cool completely before serving.

These cookies will keep in an airtight container for up to 2 days. If it's especially humid, wrap the container with plastic wrap for additional protection. Wrapped and sealed tightly, the dough can also be stored in the freezer for up to 3 months.

## baking sheets

A good-quality baking sheet is invaluable. It should distribute heat evenly and shouldn't warp. If your pans are bent or misshapen, your cookies will not bake evenly, and they can change shape during the baking process.

In the restaurant, good baking sheets are a hot commodity. Cooks, especially pastry cooks, are known to hide their baking sheets from each other. Even at home, I hide my baking sheets from Colby.

summer

# As chefs, we live for summer.

## Owing to its length and intensity, summer in the Midwest is a celebration of abundance.

What doesn't grow here in any other season will probably grow—and grow prolifically—in the summer, when our region basically turns into a gigantic hothouse. At its best, summer is an assault of produce. Farmers' trucks crowd with watermelons, and farm stands overflow with tomatoes, squash, cherries, peppers, corn, peaches, melons, snap beans, potatoes, and countless greens—all of which you'll find on the menu at Bluestem.

In this season, we focus on lighter, cleaner flavors and simpler cooking techniques to highlight the natural flavors in the produce.

There are cold salads that call for little more than quick blanching (the snap beans on page 70 and marinated melon on page 76); stripped-down pastas with quickly cooked "sauces"; and uncomplicated, middle-American flavors, like catfish with tartar sauce (page 99), trout with summer beans (page 96), chicken with pistou (page 101), and pork with syrupy glazed peaches (page 103).

And despite the often oppressive heat and humidity during summers in the Midwest, you'll never find us failing to exercise our God-given right to fire up our grills and smokers. So we've included a few dishes that will give you a reason to enjoy a couple beers or cocktails on the patio while you wait for your coals to heat up.

# summer

# menu

# wine

A chilled, dry rosé is the next best thing to air conditioning. On a hot, muggy summer day, a blushing Marsannay, for example, will help drop the temperature around any table. If it's summer, you can bet there's a bottle or two near me.

Rosés have gotten a bad reputation, one that I'm constantly trying to rewrite. They're fragrant with a good balance of acidity and tannins, and usually drier than you'd assume.

In this section, a nice rosé will pair well with the snap bean salad (page 70), picking up the brighter notes in the grassy greens and the tangy goat cheese, and highlight the more delicate flavors in the wild coho salmon recipe on page 93.

Colby's gazpacho (page 72) is amazingly versatile. At Bluestem, we incorporate the gazpacho into a cocktail, shaking it with the vodka and pouring it into a frosty martini glass. Pairing wine with the gazpacho in the dining room is a little trickier. Because it is unusually acidic, the gazpacho tends to overpower most white wines. My solution: a high-quality, unfiltered junmai sake, which has a creamy texture and a fruity finish that complements the soup without being overwhelmed by it.

# notes

The tropical fruit flavors in a white wine from the French Rhône region will pair nicely with the sweet and sour peaches that Colby serves with the pork tenderloin on page 103. The fatty texture of a white Rhône will also hold up well against the meat.

Megan's mulberry-pinot sorbet (page 116), served with linzer wafer cookies and a honey custard, will pair especially well with Brachetto d'Acqui, a sweet red wine from the Piedmont region of Italy. Effervescent and rosy, it tastes like an adult version of strawberry cream soda.

# watermelon shots

**Serves 8 to 10 as an amuse-bouche**

### watermelon juice

2 cups coarsely chopped seedless watermelon

1½ teaspoons saba

⅛ teaspoon sea salt

### domaine de canton foam

½ cup Domaine de Canton liqueur

½ cup dry white wine, such as Pinot Blanc or Sauvignon Blanc

½ teaspoon powdered gelatin

When I worked at Tru under chef Rick Tramonto, the innovative chef José Andrés came to Chicago and cooked with us for a week. Among his many creative ideas was filling mini watermelon cups with aged balsamic vinegar. Equally taken by Andrés's striking presentation and inspired by its simplicity, I was excited by the dish's refreshingly tangy crispness.

I borrowed Andrés's idea and transformed it into a little shot of juice for a cool summer starter. We use saba, an uncooked grape must similar to but thicker than balsamic vinegar, in the juice and cap it off with a frothy head made of Domaine de Canton, a ginger liqueur that originated in the former Indochina.

*Note on iSi Canister:* An iSi canister is a metal canister that is charged with nitrous oxide ($N_2O$). Once charged, its liquid contents can be dispensed from the canister in the form of a frothy foam (in order for this to work properly, the contents must contain some kind of gelling agent or protein). The most common, commercial form of this type of mechanism is the good old can of whipped cream. In the restaurant, we fill our canisters with everything from horseradish potatoes to the Canton foam in this recipe. You can buy an iSi canister and the nitrous oxide chargers at most specialty kitchenware stores, including Williams-Sonoma and Sur La Table, or locally in Kansas City at Pryde's Old Westport (see Sources, page 272).

---

**Make the watermelon juice:** Juice the watermelon with a juicer. Strain the watermelon juice through a double layer of cheesecloth. Discard the frothy pulp residue. Stir in the saba and salt. Cover and chill for 2 hours, or until ready to serve.

**Make the Canton foam:** Pour the liqueur and wine into the top of a double boiler.

Sprinkle the gelatin evenly over the top and let it sit for 5 minutes to bloom.

Gently heat the mixture over low heat, just until the gelatin has dissolved. Remove from the heat and let it cool completely.

Transfer the mixture to an iSi canister. Seal the canister and charge it with a $N_2O$ cartridge according to the manufacturer's instructions. Chill the canister for at least 4 hours or, for the best results, overnight, before discharging the foam.

**To serve:** Pour the chilled watermelon juice into shot glasses, filling them about two-thirds full. Shake the charged iSi canister vigorously and dispense the Canton foam into the shot glasses, filling them to the brim. Serve immediately.

# sweet corn soup, maryland blue crab

**Serves 4**

3 ears corn, husks and silk removed

2 tablespoons unsalted butter

Salt and freshly cracked black pepper

2 large shallots, finely chopped

4 cloves garlic, finely chopped

1 cup rye whiskey

½ cup dry white wine

1½ cups heavy cream

4 ounces jumbo lump crabmeat, picked over for shells and cartilage

Freshly squeezed lime juice, for garnish

Sweet corn is just about as abundant in the Midwest in the summer as blue crabs are along the Eastern coast of the United States. Every summer, Megan and I try our best to visit my relatives in Delaware. There's nothing I relish more than sitting out on the docks with a bib, cracking freshly steamed crabs.

Fresh crabs are a luxury here in the Midwest, but once in a while, when I have a yen for the shore, I'll order some and pair them with corn freshly picked by our local farmers. Depending on how good you are at picking crabmeat, you'll need at least 2 pounds of whole live crabs to yield 4 ounces of meat. If you can't get fresh crabs, you can substitute unpasteurized crabmeat.

---

Rub the ears of corn with 1 tablespoon of the butter to coat. Liberally season them with salt and pepper.

Over a preheated charcoal or gas grill, or directly on the open flame of a gas stove, roast the corn, rotating the ears every 20 seconds, until the kernels begin to char. When the kernels have developed an even speckling of black char spots, set the ears aside to cool.

Cut the kernels off the cobs and set them aside in a bowl. Working over a separate bowl, "milk" the cobs by running the back of your knife, while pressing against the corncobs, down the length of the cob. Reserve the liquid and discard the cobs.

In a medium saucepan heat the remaining tablespoon of butter over medium-high heat. Add the shallots and garlic and sauté them for 1 minute. Stir in the corn and

cook for 1 more minute. Add the rye whiskey, white wine, and reserved corn milk and season with salt and pepper to taste. Let the mixture simmer for 5 minutes. Add the cream, return to a simmer, and let the soup reduce for 10 minutes. Remove the pot from the heat and let it stand for 10 minutes to cool.

Carefully pour the hot mixture into a blender. With a towel-wrapped hand held firmly over the lid, puree the soup on high speed until smooth and liquefied, about 5

minutes. Strain the soup through a fine-mesh sieve or a double thickness of cheesecloth. Press down on the pulp with the back of a ladle or flat spoon to yield as much liquid as possible. Discard the pulp.

To serve, if the soup has cooled, reheat the soup in a small pot over medium-low heat. Divide the crabmeat among 4 small cups or bowls and pour about ¼ cup soup into each one. Garnish each serving with a dash of lime juice.

# snap beans, speck, green dirt farm's cheese, champagne vinaigrette

**Serves 4**

12 ounces assorted snap beans, trimmed

½ cup baby arugula

¼ cup Champagne Vinaigrette (page 253)

Salt and freshly ground white pepper

4 ounces goat cheese

2 ounces speck, thinly sliced

In the Midwest, one simply can't escape the green bean. Every Aunt Susie, Mae, and Fanny has a signature plate of buttered beans, green bean salad, or a green bean casserole to show at the church picnic.

When I was a child, green beans were a staple in our household. To this day, my dad cans a bushel of them every summer to give away during the holiday season.

At Bluestem, I celebrate all the cooking aunties and canning dads out there with this light, fresh, and crisp salad. The beans are quickly blanched, just enough to take the snap out of them, leaving them sturdy but tender. Tossed with a little Champagne vinaigrette, the beans pick up a bit of creamy tanginess from goat cheese and a salty, smoky meatiness from strips of thinly shaved speck, a cured ham. If you can't find speck, prosciutto is a good substitute.

---

Bring a large stockpot of heavily salted water to a rolling boil. While the water is heating, prepare a large ice bath (see the User Manual, page xxv). Blanch the beans for 2 to 3 minutes, grouping them according to size and thickness if necessary, and cool them in the ice bath (for blanching instructions, see the User Manual, page xxiv). Drain the beans and slice them into ¾-inch lengths.

Toss the beans with the arugula and vinaigrette to coat. Season with salt and pepper to taste.

Divide the beans and greens among 4 plates. Dot each plate with some goat cheese and a few slices of speck. Serve immediately.

# snap beans

Snap beans grow on either a bush plant or a vine plant (beans from the latter are also called pole or runner beans because the plant must be staked or trellised). They include the common green bean and yellow wax beans and the flamboyantly streaked Dragon Tongue bean. A variety of different-colored snap beans will make this salad particularly beautiful.

Sadly, one of the most beautiful snap beans, the Royal Burgundy, loses its striking purple color when cooked (the Dragon Tongues also lose their beautiful streaks).

# gazpacho

**Serves 4**

### gazpacho

4 red bell peppers, cored and finely chopped

1 red onion, finely chopped

2 large cucumbers, finely chopped

6 cloves garlic, peeled

6 large tomatoes, coarsely chopped

Juice of 1 lemon

¾ cup extra-virgin olive oil

1 cup red wine vinegar

1 teaspoon cayenne pepper

1½ teaspoons salt

Freshly cracked white pepper

### gazpacho foam

3 cloves garlic, peeled

3 cups white grapes

1 cup blanched almonds

¼ cup Champagne vinegar

½ cup water

½ cup heavy cream

Salt and freshly ground white pepper

### garnishes

8 cherry tomatoes

8 seedless white grapes

1 radish, thinly sliced

Basil blossoms

This is a marriage of two Spanish cold soups: gazpacho—the often chunky puree of tomatoes, bell peppers, onions, and vinegar—and *ajo blanco*—a thick, white soup made by blending together bread, almonds, garlic, and oil.

To make this soup a little more refined for our restaurant, I strain the gazpacho to yield a clear broth and transform the *ajo blanco* into a foam, which I float over the soup right before sending it out to the table. The clear gazpacho broth also does double duty in a gazpacho martini, which we serve in our lounge (equal parts gazpacho and vodka). People seem to siphon it by the gallon.

**Make the gazpacho:** Line a colander with eight layers of cheesecloth (this can be one large sheet folded over eight times) and set it over a large, deep bowl.

Combine all of the gazpacho ingredients in a blender and puree until the contents are liquefied.

Strain the puree through the cheesecloth-lined colander. A clear gazpacho liquid should strain through to the bowl underneath. When most of the liquid has strained through, use the back of a ladle to push the pulp down to extract as much liquid as possible. Discard the pulp.

Stored tightly covered in the refrigerator, the gazpacho will keep for 3 days.

**Make the gazpacho foam:** Combine all of the ingredients in a blender and puree until liquefied.

Pour the strained liquid into an iSi canister and charge it with a $N_2O$ cartridge according to the manufacturer's instructions (see headnote on page 66). Chill the canister for at least 1 hour before discharging the contents.

If you don't have an iSi canister, you can omit the foam, or you may serve the blended foam ingredients in a separate bowl along with the clear gazpacho.

**Blanch and peel the garnishes:** Prepare an ice bath (see the User Manual, page xxv). Bring a pot of water to a boil and blanch the cherry tomatoes for 30 seconds (for blanching instructions, see the User Manual, page xxiv). Cool them immediately in the ice bath. Blanch the white grapes for 2 minutes. The ice bath will not only stop the cooking process for the tomatoes and grapes but also help loosen the skin.

Carefully, peel the skins off of the tomatoes and grapes, leaving them whole.

**To serve:** Slice the grapes into thirds and halve the tomatoes lengthwise. Divide and arrange them in 4 soup bowls. Pour the gazpacho over the garnishes and discharge a large dollop of white gazpacho foam over the soup (or serve the blended ingredients in a separate bowl alongside to make a gazpacho duo). Serve immediately.

# crum's heirlooms

She's one of the most passionate and emotional fruit and vegetable enthusiasts you'll ever meet: Set a ripe peach in front of Debbie and the world around her disappears. He's a diligent, no-complaints worker on a steady and even keel: Give Jim a watermelon and he'll spit out the rind and plant the seeds. Together, the Crums have become, to Kansas City's chefs, the beloved king and queen of summer.

The Crums spoil us. Thanks to them, we are less reliant upon and less interested in produce from outside our region.

## tomatoes. lots of tomatoes.

It was an unexpected bumper crop in the summer of 2002 that got the couple thinking. Their son Dave, who was working as a chef in Minneapolis at the time (and who later became chef de cuisine at Bluestem), suggested that they sell them. And that's how Crum's Heirlooms was born.

What started as a small, ⅓-acre garden has now expanded to a 12-acre plot of land near Bonner Springs, Kansas, that is responsible for some of the finest organic produce in our area. It's taken on a life of its own, growing every year. Every summer there's something new and exciting happening at the farm. We are already anxiously anticipating their yield in the coming years.

Although both of them have daytime jobs—Debbie is a substitute teacher and Jim works in technology sales—the Crums always find energy to tend their farm. Taking full advantage of the long summer days, they squeeze every ounce of sunlight out of the sky and put it into their produce.

We feature the Crums' vegetables wherever and whenever possible. We're proud to share their beautiful bounty with our diners. Their heirloom tomatoes—for which they've become famous—are juicy and sweet (and come in more shapes, sizes, and colors than you can imagine). From them, we make a summer gazpacho (page 72) that's light and refreshing. Dave also developed a recipe for ketchup, which we serve—seemingly by the bowlful—in the lounge as a condiment for burgers and *pommes frites*. It's immensely popular.

The Crums bring dozens of varieties of carrots, beets, peppers, and radishes to the table as well. Spring onions, pearl onions, large onions—you name it, they grow it. At the height of summer, they shower us with baskets of squash blossoms, which we fill with goat cheese or scallop mousse and deep-fry. In the colder months, they keep us going with root vegetables, such as turnips and potatoes.

The couple now provides produce to more than 30 restaurants in Kansas City. Bluestem is lucky to be one of them.

# marinated **melon**, tomato, tomato jam, saba, fennel, cilantro

**Serves 4**

### pickled watermelon rind

4 cups watermelon rind trimmed of pink flesh and outer green skin and cut into 1-inch chunks

3 cups water

3 tablespoons salt

1 cup Champagne vinegar

2 cups sugar

2 teaspoons coriander seeds

¼ teaspoon mustard seeds

1 small fennel bulb, trimmed and chopped

### vinaigrette

¼ cup saba

½ cup extra-virgin olive oil

### tomatoes and melon

2 pounds heirloom tomatoes in assorted sizes, preferably golf ball size or smaller

1 pound ripe melons (an assortment of watermelon, cantaloupe, and honeydew)

Sea salt and freshly cracked black pepper

¼ cup Tomato Jam (page 109)

Chopped fresh chives, basil blossoms, and mint leaves, for garnish

I grew up hating tomatoes, eggs, and milk. Although I'm still working on eggs, I eventually graduated to milk and the tomato. In fact, I now love tomatoes so much that I eat them plain with a dash of salt.

In the Midwest, when the tomatoes are good, they're exceptional. It's hard to justify doing anything to them at all. This salad brings them together with another Midwestern summer treasure: ripe melons, a fleshier and slightly sweeter counterpart to the acidic tomato. The presentation is particularly beautiful when you use a mismatched patchwork of different-colored tomatoes and melons.

---

**Pickle the watermelon rind:** Combine all of the ingredients for the pickled rind in a medium pot and bring to a boil over high heat. Boil for 8 to 10 minutes, until the liquid thickens into a light syrup. Lower the heat to medium and let the rinds simmer in the syrup for about 50 minutes, or until they soften and turn translucent. Remove the pot from the heat and let cool completely.

**Make the vinaigrette:** Whisk together the saba and olive oil.

**Prepare the tomatoes and melons:** Bring a pot of heavily salted water to a rolling boil. While the water is heating, prepare an ice bath (see the User Manual, page xxv). Blanch the tomatoes in two batches for 10 seconds.

Drain, then cool them in the ice bath (for blanching instructions, see the User Manual, page xxiv). Carefully peel the skins off the tomatoes. Discard the skins and set the tomatoes aside.

Using a melon baller, scoop out 24 melon balls (at the restaurant, we use a ¼-inch melon baller, but a sturdy metal ¼-teaspoon measuring spoon will also work).

**To serve:** Season the melon balls and tomatoes with salt and pepper to taste and toss them in some vinaigrette to coat.

Divide the pickled watermelon rinds and dressed tomatoes and melon balls among 4 plates. Dot each plate with a couple of teaspoons of tomato jam and garnish the salad with the herbs. Serve immediately.

# braised **artichoke**, potatoes confit, german-style dressing

**Serves 4**

**artichoke hearts**

Juice of 1 lemon

8 large globe artichokes

4 cups water

2 cups dry white wine

½ cup olive oil

1 small white onion, coarsely chopped

1 medium carrot, diced

6 cloves garlic, chopped

1 bay leaf

**artichoke dressing**

2 tablespoons white wine vinegar

1 tablespoon Dijon mustard

1 tablespoon grainy mustard

Pinch of salt

4 prepared artichoke hearts, quartered

½ marinated white anchovy fillet

½ cup olive oil

¼ red onion, thinly shaved

½ Preserved Lemon, homemade (page 263) or store-bought

6 Potatoes Confit (page 260)

No Midwestern gathering is complete without potato salad. Megan and I are both of German stock, which is perhaps why we gravitate toward versions with a tart and tangy dressing. In this recipe, I incorporate into the potato salad one of my favorite summertime foods: the artichoke.

The edible artichoke is actually the bud of a giant thistle plant. It takes some work to trim and clean them, but the result is well worth the trouble. The tender heart and stem has a slightly grassy flavor that pairs particularly well with tart and creamy foods. (Artichokes also contain the chemical compound cynarin, which enhances your ability to perceive sweetness.) This recipe calls for a total of eight artichoke hearts. The four required for the dressing are included in the eight hearts you have prepared at the beginning of the recipe.

You can find white anchovies at any gourmet food store. Do not substitute canned anchovies.

---

**Prepare and cook the artichoke hearts:** Fill a medium bowl with cold water and acidulate it with the lemon juice.

Peel off the hard outer leaves of the artichoke. Cut off the top cone of leaves, revealing the furry choke. Using a sharp paring knife, trim off the hard outer skin of each artichoke around the stem and base of the artichoke

where the leaves attached, exposing the whitish flesh of the artichoke base. Scoop out the choke with a spoon, scraping the inside clean of fuzz. Soak the trimmed artichokes in the acidulated water to prevent them from browning.

Cut out a round of parchment paper to fit snugly over the opening of a large stockpot. In the stockpot, combine the water, wine, olive oil, white onion, carrot, garlic, bay leaf, and trimmed artichoke hearts. Cover the pot with the parchment lid and bring the liquid to a simmer over medium-high heat. Cook until the artichoke hearts are tender, about 10 minutes (a skewer or sharp knife should slip in and out of them easily). Remove the stockpot from the heat and let cool. Chill and store the artichoke hearts in their braising liquid for up to 2 days. When you are ready to use the artichokes, drain them, discard the aromatics and liquid, and cut the artichoke hearts into quarters.

**Make the dressing:** Combine the vinegar, the Dijon and grainy mustards, salt, artichokes, and anchovies in a blender and puree together until slightly chunky. With the blender running, slowly drizzle in the olive oil through the top of the blender in a thin stream until the dressing emulsifies and turns smooth.

**To serve:** Soak the red onion shavings in ice water for several minutes. This takes the bitterness out of the onion and makes them curl. Drain well before using.

Scoop out and discard the pulp of the preserved lemon. Rinse the rind well with cold water to remove excess salt. Pat the rinds dry with a paper towel and dice them.

Cut the potatoes confit into coins. Toss the artichoke wedges, potatoes, and preserved lemon with ⅓ cup of the dressing. Divide the mixture among 4 plates. Garnish each plate with some shaved onions and serve.

# jonah crab, cucumber gelée, avocado

**Serves 4**

### cucumber gelée

2 cups cucumber juice (see box)

Juice of 1 lime

2 tablespoons Tanqueray Rangpur (lime-flavored gin) or regular gin

1 teaspoon salt

1 teaspoon powdered gelatin

### crab salad

1 pound Jonah crabmeat, picked over for shells and cartilage

¼ cup Aïoli (page 252)

2 teaspoons togarashi (Japanese seven-spice blend)

Salt and freshly ground white pepper

### avocado

2 Hass avocados, pitted, peeled, and diced

Juice of ½ lime

Pinch of salt

Freshly ground white pepper

Edible flowers, for garnish

---

Let's be honest: There really isn't anything Midwestern about this dish. I mean, a Kansan making seafood salad is just about as irresponsible as a Carolinian making barbecue. Yet "seafood salads" make a regular appearance at summer outings. They're usually made with imitation crab, baby shrimp, and a lot of mayonnaise.

At Bluestem, we try to show that Midwesterners can make crab salad just as well as we make barbecue. Here is a more elegant version with sweet Jonah crabmeat set over a cucumber gelée and diced avocados. If you can't find Jonah crabmeat, you can use another unpasteurized lump crabmeat.

With its emerald green base of cucumber juice, this salad is particularly pretty when garnished with brightly colored edible flowers. You don't want to use anything too herbal or floral, so we suggest using impatiens, nasturtiums, pansies, and Johnny-jump-ups.

---

**Make the cucumber gelée:** Put the cucumber juice, lime juice, gin, and salt in a small saucepan. Sprinkle the gelatin powder over the juice and let it bloom for 5 minutes. Gently heat the cucumber juice over low heat, stirring the gelatin until it completely dissolves. You want to warm the juice only enough to dissolve the gelatin, not heat it.

Divide the juice among 4 small, shallow bowls. Set them on a level shelf in the refrigerator and chill them for 2 hours, or until the gelée has set.

**Make the crab salad:** Toss the crabmeat with the aïoli and togarashi. Season with salt and pepper to taste.

**Prepare the avocado:** Gently toss the avocado with the lime juice, salt, and pepper to taste.

**To serve:** Remove the chilled bowls of gelée from the refrigerator. Mound one-quarter of the crab salad onto the center of each bowl of gelée. Garnish each salad with the diced avocado and edible flowers. Serve immediately.

## green

To get a dark, emerald-green color for the cucumber gelée, juice the cucumbers with the skin on. However, make sure you are using cucumbers that have not been waxed.

# foie gras au torchon, bing cherry mostarda, crispy toast

**Serves 4**

### bing cherry mostarda

1 cup Simple Syrup (page 265)

2 cups Bing cherries, stemmed and pitted

10 drops mustard essence, or ¼ cup dry mustard dissolved in ¼ cup white wine vinegar to make a paste

### foie gras

1½ teaspoons fine sea salt

½ teaspoon *sel rose* (see box)

¼ teaspoon finely ground white pepper

¼ teaspoon sugar

1½ pounds foie gras (about 1 lobe), preferably Grade A (see box), cleaned and deveined (see Note)

2 teaspoons Grand Marnier

12 to 16 cups kosher salt (about 3 3-pound boxes)

4 slices brioche bread

Along with the beef tartare on page 16, foie gras *au torchon* is always on the Bluestem menu. Although I change the accompaniments throughout the year, this version, served with mustard-spiked cherries, is my favorite.

Mustard essence, the distilled oil from mustard seeds, is the ingredient that gives *mostarda* its nose-clearing bite. Mustard essence is extremely powerful; mishandled, it can even be dangerous. Never smell it directly (think fistful of wasabi or horseradish jammed up your nose coupled with a punch in the face). As a result, mustard essence—*essenza di senape* or *essenza di mostarda*, as it is known in Italy—is extremely difficult to find in the United States. You can sometimes find it in Indian food markets, labeled mustard oil. Fortunately, I have a contact in Italy who sends it to me. If you can't find mustard essence, you can use dry mustard instead.

**Make the mostarda:** Heat the simple syrup in a small saucepan over medium-low heat. When the syrup begins to simmer, turn off the heat and remove the pot from the stove. Add the cherries and toss them to coat. Let the mixture cool and stir in the mustard essence. Let the *mostarda* cool completely before transferring it to an airtight container. Cover and chill in the refrigerator overnight before serving. Tightly sealed, the *mostarda* will keep in the refrigerator for up to 3 months.

**Season and cure the foie gras:** In a small bowl, combine the sea salt, *sel rose*, pepper, and sugar. Put the foie gras in a large bowl. Sprinkle the seasonings and Grand Marnier over the foie gras and, using your hands, rub them all over the surface of the liver. It's okay if the foie gras breaks up

# "fwah grah"

Don't be intimidated by foie gras. It's not difficult to work with. It's just expensive. The hardest part of curing foie gras in a *torchon*—French for "rag"—is rolling it into a neat log and securing it tightly at both ends with twine. You'll find that this is easier to do when the foie gras is cold and, therefore, firmer.

At Bluestem, we use Grade A foie gras, which in addition to having a higher level of fat has the least amount of blemishes and veining of the three grades sold in the United States (Grades B and C are the other two). The integrity of Grade A foie gras makes it particularly good for making cured foie gras. Since cured foie gras is not cooked or heated, the top grade's natural, extra-creamy, and ultra smooth consistency can be fully appreciated, and, cosmetically, its flawless appearance makes a more attractive presentation. Save Grade B foie gras, which is slightly less expensive but also less spotless, for recipes where the foie gras is cooked. Since the surface of the foie gras will be charred in the cooking process and the inside will be softened, blemishes won't be noticeable.

# sel rose

*Sel rose*, or "pink salt," is a pink curing salt containing nitrates that retards oxidation and helps preserve the integrity and rosy color of meats and charcuterie products, like foie gras. If you can't get or don't want to use *sel rose*, you can use pickling salt instead. However, expect the foie gras to discolor over time.

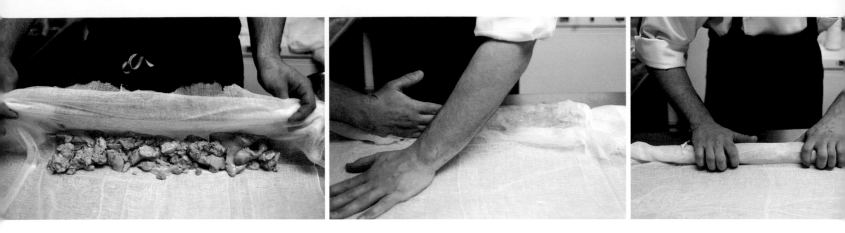

# "the roll"

This is a technique that we use in the restaurant to form meats and other ingredients into a log for curing or cooking and then slicing. Once you master it, you'll have a very useful skill in your pocket. Depending on the amount and type of filling you're rolling, and whether you're curing or cooking the filling, you'll need varying amounts of cheesecloth or plastic wrap. The instructions given here are specifically for this recipe. Other recipes in this cookbook that employ this technique will specify the amount and type of wrapping to be used. If you want to practice this technique with less-expensive ingredients first, try making the knödel on page 167.

slightly; the point is to make sure that the surface of the foie gras is coated with the seasonings and liqueur. Chill the foie gras in the refrigerator for 10 to 15 minutes, to help firm it up a little in preparation for the rolling it in the *torchon*.

Spread a large sheet of cheesecloth, about 24 by 12 inches, on a clean work surface with one of the short ends nearest you. Leaving a 2-inch margin on the edge of the cheesecloth nearest to you, form the seasoned foie gras roughly into a log shape across the width of the cheesecloth. Leave a 3-inch margin of cloth on either end of the log.

Roll the log of foie gras in the cheesecloth away from you, trying to keep the cloth as taut and tight against the foie gras as possible. Twist the overhanging cloth on both ends of the log, firmly squeezing inward from both sides as you twist, to form a rounded, tight, sausage-like log. Secure both ends with kitchen twine, looping the twine tightly around a few times. Cut off the extra twine.

In a large Dutch oven or deep casserole dish, completely bury the rolled foie gras in the kosher salt. Let the foie gras cure in the refrigerator for 16 hours.

Remove the foie gras from the salt cure and brush off all of the salt from the cheesecloth.

Working quickly, before the foie gras warms and softens, unwrap the cheesecloth and reroll the foie gras tightly in multiple layers of plastic wrap (at least three turns), using the same rolling technique you used with the cheesecloth. Twist and secure both ends with kitchen twine, leaving an extra 1-foot-long length of twine on one side.

Let the *torchon* chill in the refrigerator for 2 hours.

**To serve:** Fill a large bowl or tall canister with hot water. Dip a sharp knife into the water to warm it slightly. Wipe the knife dry with a kitchen towel and, slicing through the plastic wrap, cut off one end of the torchon. Slice the torchon into ½-inch-thick rounds, dipping and wiping the knife after each slice.

Place a slice of foie gras on each plate, along with a spoonful of the *mostarda*. Toast the brioche slices and serve them warm alongside the foie gras.

Store the unused foie gras, wrapped in plastic wrap, in the refrigerator. Seasoned with *sel rose*, the foie gras will keep for at least 1 week. If you are using pickling salt instead, it will keep for up to 3 days.

**NOTE:** An extremely fatty liver, foie gras comes with a network of veins running throughout it. These must be removed before you can use the foie gras—they are stringy and unpalatable.

I let the foie gras come almost to room temperature so that it softens a bit. There are two parts to the liver, one larger than the other, divided by a conspicuous seam. Gently, separate the two parts. The larger half of the lobe will have a vein peeking out of the top. Insert a paring knife into the lobe at the vein. Cutting halfway into the lobe, slice it open down its length. Parting the lobe along the cut, open it up like a book. A network of veins should be plainly visible. Using the paring knife and your thumb, lift up the large end of the vein at the top of the lobe and gently pull out the network of veins; it should come out in one piece. You may need to scrape away some of the foie gras to loosen some of the smaller strands. Once the large network of veins has been removed, look for smaller veins that may have been left behind—look for red streaks and spots. Repeat the process with the smaller half of the liver. You won't find a vein readily visible on its surface like the larger half. Instead, just slice it open and work through it in a similar fashion. If, at any time, the foie gras becomes too soft, stick it in the icebox for a few minutes to let it firm up a bit before continuing.

# warm **eggplant** salad, caperberries, lemon vinaigrette

**Serves 4**

**eggplant**

8 ounces baby eggplant

Salt

**lemon vinaigrette**

½ cup extra-virgin olive oil

Juice of 2 lemons

2 tablespoons Champagne vinegar

½ teaspoon sugar

Salt and freshly ground white pepper

**salad**

5 tablespoons vegetable oil

4 ounces okra, ends trimmed and halved lengthwise

1 shallot, minced

2 cloves garlic, minced

8 caperberries, halved

Watercress, for garnish

They say that eggplant has no nutritional value. But its porous flesh is a chameleon, having the ability to take on the flavor of its companions magnificently when cooked.

In this warm salad, baby eggplant is pan-fried and tossed with seared okra and lemony vinaigrette. Together, it's meaty, it's bright, it's warm, and it's sophisticated.

**Prepare the eggplant:** Slice the eggplants on the bias into thirds. Put the slices on a baking sheet and salt them liberally, rubbing the salt over the cut sides of each slice. Spread them out on a baking sheet lined with a kitchen towel and let drain for at least 1 hour, or overnight if possible. This not only draws out the liquid but also removes any bitterness the eggplant might have.

**Make the vinaigrette:** Whisk together the olive oil, lemon juice, vinegar, and sugar. Season the vinaigrette with salt and pepper to taste.

**Cook the vegetables:** Rinse the eggplant under cold water to wash away the salt. Pat the eggplant dry with kitchen towels. Line a large platter with paper towels.

Heat 3 tablespoons of the vegetable oil in a large sauté pan over medium-high heat. Sear the eggplant slices on both sides until golden brown, about 4 minutes. Spread the eggplant out on the lined platter to drain.

Return the sauté pan to the stove and heat the remaining 2 tablespoons vegetable oil over medium-high heat. Sear the okra on both sides, cut side down first, until brown, about 1 minute per side. Transfer the okra to the lined platter, leaving as much oil in the pan as possible.

Return the sauté pan to the stove over medium-low heat. Add the shallot and garlic and cook for 1 minute, or until the shallots become translucent. Add the vinaigrette and caperberries and bring to a slow simmer. Add the eggplant and okra to the skillet and gently toss to coat the vegetables with the vinaigrette.

**To serve:** Divide the eggplant, okra, and caperberries among 4 plates, leaving as much vinaigrette in the sauté pan as possible. Garnish each plate with watercress. Drizzle a spoonful of the warm vinaigrette over each plate and serve. The extra vinaigrette can be cooled and stored in an airtight container in the refrigerator for up to 1 week.

# sausage, rye whiskey plums

**Serves 4**

**pork sausage**

1 (2-ounce) package salted pork casing (or approximately 10 feet of casing)

3 pounds ground pork butt

2 tablespoons salt

2 teaspoons freshly ground white pepper

½ cup chilled dry white wine

¼ cup vegetable oil, plus more for brushing

**whiskey plums**

3 cups rye whiskey

1¾ cups port

1½ cups freshly squeezed orange juice

1 cup sugar

1½ tablespoons grated orange zest

4 juniper berries

2 star anise

2 firm but ripe plums, halved and pitted

Making sausage isn't difficult at all, as long as you have the proper tools. You could even skip the step of stuffing the meat into casings to make links and just cook sausage patties.

While this recipe calls for poaching only two plums, you could poach up to six plums in the amount of liquid that is called for. The extra stewed plums can be served at room temperature with the foie gras *au torchon* (page 82) and some chopped almonds or warmed and served with honey ice cream (page 266) and a drizzle of the plum syrup.

**Prepare the casing:** Rinse the casing under running water to wash off the salt. Open one end of the casing and run the water through the casing. Soak the casing in room-temperature water for 1 hour.

**Make the stuffing:** Freeze the meat for 15 minutes to make sure the meat is cold.

Combine the chilled meat, salt, and pepper in the bowl of a stand mixer fitted with a paddle attachment. Mix on medium speed for 1 minute. With the mixer running, drizzle in the wine and continue to beat until the meat is sticky, about 2 minutes.

Since you won't be able to season the meat once it's in the casing, you'll want to taste it and adjust the seasoning before you stuff the sausage. Pinch off a golf ball–size

piece of meat. Roll the meat together between your palms and flatten it slightly to make a small patty. Heat 2 tablespoons of the vegetable oil in a sauté pan over medium-high heat. When the oil is hot, add the sausage patty and cook for 2 minutes on one side, then flip the patty and cook for another minute or two, until the meat has browned (if you want to be extra cautious, check to see that the internal temperature registers 160°F on an instant-read thermometer). Taste the sausage and make any seasoning adjustments necessary to the whole batch accordingly.

At this point, if you don't want to stuff the sausage into the casing, you can form the rest of the meat into patties and fry them in a little vegetable oil just as you did with the tester patty.

**Stuff the sausages:** Brush the nozzle of a sausage stuffer with vegetable oil. Thread the casing onto the nozzle, leaving a 6-inch tail at the end (which will be used to tie the sausage off).

Feed a fistful of ground meat into the sausage stuffer. Stuff the sausage according to the manufacturer's instructions (depending on the device you use, this could be as simple as flipping a switch, or it may require cranking by hand).

Tie the two ends of the sausage with butcher's twine. Trim off any excess casing at either end. Twist the sausage—four or five turns—at intervals to form individual links (we recommend 3- to 3½-inch lengths).

**Cook the plums:** In a saucepan combine the whiskey, port, juice, sugar, zest, juniper berries, and star anise and bring them to a boil over medium-high heat. Lower the heat to a simmer and add the plums.

Cook the plums until the skins have loosened just enough to pull away, about 5 minutes.

Remove the plums with a slotted spoon and let them cool on a plate. Strain the stewing liquid through a fine-mesh sieve to remove any solids. Reserve 4 cups of the stewing liquid; return the remaining liquid to the pot and bring it to a simmer over medium-low heat. Let the liquid reduce until it thickens into a syrup, about 10 minutes. Keep an eye on it to make sure it doesn't bubble over.

When the plums have cooled enough to handle them, peel the skins off, being careful not to destroy the shape of the plums. Discard the skins and store the plums in the reserved stewing liquid. Covered and refrigerated, they will keep for up to 1 week.

**Cook the sausages:** Using small scissors, cut the sausage at each twist to separate the links. Depending on the size of the sausages, you will need one or two per person for a first-course portion.

Heat the remaining 2 tablespoons of vegetable oil in a small sauté pan over medium-high heat. Fry the sausages for 4 to 5 minutes, turning them every 30 seconds or so to get them evenly browned.

**To serve:** Divide the sausages and stewed plums among 4 plates. Drizzle a spoonful of the plum syrup around each plate and serve immediately. Loosely covered, extra sausages will keep for up to 1 week in the refrigerator. Tightly wrapped and stored in the freezer, they will keep for up to 2 months.

# chitarra, tomatoes, chard

**Serves 4**

2 tablespoons olive oil

8 ounces cherry tomatoes

12 ounces chitarra pasta

3 cloves garlic, thinly sliced

8 ounces young Swiss chard, leaves and stems separated and chopped

2 tablespoons white wine

Salt and freshly ground black pepper

2 ounces goat cheese

## Tomatoes! Tomatoes! Tomatoes!

Some summers, we get more than we could dream of using. It's an onslaught most desired. Other summers, they come and go in the blink of an eye, plagued by too much rain or fungal growth or ruined by unseasonably cool temperatures.

This recipe is stripped down and simple, an ideal showcase for great summer produce. You can use any fleshy green-leaf vegetable instead of chard. The important thing is that you use something fresh, with good natural flavor. If you cannot find *pasta alla chitarra*, which is similar to spaghetti except that the strands are square instead of round, substitute regular spaghetti.

Heat 1 tablespoon of the olive oil in a large sauté pan over high heat. When the oil is smoking hot, add the tomatoes. They will blister immediately. Shake the pan to roll the tomatoes around until they're blistered all over, less than 30 seconds. Transfer the tomatoes from the pan to a plate.

Bring a large stockpot of water to a rolling boil over high heat. Heavily salt the water, stirring it in to dissolve it. Cook the pasta until just short of tender—you will cook the pasta a little more with the chard. Drain the pasta, reserving a bit more than ¼ cup of the pasta water, and set the pasta aside, keeping it warm.

Heat the remaining tablespoon of oil in the sauté pan over low heat. Add the garlic and chard stems and cook until they start to turn translucent, about 1 minute. Stir in the chard leaves, ¼ cup of the reserved pasta water, and the wine and continue to cook until the greens have wilted, about 1 minute. Add the pasta, tossing to coat, and then the tomatoes. Add a bit more reserved pasta water to keep the pasta moist, if necessary, and let it simmer for 30 seconds. Season with salt and black pepper to taste.

Divide the pasta and vegetables among 4 bowls, top each with some goat cheese, and serve immediately.

# orecchiette, pattypan squash, brown butter, sage

**Serves 4**

12 ounces orecchiette

8 tablespoons (1 stick) unsalted butter

12 ounces pattypan squash, cut into ¼-inch slices

6 cloves garlic, thinly sliced

⅓ cup fresh sage leaves, finely chopped

4 ounces cherry tomatoes

Salt and freshly ground white pepper

If you doubt the saying "butter makes everything better," then try this dish. It's a super-easy and delicious way to use up extra squash and tomatoes, which can seem almost over-abundant at the height of summer.

It goes without saying that using good-quality ingredients makes good dishes great. And that couldn't be truer here. Good-quality butter will give this dish a fuller, rounder toastiness that will balance the bright acidity of the tomatoes. Orecchiette is a small, round pasta shape whose name translates from the Italian as "little ears."

---

Bring a large stockpot of water to a rolling boil over high heat. Heavily salt the water, stirring it in to dissolve it. Cook the pasta until just short of tender—you will cook the pasta a little more with the brown butter and squash. Drain the pasta, reserving ¼ cup of the pasta water, and set the pasta aside, keeping it warm.

Heat 1 tablespoon of the butter over high heat in a medium sauté pan. Add the squash and sauté until the slices develop a toasty, golden surface, about 3 minutes.

Add the garlic and cook just to warm through. Add the pasta and the remaining butter and lower the heat to medium. Continue to cook the pasta and vegetables until the butter begins to brown and gives off a nutty aroma, about 2 minutes. Add the sage and tomatoes and stir to warm through. Season the mixture with salt and pepper to taste.

Divide the pasta and vegetables among 4 bowls and serve immediately.

# poached **wild coho salmon**, champagne–trout roe vinaigrette, braised endive

**Serves 4**

### endive

4 Belgian endives, halved

1 medium grapefruit

1 tablespoon peeled and grated fresh ginger

½ teaspoon sugar

1 cup dry white wine

2 cloves garlic, peeled

1 cup Fish Stock (page 255)

Salt and freshly ground white pepper

1 English cucumber, peeled and shaved lengthwise into ribbons

### salmon

3 cups Fish Stock (page 255)

¾ cup dry white wine

2 cloves garlic, chopped

2 sprigs fresh tarragon

1 bay leaf

1 shallot, sliced

2 teaspoons salt

¼ teaspoon freshly ground white pepper

4 (6-ounce) wild coho salmon fillets

### champagne and roe vinaigrette

¼ cup reserved endive broth

¼ cup reserved salmon broth

¼ cup Champagne vinegar

2 heaping tablespoons trout roe or salmon roe

Salt and freshly ground white pepper

Fresh tarragon leaves, for garnish

Since fish spend their whole lives in water, it seems quite natural to cook them in water. I know many home cooks who get nervous about poaching fish because the results can be disappointing. The fish can turn out dry, crumbly, and flavorless, the flavor having leached out of the fish and into the poaching liquid. But done well, poaching is a gentle method of cooking that leaves the fish moist and silky. In fact, I prefer the light flavor of nicely poached fish to that of a seared or roasted piece of fish.

Any salmon will work for this recipe, though I especially love using wild-caught coho salmon from Alaska, which is available all summer. Wild coho salmon has a high amount of fat, which gives it a naturally rich flavor. You'll be surprised at how buttery this dish tastes, despite the fact that there is no butter in the recipe.

**Braise the endives:** Cut out a round of parchment paper just large enough to fit snugly over the opening of a large sauté pan. Arrange the endive halves in the sauté pan, cut side down, so that they're fanned out with the cores facing the middle.

Remove the zest of the grapefruit with a vegetable peeler (a Y-peeler works particularly well), trimming off all the bitter white pith. Slice the zest into thin strips and sprinkle them over the endives. Slice the grapefruit in

half and juice it over the endives, straining out the seeds. Discard the grapefruit rinds.

In a bowl, whisk together the ginger, sugar, wine, garlic, and fish stock and season it with salt and pepper to taste. Pour this mixture over the endives and cover the pan with the parchment paper. Bring the endives to a gentle simmer over low heat and cook for 20 to 25 minutes, until the endives have softened. Transfer the endives and grapefruit zest from the braising liquid (a slotted spatula or spoon is especially useful here) to a plate and set aside.

Bring the braising liquid back to a simmer over medium-high heat. Drop in the cucumber ribbons and blanch them for 30 seconds. Again using a slotted spatula, transfer the cucumbers from the pan to the plate of endives to drain. Reserve ¼ cup of the endive braising liquid.

**Poach the salmon:** Combine the stock, wine, garlic, tarragon sprigs, bay leaf, shallot, salt, and pepper in a large saucepan or sauté pan with high sides. Heat the ingredients over low heat until the liquid reaches 135°F on an instant-read thermometer (the liquid should be just hot enough that you can barely stand to keep your finger in it). Season the fish with salt and pepper. Put the fillets in the poaching liquid and cover the pot loosely with aluminum foil. Poach the fillets for 6 to 7 minutes, trying to maintain the temperature as close to 135°F as possible. Carefully transfer the fish fillets to a plate to drain and cool. Reserve ¼ cup of the poaching liquid.

**Make the vinaigrette:** Combine the reserved endive braising liquid and reserved salmon poaching liquid in a bowl. Whisk in the Champagne vinegar. Add the trout roe and season with salt and pepper to taste.

**To serve:** Divide the endives and grapefruit zest evenly among 4 shallow bowls. Top each portion of endives with a fish fillet. Season the fish with salt and pepper to taste. Spoon a bit of the vinaigrette and roe over the fish and garnish each plate with tarragon leaves. Serve immediately.

# trout, pistachio, summer beans, coriander butter sauce

**Serves 4**

### sauce

2 trout heads and trimmings
(see headnote)

6 cloves garlic, smashed

1 large carrot, coarsely chopped

2 celery stalks, coarsely chopped

1 medium onion, coarsely chopped

2 cups white wine

2 cups water

1 bay leaf

2 sprigs fresh thyme

2 sprigs fresh tarragon

¼ cup coriander seeds, toasted

### beans

8 ounces green beans, trimmed and
strings removed

5 ounces slab bacon, cut into 1-inch
cubes

2 tablespoons unsalted butter

1 cup White Beans (page 261)

Salt and freshly ground white pepper

### trout

1 medium onion, finely diced

2 carrots, finely diced

2 celery stalks, finely diced

4 sprigs fresh thyme

4 (6- to 8-ounce) trout fillets, such as
brook, lake, or rainbow trout

Salt and freshly ground black pepper

¼ cup vegetable oil

½ cup heavy cream

¼ cup unsalted pistachios, toasted and
chopped

Young parsley leaves, for garnish

Trout is abundant all over the Midwest, particularly in the Upper Great Lakes region. In Missouri, our lakes in the Ozarks are a haven for trout anglers.

My dad was the head of my Cub Scout pack, so outdoorsmanship was inescapable. While I loved camping, sadly, I might have been the only Midwestern boy who hated fishing. I didn't have the patience for it, a claim my dad finds dubious every time he sees me cleaning and filleting fish.

Unless you are very good at filleting fish, with its small bones and delicate flesh, it's best to have your fishmonger fillet trout for you. Ask for the heads and trimmings to be wrapped up and included — you'll need them for the sauce. If you are filleting the fish yourself, make sure that you remove and discard the gills and that you pull out all of the tiny pin bones in the fillets with tweezers.

**Make the sauce:** Bring the trout trimmings, garlic, carrot, celery, onion, wine, water, bay leaf, thyme, tarragon, and coriander seeds to a boil in a large stockpot over high heat. Lower the heat to medium and let the stock simmer and reduce by three-quarters to yield about 1½ cups of stock, about 10 minutes. Remove the stock from the heat, cover, and keep warm until ready to serve.

**Make the beans:** Bring a pot of water to a boil. While the water is heating, prepare an ice bath (see the User Manual, page xxv). Blanch the snap beans for 1½ minutes. Drain, then cool them in an ice bath, drain, and set aside (for blanching instructions, see the User Manual, page xxiv).

In a small sauté pan over high heat, cook the bacon until the bacon cubes develop a light brown crust. Transfer the bacon cubes to a plate lined with paper towels to drain. Pour off the rendered bacon fat, reserving it for another use.

Heat the butter in a large sauté pan over high heat. When the butter begins to foam, add the snap beans and white beans and cook them for a minute, stirring to coat them with the butter. Add the cooked bacon and continue to cook for a minute. Season the beans with salt and pepper to taste. Remove the pan from the heat and set aside, keeping the beans warm until ready to serve.

**Cook the trout:** Preheat the oven to 300°F.

Spread the onion, carrots, celery, and thyme evenly over a large baking sheet or pan. Position a rack over the vegetables, making sure that it is level, and spray the rack with nonstick cooking spray. Season both sides of the fillets with salt and pepper and set them on the rack, skin side down. Roast the trout in the oven for 5 minutes.

Remove the fillets from the rack, being careful not to tear the skin. Discard the vegetables. Pat both sides of the fillets dry with paper towels. Heat 2 tablespoons

of the vegetable oil in a large sauté pan over high heat. When the oil begins to smoke, add 2 fillets, skin side down, and pan-fry them just long enough to crisp the skin, about 30 seconds. Transfer to a plate. There should be enough oil left in the pan to fry the remaining fillets. If not, add up to 2 more tablespoons of vegetable oil for frying the second batch of fish.

**To serve:** Stir the cream into the warm stock. Using a handheld blender, froth the stock by holding the spinning blades near the surface of the liquid, just barely submerging the blades.

Lay a fillet of fish, skin side up, on each plate. Divide the beans among the 4 plates. Top each serving with a heaping spoonful of frothed stock. Garnish each plate with chopped pistachios and parsley. Serve immediately.

# catfish sticks, corn nuts

**Serves 4**

3 cups corn nuts

1 cup all-purpose flour

2 cups whole milk

1½ pounds freshwater catfish fillets

Salt and freshly ground white pepper

2 tablespoons vegetable oil

Tartar Sauce (recipe follows)

4 ounces radishes, trimmed and thinly sliced

Raise your hand if you grew up eating fish out of a box in stick form. Yes, that grizzled, most-interesting-man-in-the-world in rain slickers was my best friend as a kid.

Rolled in crushed corn nuts, these fish sticks are a fun take on a childhood favorite. Although you could use a white fish from the ocean, at Bluestem we use freshwater catfish, which is probably the most commonly found fish item on menus across the Midwest. Here I've simplified the recipe so that it's more like fish strips.

---

Toast the corn nuts in a dry sauté pan over medium-high heat, 3 to 5 minutes. Shake the pan to prevent them from burning.

Remove the corn nuts from the pan and let them cool completely. Pulverize the corn nuts in a food processor until they are coarsely ground. Set aside 2 tablespoons of the ground corn nuts to use as garnish.

Put the flour in a shallow dish. Pour the milk into another shallow dish. Put the ground corn nuts in a third shallow dish.

Line a large plate or baking sheet with paper towels.

Pat the fish dry. Slice the fillets lengthwise into 1-inch-wide strips. Season them with salt and pepper.

Toss the fish strips in the flour to coat. Knock off the excess flour. Dip the fish strips in the milk, and then roll them in the ground corn nuts to coat. Transfer the crusted fish strips to the lined plate or baking sheet.

Heat the vegetable oil in a large sauté pan over medium-high heat. Carefully add the fish strips to the pan and fry, undisturbed, until the corn nut crust turns dark golden on the bottom, about 2 minutes. Flip the strips over and fry on the second side until the crust darkens and the fish is cooked through, about 1 minute more.

To serve, smear a spoonful of tartar sauce across the center of each of 4 plates. Divide the fish strips among the plates and garnish with the radish slices and reserved ground corn nuts. Serve immediately.

## *tartar sauce*  Makes about 2 cups

½ cup Crème Fraîche (page 251)

½ cup mayonnaise, homemade (page 252)
or store-bought

2 hard-boiled eggs, finely chopped

10 cornichons, drained and minced

2 tablespoons drained capers, minced

1 tablespoon Champagne vinegar

Juice of 1 lemon

2 tablespoons Dijon mustard

1 tablespoon chopped fresh flat-leaf parsley

1 tablespoon chopped fresh tarragon

Salt and freshly ground white pepper

Whisk the crème fraîche and mayonnaise together until smooth. Stir in the eggs, cornichons, capers, vinegar, lemon juice, and mustard. Add the parsley and tarragon and season with salt and pepper to taste.

**NOTE:** This sauce tastes better when made 1 day ahead to allow the flavors to blend. If you do make it ahead, leave the parsley and tarragon out of the sauce until just before serving.

# campo lindo **hen**, pistachio pistou

**Serves 4**

**pistou**

1¼ cups Chicken Stock (page 256), chilled

½ cup unsalted pistachios, toasted and chilled

1½ ounces Parmigiano cheese in one chunk, chilled

2 garlic cloves, coarsely chopped and chilled

1 small shallot, coarsely chopped and chilled

8 cups loosely packed fresh basil leaves

¼ cup fresh flat-leaf parsley

½ cup fresh oregano

½ cup ice cubes

**vegetables**

2 teaspoons extra-virgin olive oil

1 small red onion, thinly sliced

1 small fennel bulb, trimmed and thinly sliced

2 cups assorted diced summer squash

2 cups assorted peeled and diced carrots

Salt and freshly ground white pepper

**chicken**

4 (6-ounce) boneless, skin-on chicken breasts

Salt and freshly ground white pepper

2 tablespoons olive oil

3 tablespoons unsalted butter

1 shallot, coarsely chopped

4 sprigs fresh thyme

1 clove garlic, coarsely chopped

2 sprigs fresh oregano

1 lemon, quartered, for serving

Thyme blossoms, for garnish

Good-quality, naturally raised chicken brims with so much natural flavor that you really don't need to do much to make it shine. This dish—one of the few that Bonjwing insisted be included in this book—proves it.

The herbaceous pistachio pistou and the gently cooked vegetables make this dish not only a summery collection of flavors but also intensely colorful, especially if you're able to find a variety of carrots—they come in almost every color of the rainbow, so keep your eyes peeled at farmers' markets.

**For the pistou:** Make sure all of the ingredients for the pistou are cold before you begin. Combine the stock, pistachios, cheese, garlic, shallot, basil, parsley, and oregano in a blender and puree until smooth. With the blender running, add the ice cubes one at a time. Transfer the pistou to a container and keep chilled until ready to serve.

**Cook the vegetables:** Heat the olive oil in a sauté pan over medium-high heat. Stir in the onion and sauté until slightly softened, about 1 minute. Add the fennel, squash, and carrots and continue to cook for 2 more minutes just to soften them—you don't want them to develop much color on the surface. Remove the pan from the heat and season the vegetables with salt and pepper. Keep the vegetables warm until ready to serve.

**Cook the chicken:** Preheat the oven to 375°F.

Pat the chicken breasts dry with a paper towel and season them on both sides with salt and pepper.

Heat the olive oil in a large ovenproof skillet over high heat. Cook the chicken breasts, skin side down, for 2 minutes to develop a light golden color. If the skin is browning too quickly, turn the heat down to medium-high. Flip the breasts over and cook for another minute.

Turn the breasts back onto the skin side, transfer the skillet to the oven, and cook the breasts for another 15 minutes, or until the internal temperature registers 165°F on an instant-read thermometer.

Return the skillet with the chicken to the stove over medium-high heat. Add the butter, shallot, thyme, garlic, and oregano. When the butter has melted, turn off the heat. Carefully tilt the skillet slightly toward you and spoon the hot butter over the breasts, basting them for about 1½ minutes.

Remove the chicken from the heat.

**To serve:** Heat the pistou in a small saucepan over low heat. Season with salt and white pepper to taste.

Slice the chicken breasts in half widthwise and serve two halves (or a whole breast) per person.

Pour about ¼ cup pistou into each of 4 shallow bowls. Divide the vegetables among the bowls, mounding them in the center. Top the vegetables with a halved chicken breast.

Squeeze a dash of fresh lemon juice over the chicken and garnish the plate with thyme blossoms. Serve immediately.

# roasted **pork**, sweet and sour peaches

**Serves 4**

**sweet and sour peaches**

2 tablespoons grapeseed oil

4 firm but ripe peaches, halved and pitted

2 young onion bulbs (or small white onions), sliced ½ inch thick

2 scallions, halved lengthwise

1½ cups bourbon

1 cup freshly squeezed orange juice

¾ cup sherry vinegar

½ cup Madeira

½ cup honey

1 tablespoon freshly ground black pepper

5 cardamom pods

**pork**

2 tablespoons salt

1 tablespoon brown sugar

½ teaspoon freshly ground black pepper

½ teaspoon chili powder

⅛ teaspoon paprika

½ teaspoon garlic salt

4 double-cut pork loin chops, attached in rack form and trussed

2 tablespoons grapeseed oil

I usually have one main course on the summer menu that casually nods toward barbecue, which is an integral part of our local culture. Kansas City barbecue relies on a combination of sweetness, smokiness, and spicy heat, with just a touch of acidity to balance it all out. You'll find all of these flavors in the sweet and sour peaches that accompany the pork.

Admittedly, the portion size and rusticity of these bone-in, double-cut pork chops wouldn't make them appropriate for our restaurant's multicourse menu. For a more elegant presentation, you can slice the meat off the bone and serve the slices alongside the peaches.

---

**Cook the peaches and onions:** Heat the oil in a large skillet over medium-low heat.

Place the peaches, onion slices, and scallions, cut side down, in the skillet. Griddle them until the peaches and onions caramelize and the scallions have just begun to soften, turning the onions and scallions as needed, about 20 minutes. Remove the skillet from the heat and transfer the peaches, onions, and scallions to a plate.

## the pits

To pit peaches, halve the peach along its seam. The peach will open with the pit lying flat, making it much easier to lever it out with a paring knife.

Make the sweet and sour glaze: Bring the bourbon, orange juice, vinegar, Madeira, honey, pepper, and cardamom to a simmer in a large saucepan over high heat. Lower the heat to medium to maintain a gentle simmer and reduce the sauce until it is thick and syrupy, about 1 hour.

**Cook the pork:** Preheat the oven to 425°F.

Combine the salt, brown sugar, pepper, chili powder, paprika, and garlic salt in a small bowl. Rub the seasoning mix over the pork, coating the meat generously with all of it.

Heat the grapeseed oil in a large skillet over high heat. When the oil begins to shimmer, brown the rack of pork, turning the meat often to prevent the rub from burning.

Place the browned rack of pork, with the bones pointing upward, on a rack set over a roasting pan. Roast the meat in the oven for 25 minutes for a slightly pink interior,

or until the internal temperature registers 140°F on an instant-read thermometer. Let the meat rest for at least 15 minutes.

**Glaze the peaches and onions:** Bring the reduced sauce to a gentle simmer in a large skillet over medium-high heat. Add the peaches and onions—but not the scallions—and let them cook in the sauce, which should thicken and bubble, for a couple of minutes. Turn the onions and peaches over to coat them with the saucy glaze.

**To serve:** Cut the pork rack into 4 equal-size "chops."

Transfer the glazed peaches, onions, and scallions from the skillet to 4 plates. Drizzle some of the syrup over and around them. Serve them with the pork chops.

**NOTES:** While it's perfectly acceptable to brine pork loins, I don't think it's necessary. Either have the butcher truss the loin or truss the loin yourself. Trussing will give it a nice shape and ensure more even cooking.

Don't be afraid to use dry seasonings to make rubs for large pieces of meat. In the Midwest, dry seasonings are an integral part of the way our barbecue tastes.

# grilled wagyu **rib eye**, sweet corn, goat cheese, speck gratin

**Serves 4**

**speck gratin**

2 tablespoons unsalted butter

½ small white onion, diced

4 cloves garlic, minced

2 tablespoons all-purpose flour

1½ cups whole milk

2½ ounces cream cheese, softened

2½ ounces goat cheese, softened

2 cups sweet corn kernels

3 ounces speck, diced

⅛ teaspoon dried red pepper flakes

**steaks**

4 (1-pound) bone-in Wagyu rib-eye steaks, at room temperature

Salt and freshly ground black pepper

⅓ cup Herb Crumbs (page 262)

In this part of the country, beefiness is next to godliness. A big hunk of steak on the grill is not only the best way to impress guests, but the mouthwatering aroma of meat-meets-fire is also the most effective way of asserting primacy over your neighbors.

Due to its intense marbling of fat, to me, the rib eye is superior in flavor to all other cuts of beef. At home, I serve this steak with a death-defyingly rich sweet corn gratin and a simple side salad of mixed greens tossed with sherry vinaigrette (page 254).

**Make the gratin:** Heat the butter in a medium saucepan over medium heat. Stir in the onion and garlic and sweat them for about 1 minute. Turn the heat to low and sprinkle in the flour, stirring to incorporate it evenly with the onion and garlic. Add the milk and let the mixture cook and thicken for 5 minutes, stirring occasionally to make sure the sauce doesn't clump or burn. Stir in the cream cheese and goat cheese until they have melted.

Add the corn, speck, and red pepper flakes and let the mixture reduce until thick and bubbly, about 10 minutes.

Transfer the sweet corn mixture to an ovenproof serving dish. Or, if you would like to serve individual portions, divide the sweet corn among 4 ovenproof 4-ounce ramekins. Keep warm.

**Grill the steak:** Preheat a charcoal or gas grill to medium-high heat. Pat the steaks dry with a paper towel. Season them on both sides with salt and pepper. Depending on the thickness of your steaks and the temperature of your grill, cooking times will vary. For a 1-inch-thick steak, grill the meat for about 4 minutes on each side for a medium rare interior. The safest way to test the meat is by taking an internal temperature reading with a meat thermometer inserted through the side of the steak into the center. For a medium-rare steak, you'll want to take the meat off the grill when the internal temperature reaches 126°F.

Let the meat rest for 10 to 15 minutes before serving, during which the residual heat will cause the internal temperature of the meat to rise another 5°F.

While the meat is resting, sprinkle the herb crumbs over the sweet corn and toast the gratin under a broiler until the crumbs turn golden brown.

**To serve:** Slice the steaks and arrange the slices, overlapping each other, on individual plates accompanied by a serving of the sweet corn gratin.

# pleasant ridge reserve, tomato jam

**Serves 4**

8 ounces Pleasant Ridge Reserve cheese

Tomato Jam (recipe follows)

**Uplands Cheese Company** in Dodgeville, Wisconsin, makes a great cow's milk, alpine-style cheese called Pleasant Ridge Reserve. It has a waxy structure and a rich, creamy nuttiness with a hint of sweetness that goes well with tomato jam. If you can't find Pleasant Ridge Reserve, substitute an alpine cheese, such as Gruyère or Beaufort.

Divide the cheese among 4 plates. Serve with a side of tomato jam and some crackers or lavosh (see page 264).

# tomato jam    Makes 2 cups

This tomato jam is slightly chunky. If you prefer a smoother jam, puree it in a blender until it reaches the consistency you desire.

---

5 medium tomatoes

3 cloves garlic, minced

2 shallots, peeled and thinly sliced

¾ cup sherry vinegar

¼ cup honey

2 tablespoons sugar

1½ teaspoons dry pectin

½ teaspoon freshly ground black pepper

1 teaspoon salt

1 teaspoon fresh thyme

¼ cup water

Combine all of the ingredients in a medium saucepan and bring them to a simmer over medium-low heat. Let the jam cook, stirring occasionally, until the tomatoes have completely softened and broken down, about 2 hours.

Remove the jam from the heat and let it cool completely. Transfer to an airtight container and refrigerate for up to 1 month.

# **chocolate** sponge cake, bing cherries, cocoa foam, "popcorn" ice cream

**Makes one
18 by 13-inch cake;
serves 6**

⅓ cup unsweetened cocoa powder

⅓ cup all-purpose flour

½ teaspoon ground cinnamon

¼ teaspoon ground cardamom

¼ teaspoon salt

9 eggs, separated, at room temperature

1 cup plus 2 tablespoons granulated sugar

2 tablespoons strong, hot brewed coffee

Chocolate Sauce (page 268)

"Popcorn" Ice Cream (recipe follows)

8 ounces bing cherries, stemmed and pitted

Cocoa Foam (optional; recipe follows)

With a cherry tree in our yard, Mom and I would spend summer afternoons picking the cherries in the hot sun. Afterward, we'd cool off in the comfort of our air-conditioned kitchen, stemming and pitting our mound of garnet gems. Then we'd bake.

For me, summer is a time for chocolate shakes, corn on the grill, and cherry pie. I know I'm not alone. This dessert, which reconfigures them all on one plate, is a runaway hit on our summer menu.

---

Preheat the oven to 325°F. Butter and line an 18 by 13-inch jelly-roll pan with parchment paper.

Sift the cocoa powder, flour, cinnamon, and cardamom together into a bowl. Add the salt and set aside.

In the bowl of a stand mixer fitted with a paddle attachment, beat the egg yolks on high speed until they achieve a thick, ribbon-like state, about 5 minutes. Transfer the egg yolks to a larger bowl and set aside.

In a clean bowl of a stand mixer fitted with a whisk attachment, whip the egg whites on high speed until frothy, about 2 minutes. Add the sugar in a steady stream and continue beating until the egg whites form stiff but not dry peaks, about 3 minutes.

Stir a dollop of the whipped egg whites into the egg yolks to lighten the yolks. Gently fold the rest of the egg whites into the egg yolks in thirds, adding the coffee with the last third. Fold in the dry ingredients until well incorporated.

Pour the batter onto the prepared jelly-roll pan and smooth the top with a large offset spatula. Slap the pan gently on the counter to get rid of any large air bubbles in the batter.

Bake the cake for 12 minutes. It should be spongy and light. Cool the cake completely. This cake is best served the day it is made, although it can be baked 1 day ahead and kept tightly wrapped in plastic wrap. It does not

freeze well. Be careful not to touch the surface of the cake, which peels off easily.

To serve, cut the cake into squares or shapes using a cookie cutter. Drizzle some chocolate sauce across each plate. Divide the cakes among the plates, topping each with a scoop of ice cream. Garnish the plate with the cherries and spoon some cocoa foam around the plate.

## cake crumbs

Cake trimmings can be used to make cake crumbs for garnishing desserts like this chocolate sponge cake. Cake crumbs are also used as "grass" on plated desserts—a bed of crumbs on which ice creams and garnishes are placed to keep them from sliding around. Leave the cake trimmings out, uncovered, for 3 to 5 days (depending on how humid it is). Once the cake crumbs are dried, blitz them in a food processor until finely ground. Sift the crumbs through a fine-mesh sieve and store in an airtight container at room temperature for up to 1 week.

## cocoa foam

3 ounces bittersweet chocolate, chopped

1 cup plus 2 tablespoons water

Place the chocolate in a large bowl.

Bring the water to a boil in a small saucepan over high heat. Pour the boiling water over the chocolate and stir in a constant circular motion until the chocolate has fully melted. Set aside to cool. Transfer the liquid to a canister or tall, narrow pitcher.

Using a handheld immersion blender, froth the chocolate mixture until it foams, like the head of a glass of beer, and the bubbles stay. It helps to tip the canister at an angle and set the spinning blade near the surface of the liquid. Use immediately.

## "popcorn" ice cream  Makes about 1½ quarts

4 ears sweet corn

2 tablespoons light brown sugar

¼ teaspoon salt, plus more as needed

2 tablespoons unsalted butter

2 tablespoons vanilla extract

6 egg yolks

2 cups heavy cream

1 cup whole milk

¾ cup granulated sugar

Shave the kernels off the cobs into a large saucepan. "Milk" the cobs into the pot by running the back of a knife down the sides of the cobs, pressing to extract as much of the corn milk as possible. Add the cobs, brown sugar, ¼ teaspoon salt, butter, and vanilla and cook slowly over medium-low heat until the sugar has dissolved and the kernels are lightly toasted and have caramelized, 5 to 7 minutes. Remove from the heat and set aside.

In a medium-size bowl, whisk the egg yolks together.

In a large saucepan, combine the cooked corn, cream, milk, and sugar. Bring the mixture to a low simmer over medium-high heat for 2 minutes, or until the sugar has fully dissolved. Watch the pot closely, as it may boil over quickly. Remove from heat and let the ice cream base steep for 2 hours at room temperature. Remove from the heat and set aside.

Remove the cobs from the ice cream base and discard. Transfer the rest of the base to a blender and puree until smooth.  Return the base to the saucepan and bring it to a low simmer over medium-high heat.

Temper the egg yolks by whisking 1 cup of the hot ice cream base into the yolks in a slow, steady stream.  You want to add the hot cream slowly to gradually increase the temperature of the egg yolks without scrambling them.

Strain the ice cream base through a fine-mesh sieve into a large bowl. Set the bowl over ice and stir the base until it has cooled.

Churn the base in an ice cream maker according to the manufacturer's instructions (this may require chilling the base before churning).  Transfer the ice cream to a freezer-safe container.  Freeze for at least 2 hours before serving.

# stone fruit cobbler

**Serves 4 to 6**

3 nectarines, pitted and chopped into ¾-inch cubes

3 peaches, pitted and chopped into ¾-inch cubes

1 cup assorted berries, hulled

½ cup sugar

½ teaspoon ground cinnamon

¼ teaspoon ground cardamom

¼ teaspoon freshly grated nutmeg

1 teaspoon vanilla extract

Juice and zest of 1 orange

1 teaspoon peeled and grated fresh ginger

2 tablespoons cornstarch

1 pound Sugar Cookie Dough (recipe follows)

¼ cup heavy cream

4 tablespooons (½ stick) unsalted butter, cut into ¼-inch cubes

Cinnamon Sugar (page 265)

Crème Chantilly, for topping (optional; recipe follows)

Stone fruit at its peak is a short-lived but extraordinary phenomenon. Peaches are great, but I think that nectarines are overlooked. It's almost a shame to do anything with a perfectly ripened nectarine other than to eat it, chin dripping with juices. But for all the barely ripened fruit that ends up at our pastry station, there's the cobbler, one of my favorite desserts. This is a very approachable dessert, both for the home cook and for guests in our restaurant. If you can master a good crisp or cobbler, you'll be set for life.

Cobblers are best when made from fruit that is slightly on the firmer side. If the fruit is too ripe, it will break down quickly during baking and result in a soupy cobbler. In this recipe, I add assorted berries to give it a splash of color. The amount of spices can be adjusted to your taste, as should the sugar and cornstarch, depending on the sweetness and ripeness of the fruit. Generally, the riper the fruit, the less sugar and more cornstarch (a thickening agent) you will need.

Preheat the oven to 350°F.

Butter four 8-ounce ovenproof ramekins or a 13 by 9-inch baking dish. Dust the buttered ramekins or dish with sugar.

In a large bowl, toss the fruit together with the sugar, cinnamon, cardamom, nutmeg, vanilla, orange juice and zest, ginger, and cornstarch. Taste the fruit; you should be able taste each ingredient, even the cornstarch (which should give the cobbler a pasty, flour-like taste).

Depending on the sweetness and ripeness of your fruit, you may need to add more sugar, or a smidge more cornstarch (not more than 1 teaspoon).

Mound the fruit mixture into the ramekins or baking dish. The fruit will collapse as it bakes, so you want to heap it so that the fruit domes beyond the top of the baking vessel, and dot with the cubed butter.

Roll the sugar cookie dough out to a ½-inch thickness. Cut the sugar cookie dough into ½-inch cubes and

top the cobbler with as many dough cubes as possible, distributing it evenly over the fruit.

Using a pastry brush, dab the dough with the cream. Sprinkle about ¾ teaspoon of cinnamon sugar over each ramekin, or distribute about 1 tablespoon over the cobbler if using a baking dish.

Bake the cobbler until the cookie dough is golden brown and the fruit begins to bubble, about 20 minutes.

Serve the cobblers warm with crème chantilly.

## sugar cookie dough  Makes 1 pound

1 cup plus 2 tablespoons flour

¾ teaspoon baking powder

½ teaspoon salt

9 tablespoons unsalted butter

¾ cup plus 2 tablespoons sugar

½ teaspoon vanilla extract

1 tablespoon freshly squeezed lemon juice

1 tablespoon finely grated lemon zest

1 tablespoon freshly squeezed lime juice

1 tablespoon finely grated lime zest

1 large egg

Sift the flour, baking powder, and salt together and set aside.

In the bowl of a stand mixer fitted with the paddle attachment, cream the butter and sugar together on medium-high speed until light and fluffy, about 3 minutes. Beat in the vanilla, lemon juice and zest, and lime juice and zest. Scrape down the sides, then beat in the egg.

With the mixer on low speed, add the dry ingredients in thirds, scraping the bowl down after each addition. Continue mixing until a loose dough forms, about 1 minute.

Shape the dough into a flat disk, wrap it tightly in plastic wrap, and chill the dough until firm, at least 2 hours or overnight.

## crème chantilly  Makes 2 cups

This is a slightly sweetened whipped cream that can be used to garnish anything from a fruit salad to cake or pie. For best results, use this (or any whipped cream) the same day that you make it.

1 cup heavy cream, well chilled

1 tablespoon confectioners' sugar, sifted

½ teaspoon vanilla extract

In the bowl of a stand mixer fitted with a whisk attachment, whip the cream, sugar, and vanilla on medium-high speed until stiff. If you are not using it right away, transfer the whipped cream to a large bowl, cover with plastic wrap, and refrigerate. Covered and chilled, it should keep for up to 3 hours.

# honey custard, **mulberry**-pinot sorbet, linzer wafer cookies

**Serves 4**

1 cup heavy cream

1 cup whole milk

4 egg yolks

2 whole eggs

3 tablespoons plus 1 teaspoon dark brown sugar

4 teaspoons honey

Mulberry-Pinot Sorbet (recipe follows)

Linzer Wafer Cookies (recipe follows)

This is my riff on the Linzer torte, an Austrian tart known by its lattice top. Here hazelnut cookies stand in for the nut crust; mulberries replace the traditional fruit fillings—red currant or apricot—and honey custard, with its mellow sweetness, gives it all a creamy body.

You can also serve any of the components—cookies, sorbet, or custard—individually as a simple, after-meal sweet.

Preheat the oven to 300°F.

Combine the cream and milk in a small saucepan. Scald the mixture over medium-high heat (bring it to just under a boil). Remove from the heat and set aside.

Whisk together the egg yolks, eggs, brown sugar, and honey in a large bowl, breaking up any lumps of brown sugar as you work.

Slowly pour the hot cream in a thin, steady stream into the egg mixture to temper the eggs. If you pour the cream in too quickly, you will scramble the eggs. Strain the custard base through a fine-mesh sieve.

Divide the custard among four 4-ounce ovenproof ramekins. Put the ramekins in a large baking dish that is deeper than the ramekins (the tops of the ramekins should be below the top of the baking dish). Pour enough water into the pan around the ramekins so that it rises halfway up the sides of the ramekins. Try not to splash any water into the custard. Cover the baking dish with aluminum foil and bake the custard for 40 minutes, opening the foil every 10 minutes to release some of the steam. Be very careful when you open the foil, as the rush of steam can burn you. The custards are done when they are firm to the touch but still slightly jiggly in the middle. Transfer to a wire rack and let the custards cool to room temperature. Chill the cooled custards overnight before serving.

To serve, top each chilled custard with a scoop of the sorbet. Serve the wafer cookies on the side.

## *mulberry-pinot sorbet* Makes 1 quart

When I worked in Los Angeles, I found the most wonderful mulberries at the Santa Monica Farmers' Market. They were in such high demand that I had to get to the market extra early just to grab a few cartons before they were sold out. They were so sweet that we served them simply with some whipped cream.

In Missouri, summer mulberries are hard to find, and so they are quite a treat when they turn up. They're not nearly as sweet as those California ones I loved so much, so I give them some extra oomph by adding Pinot Noir to this sorbet.

---

1 pint mulberries

1½ cups water

1½ cups sugar

⅓ cup Pinot Noir or any fruit juice (optional)

Juice of ½ lemon

Bring the berries, water, and sugar to a rapid boil in a small pot over medium heat. Remove from the heat. Carefully transfer the hot mixture to a blender and puree. Strain the mixture through a fine-mesh sieve.

Whisk in the wine and lemon juice.

Freeze the sorbet base in an ice cream maker according to the manufacturer's instructions. (This may require chilling the base before churning.)

# linzer wafer cookies   Makes about 3 dozen 2½-inch cookies

¾ cup all-purpose flour

½ teaspoon baking powder

¼ teaspoon salt

½ teaspoon ground cinnamon

6 tablespoons (¾ stick) unsalted butter, softened

2 tablespoons sugar

½ teaspoon vanilla extract

1 large egg

⅓ cup hazelnuts, toasted and finely ground
(about 3 ounces)

Cinnamon Sugar (page 265)

Preheat the oven to 325°F. Line 1 or 2 baking sheets with parchment paper. You can bake 2 sheets at a time, rotating them halfway through.

In a bowl, combine the flour, baking powder, salt, and cinnamon.

In the bowl of a stand mixer fitted with a paddle attachment, beat the butter, sugar, and vanilla together on medium-high speed until the butter is pale and fluffy, about 8 minutes. Scrape down the bowl with a spatula.

With the stand mixer set on medium speed, add the egg, scraping the bowl down as needed. With the mixer on low speed, add the flour mixture. Scrape the bowl down again and add the ground hazelnuts. Continue mixing until the nuts are fully incorporated, forming a soft, sticky dough.

Divide the dough in half and form each half into a flat round. Wrap the rounds separately in plastic wrap. If you are making the cookies the same day you intend to serve them, freeze the dough for at least 30 minutes. If you are making the dough a day ahead, chill the dough overnight in the refrigerator. Wrapped tightly in two or three layers of plastic wrap, the dough will keep in the freezer for up to 1 month.

Roll one round of the chilled dough out to about ⅛-inch thickness and cut into shapes as desired. The dough is quite sticky, so dust your board and rolling pin generously with flour. Repeat with the second dough round, if desired.

Arrange the cut cookies on the prepared baking sheet, leaving at least ½ inch between them. Dust the cookies with cinnamon sugar and bake for 8 to 10 minutes, until they take on a light, golden brown color. Transfer the cookies to a wire rack to cool. Stored in an airtight container, the cookies will keep for up to 1 week.

I used to go camping every summer with my family in Manitowoc, Wisconsin. At least one night of the trip, we'd pile into the car and go to Beerntsen's, a time capsule of a soda fountain and candy store right on Lake Michigan. Like a page from the *Saturday Evening Post*, perched on a stool at the counter, I'd lose myself in an enormous banana split and a tall glass of chocolate soda. The three summer petits fours that follow were inspired by those blissfully unedited moments at the soda fountain.

# amarena **cherry** soda

**Makes 4 cups; serves 8**

3½ cups water

¼ cup sugar

¼ cup unsweetened cocoa powder

2 tablespoons amarena cherry syrup

This little shot of bubbly is quite sweet, so it's perfect as a petit four. Amarena cherry syrup isn't easy to find. At the restaurant, we strain it from a bottle of amarena cherries, which you can find in specialty and gourmet markets.

Combine all of the ingredients in a medium saucepan and bring them to a boil over medium-high heat to dissolve the sugar. Remove the saucepan from the heat and let the syrup cool slightly.

Strain the hot syrup through a fine-mesh sieve. Pour the strained syrup into an iSi soda canister, making sure not to exceed the fill line (see page 66). Charge the iSi soda canister according to the manufacturer's instruction and refrigerate for at least 2 hours and preferably overnight if possible.

When you are ready to serve, dispense the charged contents into shot glasses and serve with swizzle straws.

# malted **strawberry** macarons

**Makes about 30 macarons**

2 tablespoons malt powder

1¼ cup confectioners' sugar

1½ cup plus 2 tablespoons almond flour

3 egg whites

¼ cup granulated sugar

Pinch of salt

1 teaspoon vanilla extract

Strawberry Buttercream (recipe follows)

I adore Sophia Coppola's film *Marie Antoinette*, which drops that ill-fated queen of France into a music video–meets–candy land court of haute couture. As a woman and a pastry chef, I gleefully imagine being smothered along with her under mountains of petticoats and petits fours.

*Macarons* are the Marie Antoinette, the *divas au courant* of the pastry world. Á la mode and fashionable, these almond meringue buttons are the ultimate designer cookie sandwich. Filled with buttercream or jam, they now dot high-end patisserie window displays with vibrant colors from Paris to Tokyo.

*Macarons* are extremely delicate. Due to their sensitivity to moisture, they are best eaten the day they are filled, though unfilled *macarons* will keep for a couple of days in an airtight container.

Here I merge the form of the French meringue cookie with the flavors of the American soda fountain.

---

Preheat the oven to 300°F. Line a baking sheet with parchment paper or a nonstick baking mat.

Sift the malt powder and confectioners' sugar together into a large bowl. Add the almond flour. Set aside.

In a clean, dry bowl of a stand mixer fitted with a whisk attachment, whip the egg whites on medium-high speed until frothy, about 2 minutes. Continue whipping, adding the granulated sugar and salt gradually in a steady stream, until medium-stiff peaks form (the tops of the peaks should hold their shape after leaning to one side, as opposed to stiff peaks, which will stand straight up).

Fold half of the dry ingredients into the whipped egg whites. Add the vanilla extract and fold in the remaining dry ingredients. Lightly rap the bowl against the counter to remove any air pockets.

Transfer the meringue to a pastry bag fitted with a plain tip (preferably a #4 tip). Pipe the meringue onto the lined baking sheet in quarter-size mounds about ½ inch apart. Bake the *macarons* for 10 minutes, rotating the baking sheet once halfway through baking.

Remove the *macarons* from the oven and allow them to cool. Carefully slip a metal spatula under each cookie to remove it from the liner.

Pipe about 1 tablespoon of buttercream onto the bottom (flat side) of a *macaron* cookie and top it with another cookie, bottom side down, to make a mini cookie sandwich. These are best served the day they are made, so pipe only as many sandwiches as you plan to consume that day. You can store the unfilled cookies in an airtight container wrapped in multiple layers of plastic wrap in the refrigerator for up to 1 week. Let them come to room temperature before filling them with buttercream.

# strawberry buttercream   Makes about 2½ cups

This pretty pink buttercream has an incredibly smooth, satiny finish. When whipped properly, it's extremely light and fluffy, making it perfect for summertime desserts. This buttercream is also extremely versatile. At the restaurant, I use it to frost cakes and fill *macarons*; at weekend teas I even serve it plain alongside warm scones. Although it is best used and eaten the day it's made, I've included instructions for storing the buttercream for later use.

3 egg whites

¾ cup sugar

1 cup plus 2 tablespoons (2¼ sticks) unsalted butter, softened

1 teaspoon vanilla extract

¼ cup Strawberry Jam (or more or less according to your taste; recipe follows)

In the bowl of a stand mixer, combine the egg whites and sugar. Set the bowl over a saucepan with about 1 inch of simmering water in the bottom. Gently whisk the mixture until the sugar dissolves, about 3 minutes. Remove the bowl from the simmering water. Using a handheld mixer or a stand mixer fitted with a whisk attachment, whip the heated egg whites and sugar on high speed until stiff peaks form, about 5 minutes. It should look very glossy, like soft marshmallow crème.

With the mixer on medium speed, slowly add tablespoon-size pieces of butter to the meringue, allowing each to disappear before adding the next. The meringue will break and turn to liquid form, but then it will rewhip into a thick buttercream. Once all the butter has been added, add the vanilla and whip the buttercream on high speed for 1 minute more.

Fold in the strawberry jam by hand.

If you are not using the buttercream the same day, transfer it to an airtight container and freeze it for up to 1 month. When you are ready to use the buttercream, let it thaw completely and rewhip it in a stand mixer fitted with a paddle attachment until soft and fluffy.

## *strawberry jam*   Makes ½ cup

1½ teaspoons dry pectin

¾ cup sugar

8 ounces strawberries, hulled and quartered

½ vanilla bean, split and scraped

1 teaspoon brandy

¼ cup water

Sift together the pectin and ½ cup of the sugar. Set aside.

Bring the strawberries, remaining ¼ cup of sugar, vanilla, and brandy to a simmer in a medium saucepan over medium heat. Continue cooking until the strawberries begin to break down and the mixture starts to bubble.

Meanwhile, prepare a large ice bath (see the User Manual, page xxv).

Add the sifted pectin and sugar to the simmering strawberry mixture along with the water. Bring the mixture to a rapid boil over high heat. Remove the vanilla pod. Remove the jam from the heat and transfer it to a nonreactive bowl. Place the bowl over the ice bath, whisking occasionally to help the mixture cool. Transfer the cooled jam to an airtight container. Sealed tightly, it will keep in the refrigerator for up to 1 month.

# banana-pineapple tea cake

**Makes 20 petits fours**

½ cup finely diced fresh pineapple or 8 ounces canned crushed pineapple, drained well

2 tablespoons vanilla rum or vanilla brandy (optional)

½ cup plus 1 tablespoon all-purpose flour

6 tablespoons granulated sugar

1 tablespoon cornstarch

½ teaspoon ground cinnamon

1 teaspoon baking powder

½ teaspoon baking soda

¼ teaspoon salt

2 very ripe bananas, peeled

3 tablespoons unsalted butter, melted

1 large egg

¾ teaspoon vanilla extract

½ cup walnuts, toasted and finely chopped (optional)

1 tablespoon turbinado sugar

Our daughter, Madilyn, is notorious for swiping these off the cooling rack when no one is looking. We call this a tea cake because it appears at our holiday tea services, along with our petit four plate. Inspired by the tropical fruit in a banana split, this faux upside-down cake features the pineapple baked atop a moist banana cake. A dash of turbinado sugar gives it crunch.

Although we suggest making these as small petits fours, with an adjustment to the baking time, the batter is suitable for making loaf cakes as well (see Note).

---

If you are using the rum or brandy, soak the pineapple in the liquor overnight, or for at least 6 hours.

Preheat the oven to 325°F.

Butter 20 petits fours molds.

In a small bowl, combine the flour, granulated sugar, cornstarch, cinnamon, baking powder, baking soda, and salt and set aside.

In a large bowl, mash the bananas with a fork until you have a chunky puree. Stir in the butter, egg, and vanilla extract and mix well.

Fold half of the dry ingredients into the banana mixture, stirring just to combine between additions. Don't overmix. Fold in the walnuts at the very end.

Divide the batter among the petits fours molds, leaving a little room at the top for the pineapple topping. Drain the pineapple well. Dot the top of each filled petit four mold with ¼ teaspoon pineapple. Sprinkle the turbinado sugar over the tea cakes. Bake for 10 to 12 minutes. They should dome slightly and take on a golden-brown color. Let the tea cakes cool on a wire rack. Stored in an airtight container, they will keep for 2 days.

**NOTE:** To adapt this recipe to make a 9-inch loaf cake, double the recipe and increase the heat of the oven to 350°F. Lightly butter and flour your loaf pan and make the batter as directed. Scrape the batter into the loaf pan and dot the top with ¼ cup of the pineapple. Bake for 45 minutes. Sprinkle the turbinado sugar over the top of the loaf, return the pan to the oven, and bake until a wooden toothpick or skewer inserted into the center of the loaf comes out clean, 10 to 15 minutes more.

autumn

# There's a moment at the end of summer when the temperature drops an octave.

The leaves lose their luster and the wind leans with a sharper edge. It's unmistakable: Autumn has arrived.

With its sepia hue and cinnamon scent, autumn evokes nostalgia more than any other season. Kids head back to school, recalling our own peanut butter and jelly years. There's cider to be mulled, pumpkins to be carved, and hayrides to be had. Homecoming, football, and hunting: Autumn in the Midwest is wonderful.

Though the garden quickly thins out, leaving us with stalk and root vegetables, winter squashes soon start to appear. Game meats come into season, including birds of all shapes and sizes. And the forest floor grows thick with mushrooms.

In the kitchen, stocks darken, sauces thicken, and everything seems to take on a heavier coat in preparation for winter.

As the temperature drops, the air begins to crisp up, which makes Megan particularly happy in the pastry kitchen. Oatmeal, spices, and dried fruits all come out of the larder to stoke our nostalgia. And vintage fruits come to the fore—apples, quinces, pears—magically transformed into delicious desserts.

# autumn

# menu

# wine

The acidity of a wine must be considered when pairing wine with food. Acid has the ability to cut through richness and highlight bright flavors. But if unbalanced, acid can destroy a dish.

Colby's beet salad (page 134) is perfect for a New Zealand Sauvignon Blanc, whose steely streak of grapefruit drills through the creamy richness of the blue cheese without killing the subtle, earthy sweetness of the beets.

The char with wild rice (page 162) will pair well with a red Burgundy or an American Pinot Noir. I would avoid overly tannic (or overly dry) wines, such as a Cabernet Sauvignon, as the tannins, which are especially pronounced in that grape varietal, often produce a metallic taste when paired with darker-fleshed fish like char and salmon.

Colby's *strozzapreti* with duck confit and orange sauce (page 154) has a fair amount of pepper in it, which makes it prime for a spicy Zinfandel. But choose one that's low in alcohol.

I really like to pair pork tenderloin (page 165) with medium-bodied Spanish red wines. The slightly earthy texture of a good Tempranillo always seems to work with the flavor of pork. The other ingredients in this dish only reinforce my choice, as they give the dish a sweet, fatty flavor that works beautifully with the spiciness common to Tempranillos.

# notes

Megan's poached apple dessert (page 181) will do very well matched with a dry, hard cider. At Bluestem, we pair it with a vintage cider from Normandy, which is slightly effervescent and has a refreshingly dry finish that rides out the lingering sweetness in the apples. Also, the cider is low in alcohol, which allows the subtleties in high-sugar foods to show better. If you are looking for a wine option, Moscato d'Asti will also work with this dish.

**A note on Thanksgiving:** I'm usually tasked with pairing wines for Thanksgiving, and quite frankly, it's an impossible task. There are usually too many flavors on the plate to select the "perfect" wine. So, instead of trying to find one, I encourage people to simply open up a bottle or two of something that everyone will enjoy. I recommend a midrange Spanish Grenache or a Southern Italian crowd-pleaser, such as a Negroamaro or Aglianico.

The roasted pheasant on page 167 is Colby's take on Thanksgiving. Notwithstanding the foregoing note, I do have a good match for that dish. Since there's Barolo in the cranberry sauce, a nicely aged Nebbiolo—with favors of red fruits, tobacco, and dried fruits—is a natural choice. (Nebbiolo is an Italian red grape varietal, but also refers to wines made from the Nebbiolo grape. Barolo is made from Nebbiolo grapes.)

# smoked salmon panna cotta, smoked salmon roe

**Serves 8 to 10 as an amuse-bouche**

2 cups heavy cream, chilled

2½ teaspoons powdered gelatin

5 ounces smoked salmon

1 tablespoon sugar

3 tablespoons smoked salmon roe

This panna cotta is a variation of an amuse-bouche that we served at Tru when I worked for chef Rick Tramonto.

Since an amuse bouche should be only one or two bites, you can set the panna cottas in small, individual molds. At the restaurant, we find it easier to pour the panna cotta base into a 13 by 9-inch pan and punch out individual rounds using small ring molds dipped in warm water.

Often, bubbles will settle on or near the surface of the panna cotta as the gelatin sets, leaving the surface slightly pockmarked. To smooth the surface for a more attractive presentation, wave the flame of a crème brûlée torch quickly over the surface from a distance. You don't want to melt or char the top, just gently warm it enough so that the surface smooths out.

Pour the cream into a small saucepan. Sprinkle the powdered gelatin over the cream and let it sit for 5 minutes to bloom.

Heat the cream over medium-high heat to dissolve the gelatin. Add the salmon and sugar and turn the heat to high. As soon as the panna cotta base comes to a simmer, remove it from the heat. Watch it closely, as dairy products have a tendency to boil over quickly.

Carefully transfer the hot panna cotta base to a blender. With one towel-wrapped hand held tightly over the lid, puree the base until liquefied. Strain the hot liquid through a fine-mesh sieve.

Pour the liquid panna cotta base into small molds, about 1 inch in diameter, or into a 13 by 9-inch pan. Chill the molds on a level shelf in the refrigerator for 6 hours, or preferably overnight.

To loosen the panna cottas from their molds or the pan, heat the molds or the bottom of the pan briefly in a shallow pan of hot water. Unmold the panna cottas from molds onto a large spoon or into a small serving dish. If you poured the panna cotta into a sheet pan, punch out cylinders with a 1-inch ring mold dipped in warm water. Top each panna cotta with a bit of the roe and serve immediately.

# warm **sunchoke** soup, hazelnuts

**Serves 8 to 10 as an amuse-bouche,
4 as a first course**

2 tablespoons vegetable oil

12 ounces sunchokes, peeled

1 small yellow onion, coarsely chopped

½ small fennel bulb, trimmed and coarsely chopped

4 cloves garlic, smashed and chopped

1 teaspoon peeled and chopped fresh ginger

1½ cups white wine

2 cups Fish Stock (page 255)

1 teaspoon salt

⅛ teaspoon freshly ground white pepper

1 tablespoon Crème Fraîche (page 251)

Juice of 1 lemon

2 tablespoons hazelnuts, toasted and chopped

Velvety and thick, this soup is a perfect opening act for a chilly autumn night. I especially love how the earthy and nutty flavors of the sunchokes blossom as the soup is heated, developing a smoky, flinty hint too.

The soup can be served in demitasse cups as an amuse-bouche or in bowls as a more substantial first course.

Left alone, sunchokes will brown after they've been peeled. To preserve their ivory color for the soup, as you peel the sunchokes, drop them into a bowl of cold water slightly acidulated with some lemon juice—about half a lemon's worth will do.

---

Heat the oil in a large saucepan over medium-high heat. Add the sunchokes, onion, fennel, garlic, and ginger and cook for 2 minutes. Add the wine and simmer until the liquid is reduced by half, about 5 minutes. Add the stock and let the soup simmer for 10 minutes.

Carefully transfer the contents of the saucepan to a blender. With one towel-wrapped hand held firmly over the lid, puree the soup until smooth. Season the soup with the salt and pepper. Add the crème fraîche and lemon juice and puree until they are incorporated. Adjust the seasonings if needed.

Serve the soup in small cups or bowls. Garnish with the hazelnuts just before serving.

# beets, whipped blue cheese, candied pecans

**Serves 4**

1 pound baby beets, trimmed of greens

Salt and freshly ground black pepper

4 ounces cream cheese, softened

2 ounces blue cheese, softened

¼ cup Champagne Vinaigrette (page 253)

⅓ cup Candied Pecans, chopped (page 254)

Baby frisée, for garnish

I can't keep Megan away from beets when the gem-like baby ones roll in. Lucky for her, beets are readily available year-round in the Midwest. Although this salad can take on one of many variations, we strip it down to its bare essentials, focusing on the beets, whose sweetness seems intensified against the salty whipped blue cheese that we pair with it. Candied pecans give the salad some needed snap, and a few tendrils of baby frisée lettuce frame it all nicely with a frilly border.

This salad is particularly pretty if you use different-colored beets. Just make sure you keep them separated before arranging them on plates so they don't stain each other.

---

Preheat the oven to 350°F.

Tightly seal the beets, whole, in a large sheet of aluminum foil. If you are using different-colored beats, package the beets separately by color so that the red ones won't stain the lighter-colored ones.

Bake the beets for 40 minutes. To test the beets for doneness, a knife should slip in and out of them without any effort. Let the beets cool. Peel the thin layer of skin from each beet. Cut the beets into quarters. Season with salt and pepper and set aside.

In a stand mixer fitted with a paddle attachment, whip the cream cheese on high speed until soft and fluffy, stopping to scrape the bowl as needed. Add the blue

cheese and continue to whip, scraping the bowl as needed, until the two cheeses are evenly mixed and fluffy. Season with salt and pepper to taste and whip a little more to incorporate.

Toss the beets with the vinaigrette. If you are using different-colored beets, toss them separately by color to prevent them from staining each other. Divide the beets among 4 plates.

Transfer the whipped cheese to a pastry bag and pipe the cheese in small mounds around the beets. Or you can simply spoon the cheese onto the plates. Garnish each salad with some pecans and frisée. Serve immediately.

# bay scallops, celery hearts, ginger-saffron vinaigrette

**Serves 4**

8 ounces bay scallops (preferably dry-pack; try to avoid wet-pack or frozen)

Salt and freshly ground white pepper

2 cups white wine

¼ cup Champagne vinegar

2 large sprigs fresh tarragon

2 shallots, sliced

3 cloves garlic, minced

1 cup crushed ice cubes

1½ cups water

1 celery heart, thinly shaved lengthwise into ribbons with a peeler

Leaves from 3 sprigs fresh tarragon

½ cup Ginger-Saffron Vinaigrette (recipe follows)

4 teaspoons Saffron Gel (recipe follows)

Leaves from 2 celery hearts

Known as "candies of the sea," bay scallops have a delicate, sweet flesh that I like best when raw or barely cooked, which is how I serve them at Bluestem. The season is very short—October through early December—so unless you live near the coast, you will most likely have to special-order these from your fishmonger.

---

Spread the scallops out evenly in a baking dish large enough to hold them snugly. Season them with salt and pepper.

Combine the wine, vinegar, 2 sprigs of tarragon, shallots, and garlic in a saucepan and bring them to a simmer over medium-high heat. Pour the hot liquid over the scallops and let them poach for 2 minutes. Stir ½ cup of the ice cubes into the poaching liquid, distributing the ice evenly to cool the poaching liquid and stop the scallops from cooking. Cover and chill.

Make a small ice bath by combining the remaining ice cubes in a small bowl with the water. Submerge the shaved celery hearts in the ice water and set aside for a couple of minutes. The ribbons should curl. Drain the celery ribbons and pat them dry with a paper towel.

To serve, toss the scallops with the curled celery heart ribbons, tarragon leaves, and vinaigrette. Smear a generous teaspoon of saffron gel across each of 4 plates. Divide the scallop mixture evenly among the plates, arranging them over the saffron gel. Season with salt and pepper and garnish with celery heart leaves. Serve immediately.

## *ginger-saffron vinaigrette*  Makes 1¾ cups

1 cup dry white wine

⅓ cup rice wine vinegar

½ cup mirin

½ teaspoon saffron

Juice of 1 lemon

¼ teaspoon peeled and grated ginger

½ cup extra-virgin olive oil

Combine the wine, rice wine vinegar, mirin, saffron, lemon juice, and ginger in a small saucepan over low heat, heating the mixture just enough to release the perfume from the saffron. Remove the mixture from the heat and let it cool completely. Whisk in the olive oil until the vinaigrette has emulsified. Transfer the vinaigrette to an airtight container and store in the refrigerator for up to 1 week.

## *saffron gel*  Makes approximately 1½ cups

This recipe uses agar-agar, a gelatin derived from seaweed, as a gelling agent. Agar-agar is used throughout Asia and can be found in most Asian markets. It comes in both flake and powder form; be sure to buy the powdered version.

---

1 cup dry white wine

1 tablespoon mirin

1 tablespoon rice wine vinegar

1 tablespoon loosely packed saffron

2½ teaspoons agar-agar

½ teaspoon salt

Freshly ground white pepper

¼ cup cold water

1 teaspoon honey

Bring the wine, mirin, vinegar, saffron, agar-agar, salt, and pepper to a simmer in a small saucepan over medium heat. Remove from the heat and let it cool slightly, about 5 minutes. Pour the gel base into a blender. With one towel-wrapped hand firmly held over the lid, puree the ingredients on high speed until smooth. Pour the gel base into a shallow pan. Cover and chill until the gelatin has set, at least 2 hours.

Scrape the gel into a blender. Add the water and honey and puree the mixture until smooth. Transfer the gel to an airtight container and refrigerate for up to 1 week.

# **pears**, pecans, grayson cheese, watercress, spinach, white grapes, banyuls

**Serves 4**

**banyuls vinaigrette**

½ cup Banyuls vinegar

¼ cup extra-virgin olive oil

1 tablespoon maple syrup

Salt and freshly ground black pepper

**salad**

2 pears, peeled, halved, and cored (d'Anjou or Bartlett)

Small handful of watercress leaves

Small handful of baby spinach leaves

4 ounces Grayson cheese, at room temperature

1 cup white grapes, cut into ⅛-inch slices (or as thin as possible)

1 cup Candied Pecans (page 254)

**If you love** stinky cheeses as much as I do, you will love Grayson, a washed-rind, cow's milk cheese from Meadow Creek Farms in Virginia. It has a pungent, buttery texture not unlike Taleggio. To bring out the full flavor and texture of this cheese, leave it out to soften at room temperature before serving.

**Make the vinaigrette:** Whisk the Banyuls vinegar, olive oil, and maple syrup together in a bowl. Season with salt and pepper to taste.

**Make the salad:** Using a mandoline or very sharp knife, slice the pear halves to a ¹⁄₁₆-inch thickness. Keep the slices from each pear half together in a group.

Toss the watercress and spinach with 1 tablespoon of vinaigrette to coat. Dip the sliced pears in the remainder of the vinaigrette.

**To serve:** Allotting half a pear per plate, spread the dressed slices of pear out onto 4 plates. Top each plate of pears with 1 ounce of cheese and some dressed greens. Garnish with the grapes and sliced pecans and serve immediately.

# foraged mushrooms, grains, "soil," ricotta, dried cranberries

**Serves 4**

**"soil" (makes about 3 cups)**

½ cup hazelnuts, toasted

½ cup sliced almonds, toasted

2 cups pumpernickel bread crumbs

½ teaspoon salt

Freshly ground black pepper

¼ cup Garlic Butter, melted (page 253)

**whipped ricotta**

1 cup ricotta cheese

1½ cups cream cheese, softened

3 tablespoons roasted garlic puree (see box)

½ teaspoon salt

Freshly ground white pepper

**grains**

About 5 cups water

⅔ cup quinoa

⅔ cup amaranth

⅔ cup barley

¼ cup dried cranberries

1 tablespoon unsalted butter

1 tablespoon Veal Stock (page 257)

2 tablespoons Chicken Stock (page 256)

Salt and freshly ground white pepper

**mushrooms**

1 pound assorted wild mushrooms, trimmed and separated according to variety

Unsalted butter

I wanted to feature mushrooms in the fall, when they are so abundant and varied. This dish evokes the autumn forest floor with a collection of beefy, earthy, and nutty flavors. A dollop of milky whipped ricotta helps to lighten and bring it all together.

Try to get an assortment of wild foraged mushrooms, like porcini, hedgehog, trumpet, and yellow foot, which will give the dish a variety of color, shapes, and textures.

This recipe calls for three different grains so there is also a variety of texture. But you can simplify things by cooking twice the amount of one type of grain. If you do this, we recommend choosing the barley, quinoa, or wild rice, but not amaranth, as those grains are extremely small and won't provide the heft you want. Remember to increase the amount of cooking water proportionally—you'll need about twice as much cooking water as grains.

**Make the "soil":** Put the hazelnuts, almonds, bread crumbs, and salt in a food processor and pulse until coarsely ground. Season with pepper to taste. Pulse the mixture a few more times, while drizzling in the garlic butter, until finely ground. It should resemble slightly damp soil. Transfer the soil to an airtight container. Covered, it will keep at room temperature for up to 1 week.

**Whip the ricotta:** In the bowl of a stand mixer fitted with a paddle attachment, beat together the ricotta, cream cheese, roasted garlic puree, salt, and pepper on high speed until fluffy and soft, about 5 minutes.

**Prepare the grains:**

**Cook the quinoa:** Rinse the quinoa in water and drain as much as possible.

Bring 1⅓ cups of the water to a boil in a medium-size saucepan over medium-high heat. Add the quinoa and return to a boil. Turn the heat down to low and simmer, covered, for 15 minutes. Check to see that the grain has absorbed most of the water. If there is still a considerable amount of water, let it simmer for a few more minutes. Remove the saucepan from the heat and let it stand, covered, for 2 to 3 minutes. Uncover and "fluff" the quinoa with a fork.

**Cook the amaranth:** Bring 1½ cups of the remaining water to a boil in a medium-size saucepan over medium-high heat. Add the amaranth and return to a boil. Turn the heat down to low and simmer, covered, for 18 minutes. Check to see that the seeds have absorbed most of the water. If there is still a considerable amount of water, let it simmer for a few more minutes. Remove the saucepan from the heat and let it stand, covered, for 2 to 3 minutes. Uncover and "fluff" the amaranth with a fork. The seeds should be tender and slightly sticky, but not wet.

# roasting garlic

You can make as much or as little garlic puree as you like.

Using a sharp knife, slice off the top third of a head of garlic (the pointed end), exposing the cloves. Rub the cut side of the head of garlic with some olive oil. Place the head cut side up on a roasting tray lined with aluminum foil. In an oven preheated to 375°F, roast the garlic until the cloves have softened, 45 minutes to 1 hour.

Squeeze the garlic cloves out of their skins and mash them together with a fork.

In addition to being blended into soups, dressings, and sauces, roasted garlic can be spread on toasted bread or used as a flavorful topping for pizza.

**Cook the barley:** Rinse the barley in water and drain as much as possible. Bring 2 cups of the remaining water to a boil in a medium-size saucepan over medium-high heat. Add the barley and return to a boil. Turn the heat down to low and simmer, covered, for 40 minutes, or until the grains are tender and the water is absorbed. If there is still a considerable amount of water, let it simmer for a few more minutes. Remove the saucepan from the heat and let it stand, covered, for 2 to 3 minutes. Uncover and "fluff" the barley with a fork. The grains should be soft and loose.

Combine the cooked quinoa, amaranth, barley, and dried cranberries in a container with a lid. Cover and set aside to keep warm.

Heat the butter, veal stock, and chicken stock together in a small saucepan over medium-low heat just to warm it

through, about 2 minutes. Stir the warm mixture into the grains, working carefully to avoid mashing or breaking the grains. Season to taste with salt and pepper. Cover and keep warm.

**Sauté the mushrooms:** Sauté each variety of the mushrooms separately using 1 to 2 tablespoons butter in a sauté pan over medium-high heat for 2 to 3 minutes, until just soft and tender. Season with salt and pepper and drain. Mushrooms tend to absorb butter and liquid, so if your sauté pan gets a bit dry, add a little more butter.

**To serve:** Mound a cup of the mixed grains and cranberries onto each of 4 serving plates. Top the grains with some mushrooms and a couple of spoonfuls of whipped ricotta. Spoon little piles of "soil" around the plate, about a tablespoon of soil per plate. Serve immediately.

# langoustines, warm garlic-champagne crema, pomegranate

**Serves 4**

16 langoustines or extra-large shrimp

**champagne crema**

1 tablespoon vegetable oil

1 large shallot, minced

4 cloves garlic, finely chopped

1½ cups dry Champagne

1 cup heavy cream

1 tablespoon honey

1 large sprig fresh tarragon

2 tablespoons Crème Fraîche (page 251)

Salt and freshly ground white pepper

**langoustines**

5 tablespoons extra-virgin olive oil

Salt and freshly ground white pepper

2 tablespoons butter

1 ripe Bartlett pear, peeled, cored, and julienned

¼ cup pomegranate seeds

Zest of 1 lemon, finely sliced

Langoustines are tiny lobsters that look like large prawns with pincers. Indigenous to Europe, fresh, unfrozen langoustines are extremely hard to get in the United States. If you can't order them, to buy the largest shrimp you can find.

The pomegranate seeds in this recipe always surprise people at first. The scarlet kernels add not only a festive splash of color but also an unexpected crunch and a burst of juicy sweetness that brings out the fruitiness in the Champagne crema. Try them!

---

**Prepare the langoustines:** Twist the pincers off the langoustines. Holding the head with one hand and the tail with another, gently twist and pull the head apart from the tail. Save the heads and pincers for stock.

Using kitchen shears, cut the underside of the tails. Pry open the shells and carefully pull out the tail meat in one piece. Save the shells for stock.

**Make the crema:** Heat the vegetable oil in a small saucepan over medium-high heat. Sauté the shallot and garlic until softened, about 3 minutes. Add the Champagne and continue to cook until the mixture is reduced by half, about 5 minutes. Add the heavy cream, honey, and tarragon. Turn the heat down to medium-low and continue to simmer for 4 to 5 minutes.

Remove the saucepan from the heat. Discard the tarragon. Transfer the hot mixture to a blender and add the crème fraîche. With one towel-wrapped hand held firmly over the lid, puree the crema until smooth. Season with salt and pepper to taste.

**Sauté the langoustines:** Heat 2 tablespoons of the olive oil in a large sauté pan over medium-low heat. Season the langoustines with salt and pepper. Roll the langoustine tails into balls. Working in two batches, sauté the langoustines in the oil for 30 seconds on each side. Add 1 tablespoon of the butter, remove the pan from the heat, and baste the langoustines with the melted butter

for about 1 minute. Transfer the langoustines to a plate, tenting them with aluminum foil to keep them warm. Pour the oil and butter out of the pan and repeat the process with another 2 tablespoons of the olive oil, the remaining langoustines and the remaining tablespoon of butter.

**To serve:** Toss the pear pieces with the remaining tablespoon of olive oil. Season with salt. Divide the langoustines and pomegranate seeds among 4 bowls. Spoon about ¼ cup of the Champagne crema over the langoustines. Top each bowl with some julienned pear and lemon zest. Serve immediately.

# roasted butternut squash soup, jowl, glazed onions, crème fraîche

**Serves 4**

### braised jowls

6 ounces *guanciale* (cured pork jowl) or slab bacon

8 cups Chicken Stock (page 256)

3 cloves garlic, smashed and chopped

1 shallot, coarsely chopped

4 sprigs fresh thyme

1 tablespoon black peppercorns

1 bay leaf

### butternut squash soup

1¼ pounds butternut squash, peeled, seeded, and cut into 1-inch cubes

1 large carrot, coarsely chopped

1 small apple, cored and chopped

1 large shallot, coarsely chopped

3 cloves garlic, smashed and chopped

2 cups apple cider

1½ cups Chicken Stock (page 256) or Vegetable Stock (page 255)

1 cup hard sparkling cider

2 tablespoons unsalted butter

½ teaspoon ground cinnamon

⅛ teaspoon freshly grated nutmeg

1 bay leaf

5 cloves

2 teaspoons black peppercorns

### maple-glazed onions

1 tablespoon vegetable oil

4 large-bulb young green onions (cipollini or shallots will also work well), trimmed of greens and roots and sliced in half lengthwise

¼ cup Vegetable Stock (page 255)

2 cloves garlic, smashed and chopped

4 sprigs fresh thyme

2 teaspoons Blis maple syrup (or Grade B maple syrup)

2 teaspoons Champagne vinegar

Salt and freshly ground white pepper

¼ cup Crème Fraîche (page 251)

Imbued with apples and yeasty hard cider, this velvety butternut squash soup brings autumn alive. Although it's quite light (there's very little fat in the soup), it's extremely satisfying, especially when served warm. On particularly cold days, I'll have it for lunch or dinner with a crusty piece of bread.

The leftover braising liquid from the pork jowl, which is quite salty, is perfect for cooking beans (see white beans, page 261). Strain the braising liquid before using it.

**Braise the pork jowl:** Preheat the oven to 350°F.

Combine all of the ingredients for the braised jowls in a small Dutch oven or a deep baking dish with a tight-fitting lid. The liquid doesn't need to completely submerge the meat, but it should cover a significant portion of it.

Cover the pot tightly and braise the pork jowl in the oven for 3 hours.

Set the pot aside to cool for 30 minutes. Chill the meat, covered, in its braising liquid overnight.

When you are ready to serve the soup, slice the chilled jowl ¼-inch thick. Reheat the meat in a small saucepan with 2 cups of the braising liquid over medium heat. The meat is quite delicate at this point, so reheat it with a gentle simmer. Cover the pot and keep the meat in the warm liquid until ready to serve.

**Make the soup:** Preheat the oven to 350°F.

In a 5-quart Dutch oven (preferably one with a tight-fitting lid) or a large covered casserole dish, combine the squash, carrot, apple, shallot, garlic, apple cider, stock, sparkling cider, butter, cinnamon, and nutmeg.

Make an herb sachet with the bay leaf, cloves, and peppercorns by tying them in a piece of cheesecloth with kitchen twine. Don't worry if the bay leaf crumbles inside the bag. Add the herb sachet to the rest of the ingredients in the Dutch oven.

Cover the Dutch oven. Bake for about 1 hour, or until the squash and carrots have completely softened. As long as the liquid doesn't escape through the lid, you can't really overcook this dish. The important point is that all of the contents be soft enough to puree in a blender. Remove the pot from the oven and set aside to cool for 15 minutes.

Remove and discard the sachet of herbs. Carefully, ladle half of the contents (liquid and solids) into a blender. Firmly holding the lid with one hand wrapped in a kitchen towel, puree the soup on high speed until it has liquefied. Transfer the soup to a separate container. Repeat with the remaining contents of the pot, adding this second batch of pureed soup to the first batch. Keep the soup warm.

**Make the glazed onions:** Heat the oil in a small sauté pan over medium-high heat. Add the onions and cook them evenly on all sides, turning them every few seconds (or, ideally, shake the pan so they roll around), until they begin to caramelize, 5 to 7 minutes.

Deglaze the pan with the stock, scraping up any browned bits and incorporating them, and then add the garlic, thyme, maple syrup, vinegar, and salt and pepper to taste. Turn the heat down to medium and continue to cook, stirring occasionally, until the liquid has thickened into a dark, thick sauce and the onions are glazed, about 10 minutes.

**To serve:** Divide the warm jowl meat and glazed onions among 4 bowls and top each with 1 tablespoon of the crème fraîche. Transfer the warm soup to a pitcher and pour the soup into the bowls, around the jowl and onions, at the table.

## adapting to vegetarians

This recipe can easily be adapted to be vegetarian or vegan. For vegetarians, simply substitute vegetable stock for chicken stock and leave out the *guanciale*. For vegans, in addition to substituting vegetable stock for chicken stock and omitting the pork jowl, substitute plain soy yogurt with a good squeeze of fresh lemon juice for the crème fraîche and swap out the butter for vegetable oil. The soup is delicious in any variation.

# thane palmberg

Salt of the earth. That's what Thane Palmberg is.

Since 1932, he and his family have had a stall at the City Market, Kansas City's largest and oldest farmers' market. Every weekend, they have hauled their sustainably raised produce all the way from DeSoto, Kansas, in a monstrous, Army-green truck that looks like it drove right off the set of *M\*A\*S\*H*. If you're at the City Market, you can't miss it.

Modest, shy, and honest to a fault, Thane is the type of farmer that chefs love to love. His produce is always fresh and beautiful. And he shows up at our restaurant's back door like clockwork. As long as he's growing something, we're calling him for orders. Throughout the year, we cook with his pumpkins and his radishes, his summer squashes, and his winter-hardy root vegetables.

# onion soup, bourbon, **oxtails**, toast, sheep's milk cheese, cipollini

**Serves 4**

### oxtail broth

2 sprigs fresh thyme

2 sprigs fresh flat-leaf parsley

4 pounds oxtails

Salt and freshly ground black pepper

¼ cup vegetable oil

2 small carrots, coarsely chopped

2 celery stalks, coarsely chopped

3 large shallots, coarsely chopped

2 cups dry red wine

4 cups Veal Stock (page 257)

5 cloves garlic, smashed and chopped

### onions

5 tablespoons unsalted butter

6 large red onions, thinly sliced

Salt and freshly ground black pepper

1 cup bourbon

12 medium cipollini onions

2 cups strained Oxtail Broth (see this page)

2 cups Veal Stock (page 257)

4 ounces soft sheep's milk cheese, softened

4 slices baguette, toasted

In the 1980s, steak soup and French onion soup were on just about every menu in Kansas City. They're Midwest favorites and a part of my childhood memory.

I've revived them at Bluestem with this refined hybrid. It combines the beefy broth from steak soup with the sweet, caramelized onions from French onion soup. Instead of a bubbly dome of Gruyère, this version includes a slice of toasted baguette spread with softened goat cheese, the chalky tang of which draws a thin line of escape through the richness of it all.

Once a butcher's cut (unable to sell them, butchers would keep these cuts for themselves), oxtails are more readily available nowadays. If you don't see them, ask for them.

---

**Make the broth:** Preheat the oven to 300°F.

Make an herb sachet with the thyme and parsley by tying them together in a piece of cheesecloth with kitchen twine.

Trim the oxtails of their excess fat and season them with salt and pepper.

Heat the oil in a Dutch oven over high heat. Working in batches so you don't crowd the pot, brown the oxtails on all sides, about 2 minutes per side. Set the browned oxtails on a plate when they're done, making room for others in the pot.

When all of the oxtails have been browned and removed from the pot, add the carrots, celery, and shallots and cook them until softened and browned, about 3 minutes. Add the oxtails back to the pot, along with the wine, stock, garlic, and the herb sachet. Bring to a simmer.

Cover the Dutch oven with a tight-fitting lid and bake for 3 hours.

Let the oxtail broth cool for 20 to 30 minutes. Remove the oxtails and any meat that may have fallen off the bones during the braising process. Pull all of the meat off the bones, discard the bones, and cover the meat to keep warm. Carefully strain the oxtail braising liquid through a fine-mesh sieve. Discard the solids and save the liquid as broth for the soup.

**Cook the onions:** Melt the butter in a large stockpot over medium heat. When the butter begins to foam, add the red onions. Cook the onions until they soften and begin to release their liquid, about 12 minutes. Stirring constantly, cook the onions until they have completely caramelized and almost disintegrated, about 1 hour more. If the onions are cooking faster than they're releasing liquid, turn the heat down to prevent them from burning. Season the onions with salt and pepper to taste. Stir in the bourbon and cipollini and continue to cook for 4 minutes more. Add the strained oxtail broth and the stock and continue to cook the onions until the cipollini have softened, about 45 minutes.

**To serve:** Spread the softened cheese on the slices of toast. Divide the oxtail meat among 4 bowls. Ladle a cup of soup into each bowl. You can either float the baguette and cheese on top of the soup or serve it on the side. Any remaining broth can be frozen for up to 2 months.

# risotto, **butternut squash**, allspice

**Serves 8 as a first course,**

**4 as a main course**

8 cups Chicken Stock (page 256) or Vegetable Stock (page 255)

3 tablespoons unsalted butter, softened

3 tablespoons unsalted butter, cold and cubed

2 shallots, finely diced

2 cloves garlic, minced

2 cups butternut squash in ½-inch cubes

2 cups Carnaroli rice

¾ cup white wine

Salt and freshly ground white pepper

1 cup freshly grated Parmesan cheese, plus more for garnish

Freshly grated allspice

If you've ever patiently stirred risotto until it's thick and creamy, you know why it is such a rewarding task when it turns out right. Despite the patience required, you'll want to make it over and over again.

Risotto is not difficult to make. But before you start, make sure that you have the correct variety of rice (long-grain rice will not yield the right results), all of the stock warm and ready to go, and, above all, the time. Don't try to rush this, or you'll end up with rice that looks cooked but is gritty and hard within. And make sure you're ready to eat it right when it's done. Risotto does not reward your patience with patience; it has a very short shelf life once it's cooked. Let it sit for more than a few minutes and it will begin to turn soft and gummy.

Any type of fleshy winter squash will work for this recipe, including pumpkin and acorn squash.

---

Heat the chicken stock in a stockpot over low heat. Cover and keep warm.

Heat the softened butter in a large saucepan over medium heat. Add the shallots, garlic, and butternut squash and stir until softened, about 5 minutes (you don't want to develop any color). Using a wooden spoon, stir in the rice, coating it with the butter and seasonings.

Continue to stir and toast the rice for about 5 minutes. Add the wine and stir until it evaporates.

Stirring the rice continuously, add the warm stock, 1 cup at a time, making sure that the liquid is completely absorbed by the rice before adding the next cup. The rice will start to release its starch and thicken into a creamy porridge, about 30 minutes. Depending on the texture of risotto you like, the grains of rice should be tender

to firm, but not gritty. Season the risotto with salt and pepper. Remove from the heat and let sit for a couple of minutes.

Beat the cold butter and Parmesan into the risotto. Serve immediately. Grate a bit of allspice over the risotto with a nut grater or Microplane zester and any additional Parmesan over the risotto at the table if you like.

# duck confit, strozzapreti, orange sauce

**Serves 4**

1 tablespoon vegetable oil

2 medium shallots, finely diced

4 cloves garlic, smashed and chopped

1 cup freshly squeezed orange juice

¾ cup Grand Marnier

¼ cup white wine

2 cups Duck Jus (page 258)

5 teaspoons sherry vinegar

Salt and freshly ground black pepper

20 pearl onions

4 Duck Confit legs (recipe follows, or store-bought)

8 ounces *strozzapreti*

Supremes of 2 oranges (see Note)

¼ cup Herb Crumbs (page 262)

Zest of 2 oranges, for garnish

I retooled one of my favorite French classics, *duck à l'orange*, into a simple pasta dish that could be served at Bluestem. Here, *strozzapreti* (Italian for "priest stranglers")—elongated strips of pasta that have been rolled to form curled lengths that look like warped tubes—become the perfect vehicle for a saucy duck jus infused with orange. Herbed bread crumbs, sprinkled over the dish at the last minute, offer a flavorful crunch.

If you don't want to make duck confit, you can buy it at specialty markets or special order it (see Sources, page 272). The duck ragu can be made a day ahead (see Note).

---

Heat the oil in a medium saucepan over medium-high heat. When the oil is hot, add the shallots and cook until softened, about 2 minutes. Add the garlic and continue to cook for another minute.

Deglaze the pan by adding the orange juice, Grand Marnier, and wine, stirring up any browned bits from the bottom of the pan. Bring the mixture to a simmer and let it reduce until *au sec* (meaning "almost dry"; you want the mixture to cook down to a thick, syrupy consistency), about 20 minutes. Add the duck jus and bring the sauce back to a simmer over medium heat. Add the sherry vinegar and adjust the seasoning with salt and pepper. Remove the sauce from the heat.

Prepare an ice bath (see the User Manual, page xx). Bring a small pot of salted water to a boil and blanch the onions for 5 minutes. Drain, then cool in the ice bath.

In a large sauté pan set over medium-high heat, combine the onions, duck confit, and 3 cups of the sauce. Bring the mixture to a simmer and cook until reduced by one-third to make a ragu, about 12 minutes.

While the ragu is reducing, cook the pasta by bringing a large stockpot of heavily salted water to a boil over high heat. Add the pasta and cook until barely tender (you want the pasta slightly undercooked at this stage, because the pasta will finish cooking with the ragu). Drain the pasta well.

Add the drained pasta and the orange supremes to the ragu. Bring the ragu back to a simmer, tossing the pasta to coat, and season with salt and pepper to taste.

To serve, divide the pasta among 4 bowls, making sure to get a bit of duck confit into each bowl. Sprinkle a tablespoon of herb crumbs and some freshly grated orange zest over each portion. Serve immediately.

**NOTE:** "Supreme" is, among other meanings, a French term for citrus wedges. Usually, you'll find the sections peeled or cut out of the fruit. To do this, cut into the fruit at one end with a paring knife, going just below the pith into the flesh. Working your way to the other end of the fruit, cut off a strip of rind, removing all of the pith and the fibrous lining, exposing the flesh of the fruit.

Repeat until all of the peel is removed and you're left with a "naked" citrus fruit. Cradling the fruit in a cupped palm, cut out the sections by slipping your knife into the fruit as closely to the section dividers as possible. Once the sections have been removed, you can squeeze the remaining "body" of the citrus fruit to extract the juices for other uses.

**NOTE:** The duck ragu can be made 1 day ahead. Let the duck ragu cool to room temperature. Transfer it to an airtight container and refrigerate overnight. When you are ready to serve the pasta, heat the ragu in a sauté pan over medium-high heat before adding the pasta and orange supremes.

## *duck confit*   Makes 4 duck confit legs

Duck confit, which can last for months if properly stored, is a useful product to have in your kitchen. Pulled from the bones, the meat can be tossed into salads or incorporated into a pasta dish. Whole, the legs can be seared in a skillet and served with some beans (like the white beans on page 261) or a fruit sauce (like the cranberry sauce on page 167).

2 cups tightly packed chopped fresh flat-leaf parsley

⅓ cup tightly packed fresh thyme leaves

¼ cup tightly packed fresh oregano leaves

2 large shallots, coarsely chopped

4 cloves garlic, coarsely chopped

¼ cup kosher salt

½ cup olive oil

4 (8-ounce) duck legs

6 cups duck fat (see Sources, page 272)

Combine the parsley, thyme, oregano, shallots, and garlic in a food processor and pulse until the ingredients are finely minced. Add the salt. With the machine running, drizzle in the oil in a steady stream until you have a fine, thick paste.

Rinse the duck legs with water, making sure to clean off any blood where the bone is exposed. Trim off the large pieces of fat, reserving them for the confit.

Season the exposed, cut side of each leg (the part that has no skin) with 1 tablespoon of duck cure. Press the legs together where the cut sides are exposed. Lay the pairs of legs in a casserole dish just large enough to fit them snugly, cover with plastic wrap, and weight them down with the bottom of another casserole dish filled with cans or bricks. Let the legs cure in the refrigerator overnight.

Preheat the oven to 300°F.

Scrape the cure off the legs and transfer them to a Dutch oven or deep casserole dish. Cover the legs with at least ½ inch of duck fat. Heat the legs and fat over medium heat until the fat comes to a slow simmer. Cover the pot with a tight-fitting lid or seal it tightly with aluminum foil. Cook the legs in the oven for 4 hours, or until the meat is tender but not falling off the bone. Take the lid

off the confit to let the steam out and then place directly in the refrigerator (on a trivet or pot holder) to cool. Refrigerated under a layer of fat, the duck confit legs will keep for up to 3 months.

To use the confit, remove the legs from the fat. Leaving the skin intact, scrape the fat off the legs with a spoon or knife back into the pot (the fat can be reused). At this point, you can either reheat the legs in a skillet over medium-high heat, searing them on both sides until the skin is browned, or pull off and discard the skin and pull the meat off the bone for other uses.

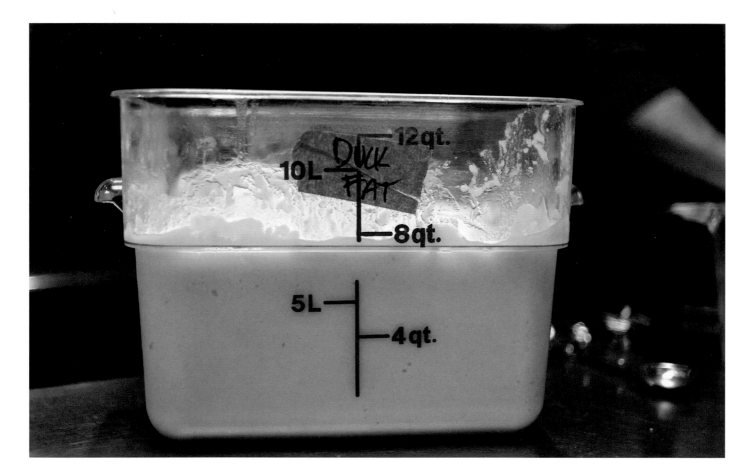

# lobster, chestnuts, cauliflower, salsify, brandy-lobster sauce

**Serves 4**

### chestnuts

16 fresh or 8 canned chestnuts

1 tablespoon olive oil

Salt and freshly ground white pepper

### salsify puree

1 pound salsify

Salt

Juice of 1 lemon, plus 2 teaspoons

⅓ cup heavy cream

1 tablespoon prepared horseradish

Freshly ground white pepper

4 (1½ pound) lobsters

### brandy-lobster sauce

2 tablespoons vegetable oil

3 cloves garlic, chopped

2 shallots, chopped

1 medium carrot, peeled and coarsely chopped

2 celery stalks, coarsely chopped

1 medium leek, trimmed of greens and coarsely chopped

1 tablespoon tomato paste

2 lobster heads (see page 158)

1 cup sherry

1 cup cognac

1 cup port

Salt and freshly ground white pepper

4 cups heavy cream

2 sprigs fresh tarragon

8 ounces cauliflower, cut into small florets

3 tablespoons unsalted butter

This dish casts lobster in a breakaway role from its familiar, sunny appearance as the virtuous luxury ingredient. With roasted chestnuts, salsify, brandy, and brown butter, this dish brings out the heartier, more serious side of lobster. You'll be surprised at how well the sweetness of the lobster meat stands up to its company. Also, together, the ingredients look like fall, an assortment of golden, earthy colors highlighted by bright orange pieces of lobster.

Salsify is a root vegetable that few home cooks use. It has a dark, hairy exterior and an ivory flesh that is somewhat fibrous. The flavor? Some call it the "oyster plant." Indeed, if you cook it with a touch of butter, you'll see why. Pureed here, it makes the perfect accompaniment for lobster. Only fresh chestnuts need to be roasted.

**Roast the fresh chestnuts:** Preheat the oven to 375°F.

Making sure to pierce through the shell, carefully score the chestnuts with a sharp paring knife. Toss the chestnuts with the olive oil and season them with salt and pepper. Roast the chestnuts on a baking sheet until the shells split open, about 25 minutes.

Let the chestnuts cool for 15 minutes. Peel the chestnuts, discard the shells, and cut the chestnuts in half.

**Make the salsify puree:** Trim and peel the salsify and soak it in cold water acidulated with the juice of 1 lemon for 5 minutes (peeled salsify can be sticky, so it might be helpful to wear gloves while trimming it). Drain the salsify and chop the stalks into 2-inch pieces.

Put the chopped salsify in a large saucepan and add enough cold water to cover. Salt the water heavily, bring it to a boil over medium heat, and cook until soft, about 25 minutes. Drain off the water and push the boiled salsify through a fine-mesh sieve. Stir in the 2 teaspoons lemon juice, the cream, and the horseradish, and season with salt and pepper to taste. Keep warm.

**Kill the lobsters:** You're going to have to kill the lobsters. For some, this will be the most difficult part of this recipe. While most recipes have you "put the lobsters to sleep" in a pot of boiling water, here you will need to blanch the different parts of the lobster separately. So you will have to kill the lobsters by hand.

The quickest and easiest way to do this is to split the head in half with a sharp chef's knife. Turn a lobster on its back, with the head facing you. Insert the knife tip into the head at the base of the head and, with a quick downward chop toward you, slice the head in half. With one hand firmly gripping the body and the other the tail, twist the tail off. Set it aside in a bowl. Twist the two claws off. Set them aside with the tail. Lift the "helmet" of the lobster head off the body. Using a spoon, scoop out the gunk from the underside of the lobster helmet. Remove and discard the feathery gills from the body. Set both the helmet and body aside for the brandy-lobster sauce. Repeat with the remaining lobsters.

**Make the brandy-lobster sauce:** Heat the vegetable oil in a large stockpot over high heat. Add the garlic, shallots, carrot, celery, leek, tomato paste, and 2 lobster heads (helmet and body, but not the tails or claws) and cook for 3 minutes. Add the sherry, cognac, and port and bring to a full simmer, mashing the heads with a wooden spoon to extract as much flavor from them as possible. Season with salt and white pepper. Reduce the stock to 2 cups, about 20 minutes. Add the cream and tarragon. Turn the heat down to medium and continue to cook and reduce the sauce for 30 minutes, to about 1½ cups. Mash the heads some more with the wooden spoon.

Strain the stock through a fine-mesh sieve. Discard the solids. Cover the stock and keep warm.

**Cook the cauliflower:** Prepare an ice bath (see the User Manual, page xxv). Bring a pot of water to a boil and blanch the cauliflower for 3 minutes. Drain, then cool in the ice bath.

**Blanch the lobster claws:** Prepare a large ice bath.

Bring a large stockpot of water to a boil over high heat. Blanch the claws and knuckles for 6 minutes. Remove the claws and knuckles with a slotted spoon and cool them in the ice bath. (See the User Manual for blanching and ice bath instructions, pages xxiv and xxv.)

When the claws and knuckles have cooled, remove the meat from the shells. Discard the shells.

**Cook the lobster tails:** Slice the lobster tails crosswise according to the segments, leaving the meat in the shell. Heat the butter in a large sauté pan over high heat. When the butter has melted, add half of the sliced lobster tails and baste the lobster with the butter for 1 minute. By now, the butter should have browned, giving off a nutty aroma. Add the cauliflower and chestnuts and toss to coat. Add the lobster claws and knuckles, making sure you don't break them, and cook for 2 more minutes to warm through.

**To serve:** Spoon about ¼ cup of the salsify puree onto each of 4 plates. Divide the cauliflower and chestnuts among the plates, arranging them around the puree. Divide the tails and claws among the plates, drizzle with a bit of the pan sauce, and serve immediately.

# potato-crusted **halibut**, mushroom, herb cream

**Serves 4**

**herb cream**

1 cup heavy cream

4 egg yolks

2 cups loosely packed fresh chervil

2 cups loosely packed fresh flat-leaf parsley

2 tablespoons fresh thyme leaves

Salt and freshly ground white pepper

**mushrooms**

2 tablespoons unsalted butter

8 ounces porcini mushrooms, trimmed and halved lengthwise

2 large shallots, finely chopped

2 cloves garlic, chopped

**vinaigrette**

1 tablespoon plus 1 teaspoon banyuls vinegar

1 tablespoon extra-virgin olive oil

Pinch of salt

**fish**

1½ pounds russet potatoes, peeled

4 (6-ounce) halibut fillets

Salt and freshly ground white pepper

¼ cup vegetable oil

This dish is uncharacteristically classic for Bluestem. And it's extremely simple too—a three-part harmony of white, meaty halibut; a rich herb cream; and beefy porcini tossed in a vinaigrette to help brighten the dish.

Porcini are my favorite mushrooms, and I await them eagerly every fall. But fresh ones are extremely hard to get in the Midwest. If you can't find them, cremini mushrooms (also known as baby portobello) will be the closest substitute.

**Make the herb cream:** Bring the cream to a simmer in a saucepan over medium-high heat. Put the egg yolks in a blender. With the blender running, drizzle the hot cream into the blender in a thin, steady stream to temper the yolks. The sauce will emulsify and thicken. Add the chervil, parsley, and thyme and puree until smooth. Season with salt and pepper to taste. Keep warm until ready to serve.

**Sauté the mushrooms:** Heat the butter in a medium skillet over high heat. Sear the porcini mushrooms, cut side down, for 1 minute, or until browned. Add the shallots and garlic and continue cooking just until they start to turn translucent. Remove the skillet from the heat.

**Make the vinaigrette:** Whisk together the vinegar, olive oil, and salt to make a vinaigrette. Set aside.

**Prepare the fish:** Grate the potatoes using a box grater. Gather the grated potatoes onto a clean kitchen towel and squeeze all the liquid out. Transfer the grated potatoes to a bowl.

Preheat the oven to 375°F. Season the fish with salt and pepper.

Season the potatoes with salt and pepper. Lay a fillet of fish over each group of grated potato. Using a sharp knife, outline the perimeter of each fillet, trimming away the excess potato around the edges.

Heat the vegetable oil in a large, ovenproof sauté pan over medium heat. When the oil is hot, carefully place the fish, potato side down, in the pan and cook until golden brown, 1 to 2 minutes. Using a wide spatula, carefully flip the fish over. The potato crust should come cleanly away from the skillet and adhere to the fish. Transfer the skillet to the oven and roast the fish for 5 minutes.

**To serve:** Toss the mushroom mixture with 2 tablespoons of the vinaigrette.

Spoon some herb cream onto each of 4 plates. Top the herb cream with a fish fillet. Divide the dressed mushrooms among the plates. Serve immediately.

# **char**, wild rice, sweetbreads, arugula-vermouth emulsion

**Serves 4**

### sweetbreads

8 ounces veal sweetbreads

Whole milk, for marinating

6 cups Veal Stock (page 257)
　　or water

### wild rice

2 cups long-grain wild rice

4 cups water

1 small carrot, coarsely chopped

1 small onion, coarsely chopped

2 celery stalks, coarsely chopped

2 bay leaves

¼ cup finely diced carrot

¼ cup finely diced celery

¼ cup finely diced onion

2 cloves garlic, finely diced

½ cup Whipped Butter (page 251)

Salt and freshly ground white pepper

### arugula-vermouth emulsion

1 tablespoon grapeseed oil

2 cloves garlic, chopped

1 large shallot, chopped

¼ fennel bulb, coarsely chopped (fronds
　　reserved)

1 cup dry vermouth

½ dry white wine

1½ cups Fish Stock (page 255)

4 cups loosely packed arugula

4 cups loosely packed spinach

2 teaspoons unsalted butter

Salt and freshly ground white pepper

### vegetables

12 baby turnips, peeled

12 Glazed Cipollini (page 259)

½ cup Whipped Butter (page 251)


Salt and freshly ground black pepper

1 cup Wondra flour

Vegetable oil, for deep frying

### fish

4 (6-ounce) arctic char fillets

Salt and freshly ground white pepper

2 tablespoons vegetable oil

4 tablespoons (½ stick) unsalted butter,
　　cut into ½-inch cubes

¼ cup fresh chervil leaves

¼ cup fennel fronds

When we first opened Bluestem, salmon flew off the menu at a breakneck speed. Although I was pleased by its popularity, the rest of my fish dishes were being neglected. So I changed the salmon to char and added sweetbreads as a speed bump, thinking it might slow down orders. That's about the time that Bonjwing came in for dinner and had this revised dish. He fell in love with it. And so did many others—it became even more popular than the salmon version. Bonjwing insisted we include it in this cookbook.

At the restaurant, we dust our sweetbreads with Wondra flour, pulverized flour that gives them a delicate crust. But you can use all-purpose flour instead. Salmon can be substituted for char in this recipe, although salmon fillets tend to be thicker than char, so you might have to increase your cooking time.

---

**Prepare the sweetbreads:** Soak the sweetbreads in milk for 4 hours, changing the liquid twice. Trim the sweetbreads of excess fat and debris, leaving the membrane intact. Divide the sweetbreads into 4 equal portions.

In a medium saucepan, bring the veal stock to a simmer over medium heat. Poach the sweetbreads for 5 minutes. Drain and cool. Set them aside.

**Make the rice:** Bring the rice, water, coarsely chopped carrot, coarsely chopped onion, coarsely chopped celery, and bay leaves to a simmer in a large saucepan over high heat. Turn the heat to low and simmer for about 6 minutes. Cover and cook until the rice grains begin to split open, about 30 minutes.

Turn the contents out onto a large baking sheet or casserole dish and remove and discard the vegetables.

Return the rice to the pot. Stir in the finely diced carrot, celery, onion, and garlic, fluffing the rice as you go. Fold in the whipped butter and season with salt and white pepper. Cover and keep warm until ready to serve.

**Make the arugula-vermouth emulsion:** Heat the grapeseed oil over medium heat. Add the garlic, shallot, and fennel and sauté for about 2 minutes. Add the vermouth and wine and simmer until reduced by half, about 10 minutes. Add the fish stock and reduce by half again. Remove the sauce from the heat and let it cool completely.

Transfer the sauce to a blender. Add the arugula and spinach and puree until smooth. Strain the sauce through a fine-mesh sieve, discard the solids, and keep warm until ready to serve. Alternatively, at this point you can refrigerate the sauce in an airtight container for up to 1 day. When you are ready to serve, reheat the sauce over medium heat. Stir in the butter until fully dissolved and season with salt and white pepper to taste.

**For the vegetables:** Bring a small pot of water to a boil and blanch the turnips for 4 minutes. Drain, then cut in half. Reheat the glazed cipollini, turnips, and whipped butter in a small saucepan over medium heat.

**Fry the sweetbreads:** Pat the sweetbreads dry and season them with salt and black pepper. Dredge the sweetbreads in the flour.

Heat 2 inches of vegetable oil in a skillet over high heat until the oil reaches 350°F. Line a plate with paper towels. Fry the sweetbreads for 2½ minutes on each side, or until golden brown. Drain the sweetbreads on a prepared plate.

**Cook the fish:** Season the fish with salt and white pepper.

Heat the oil in a sauté pan over medium-high heat. Place the fillets, skin side down, in the pan and cook until the skin is brown, about 1 minute. Flip the fillets over and add the butter. Baste the fish with the melted butter for another minute. Remove the pan from the heat.

**To serve:** Divide the rice and vegetables evenly among 4 plates. Top the rice with a fish fillet and a portion of sweetbreads. Spoon the arugula-vermouth emulsion around the plate, garnish with fresh chervil and fennel fronds, and serve immediately.

# pork tenderloin, piquillo peppers, fingerling potatoes

**Serves 4**

12 canned piquillo peppers

1 clove garlic, thinly sliced

¾ cup plus 1 tablespoon olive oil

1 cup fresh flat-leaf parsley leaves

12 Potatoes Confit, halved lengthwise (page 260)

2 tablespoons vegetable oil

2 pounds pork tenderloin

Salt and freshly ground white pepper

Dave Crum, whose parents own Crum's Heirloom Farm (see page 74), was my first chef de cuisine at Bluestem. He's one of the most talented cooks I know—his execution is always precise, his compositions always satisfying.

Having traveled and cooked throughout South America, Dave has a particular fascination with Latin culture and cuisine. This recipe is representative of the dishes he would create at the restaurant—hearty and rustic in flavor, yet refined in presentation.

Dave left the professional kitchen to pursue his passion: meat. He now works for a specialty meat company in Kansas City. For this recipe, Dave recommends Duroc pork, also known as the "Black Angus of pork," which is particularly succulent, with superior marbling.

---

Preheat the oven to 325°F.

Brush a thin coat of olive oil over the surface of a small baking sheet or shallow baking dish. Spread the piquillo peppers on the sheet and scatter the garlic over the peppers. Pour ¾ cup of the olive oil over all of it—there should be just enough oil to cover the peppers.
Bake the peppers in the oven for 30 minutes. Remove the peppers and garlic from the sheet, cover, and keep warm. Reserve the oil.

Put the reserved pepper oil in a blender along with the parsley. Puree the mixture until thick. Set aside.

Heat the remaining 1 tablespoon olive oil in a sauté pan over medium-high heat. Add the potatoes and cook, stirring them occasionally, until a golden brown crust forms, about 7 minutes. Set aside.

Raise the oven temperature to 375°F. Heat the vegetable oil in a large skillet or ovenproof sauté pan over high heat.

Season the pork with salt and pepper. Add the pork tenderloin and sear until browned, about 3 minutes per side.

Transfer the pork to the oven to finish cooking, about 8 minutes for a warm, pink center (it should register 145°F on a meat thermometer for medium). Let the pork tenderloin rest for 12 minutes before slicing it into ½-inch-thick slices.

To serve, divide the peppers and potatoes among 4 plates, gathering them in a cluster in the center of each plate. Lean a few slices of meat against the vegetables and drizzle parsley oil in a circle around the edge of each plate. Serve immediately.

# roasted **pheasant**, cranberry, pumpernickel bread pudding, barolo

**Serves 4**

### bread pudding

8 cups pumpernickel bread in ½-inch cubes

¾ cup heavy cream

⅓ cup whole milk

1 tablespoon vegetable oil

2 shallots, diced

4 cloves garlic, chopped

Salt and freshly ground black pepper

4 large eggs, lightly beaten

2 tablespoons chopped fresh flat-leaf parsley

3 tablespoons chopped fresh oregano leaves

### cranberry sauce

12 ounces cranberries

¾ cup sugar

½ cup Barolo

3 (2-inch) strips orange zest

Juice of 1 orange

½ cup Veal Stock (page 257)

Salt

### pheasant

4 (4- to 6-ounce) pheasant breasts

4 pheasant "oysters"

Salt and freshly ground black pepper

¼ cup vegetable oil

3 tablespoons unsalted butter

I grew up hunting pheasant, and I can tell you that wild pheasant in the Midwest is lean and unforgiving. If you're not used to cooking wild pheasant from your area, buy farm-raised ones, which are available commercially.

I dreamed up this dish as a more refined alternative to the traditional Thanksgiving turkey. The pumpernickel bread pudding is my version of knödel, a German dumpling made from either potatoes or bread. I first made knödel while working for Hans Röckenwagner in Los Angeles. Since then, it has become one of my go-to accompaniments for meat and fowl dishes in the colder months.

The "oysters" are tender rounds of dark meat nestled between the small of the bird's back and its thigh. Ask your butcher to carve out the oysters.

**Make the bread pudding:** Put the bread in a large heatproof bowl. Bring the cream and milk to a simmer in a small saucepan over medium heat. Remove from the heat and pour it over the bread. Let the bread soak up the liquid for 10 minutes.

Heat the oil in a small sauté pan over medium-high heat. Add the shallots and garlic and sauté until softened, about 2 minutes. Add the shallots and garlic to the bread mixture. Season with salt and pepper and set it aside to cool slightly. Then stir in the eggs, parsley, and oregano.

Roll the bread mixture tightly into a log in multiple layers of plastic wrap (see "The Roll" on page 84). Try your best to prevent air pockets from forming and to seal the packet well. Twist the plastic wrap on both ends tightly and secure them with kitchen twine. The log should be roughly 3 inches in diameter and about 12 inches long. If there are large air pockets under the surface of the plastic wrap, pop them with a small pin.

Fill a large roasting pan or stockpot with water deep enough to submerge the bread pudding and bring to a simmer over high heat. Lower the bread pudding into the water and turn the heat down to medium. Keep the package submerged with a plate or a light weight. Return the water to a simmer and poach the bread pudding for 25 to 30 minutes.

When the knödel it is almost done poaching, prepare a large ice bath (see the User Manual, page xxv). Remove the package from the simmering water and submerge it in the ice bath to cool. Then remove it from the ice bath and set aside.

**Make the cranberry sauce:** In a medium saucepan, bring the cranberries, sugar, wine, orange zest, and orange juice to a boil over medium-high heat. Turn the heat down to medium and simmer the sauce until the juices have reduced to a thick syrup, about 25 minutes. Stir in the veal stock. Season with salt to taste. Cover and keep warm.

**Cook the pheasant:** Preheat the oven to 375°F. Season the pheasant meat with salt and pepper.

Heat the oil in a large ovenproof skillet over high heat. When the oil is hot, add the pheasant breasts, skin side down, and the pheasant oysters. Brown them for about 2 minutes. Transfer the skillet to the oven and roast the meat for 6 minutes. Remove the oysters, keeping them warm until ready to serve. Return the skillet to the oven and cook the breasts for 6 minutes more. Take the skillet out of the oven, flip the breasts over, add 2 tablespoons of the butter, and let them rest for 5 minutes in the hot pan with the melting butter.

**To serve:** Using a sharp knife, slice the bread pudding through the plastic wrap into ½-inch-thick slices (you will need 4 slices for this recipe; extra knödel will keep refrigerated for up to 1 week).

Heat the remaining 1 tablespoon butter in a sauté pan over medium heat. When the butter begins to foam, fry the bread pudding slices on both sides until golden brown.

Divide the pheasant breasts, pheasant oysters, and bread pudding slices among 4 plates. Spoon some of the cranberry sauce over the pheasant and serve immediately.

# hen, posole, peppers

**Serves 4**

**posole**

¼ cup vegetable oil

1 small onion, diced

½ red bell pepper, diced

6 cloves garlic, thinly sliced

4 teaspoons chili powder

1 cup canned San Marzano tomatoes, with liquid

2 cups posole, soaked overnight in 8 cups water

9 cups Chicken Stock (page 256)

4 ounces linguiça sausage, diced

¼ cup Crème Fraîche (page 251)

Salt

**chicken**

1 tablespoon cumin seeds

1 tablespoon dried red pepper flakes

1½ tablespoons coriander seeds

1 tablespoon black peppercorns

1 tablespoon hot paprika

1 (3-pound) chicken, skin on, boned and halved

1 tablespoon fresh thyme leaves

4 cloves garlic, minced

Finely grated zest of 1 lime

2 shallots, sliced

2 tablespoons freshly squeezed lime juice

¾ cup sherry vinegar

1 cup olive oil

2 limes, halved, for garnish

At a charity dinner event that I attended as one of a few guest chefs, my good friend Ted Habiger, who owns Room 39, a restaurant in Kansas City, served a beautifully cooked guinea hen with posole that inspired me to make my own version.

Traditionally, posole is a brothy stew with hominy, chiles, and usually pork. This posole is thicker and saucier. At the restaurant, I also add a dark chocolate mole to the plate to give it another flavor and another texture. But here I've simplified the recipe, stripping it down to a skillet-smashed chicken and a hearty hominy stew with linguiça sausages.

In the Midwest, bell peppers grow right up until the first frost, making the local varieties available through the early autumn.

You can ask your butcher to debone and halve the chicken.

**Cook the posole:** Heat 3 tablespoons of the vegetable oil in a large saucepan over medium-high heat. Stir in the onion, bell pepper, and garlic and cook until the vegetables have softened and begun to caramelize, about 5 minutes. Stir the chili powder and cook for about 30 seconds, stirring to coat the vegetables with the spice.

Stir in the tomatoes and cook to soften, about 2 minutes. Add the posole and 3 cups of chicken stock and cook for about 2 hours, adding the rest of the chicken stock periodically as the posole soaks it up.

Heat the remaining 1 tablespoon vegetable oil in a small sauté pan over medium-high heat. Brown the linguiça, about 3 minutes. Add the linguiça to the posole and cook for another 5 minutes. Stir in the crème fraîche and season the posole with salt to taste.

**Make the chicken:** Toast the cumin seeds, red pepper flakes, coriander seeds, and peppercorns in a small skillet over low heat for about 2 minutes, or until the aroma starts to emerge. Pulse the spices in a spice grinder until coarsely ground. Add the paprika and mix to combine.

Rub the chicken all over with the spice mixture, thyme, garlic, lime zest, and shallots in a shallow baking dish. Add the lime juice, sherry vinegar, and oil. Let the chicken marinate, covered, for 2 to 4 hours in the refrigerator, but no longer.

Preheat the oven to 350°F. Heat a large griddle over medium-high heat.

Wipe the chicken clean of the marinade, reserving ¼ cup of the marinating liquid. Lay the chicken halves on the griddle and flatten them with a large, heavy skillet or bricks wrapped with aluminum foil. Let the chicken brown on both sides under the weight, searing them for about 3 minutes per side.

Pour the reserved marinade into a roasting pan. Place the chicken halves, skin side up, in the roasting pan and roast them in the oven for 20 minutes.

**To serve:** Cut each chicken in half—you will have two breasts and two thighs. Divide the posole and chicken among 4 plates. Garnish each plate with a half of lime.

# **strip loin**, chanterelles, mustard-glazed brussels sprouts, pecans

**Serves 4**

**butter-mustard sauce**

⅓ cup dry white wine

5 tablespoons unsalted butter, chilled and cut into ½-inch pieces

1 tablespoon Dijon mustard

1 tablespoon grainy mustard

Salt and freshly ground pepper

**steaks**

½ cup pecans

1 teaspoon olive oil

Salt and freshly ground black pepper

4 (8-ounce) strip steaks

4 tablespoons (½ stick) unsalted butter

1 cup Veal Stock (page 257)

**chanterelles and brussels sprouts**

8 ounces brussels sprouts, trimmed and leaves plucked (see Note)

1 tablespoon unsalted butter

8 ounces fresh chanterelle mushrooms, trimmed

Salt and freshly ground black pepper

---

Although there's no whiskey in this recipe, it's the flavor of fall and the inspiration for this dish, which combines some of my favorite ingredients, all of which remind me of the dark, toasty liquor. But if you want a taste of whiskey, pour yourself a shot and sip it while making this dish.

You won't find any surprises in this recipe—it's extremely straightforward and a sure crowd-pleaser. The mustard-glazed brussels sprouts will convert those who claim to dislike this unfairly maligned vegetable, like my wife, Megan.

---

**Make the butter-mustard sauce:** In a medium saucepan, bring the wine to a simmer over medium-low heat and reduce by half. Remove from the heat and whisk in the butter, one piece at a time, waiting for each piece to melt before adding the next.

Whisk in the two mustards and season the sauce with salt and pepper. Keep the sauce in a warm place, like near the stove or above the stove, but do not heat it again or the emulsion will break (the butter will separate from the liquid).

**Prepare the steaks:** Preheat the oven to 350°F.

Toss the pecans with the oil and salt and pepper to taste and spread them out on a small baking sheet. Toast the nuts in the oven for 7 minutes, stirring them at least once to prevent them from burning. Set aside to cool.

Raise the oven temperature to 375°F. Season the steaks with salt and pepper.

Heat the butter in a large ovenproof skillet over high heat. When the butter is very hot, sear the steaks for 1 minute on each side. Depending on the size of your skillet, you may have to do this in batches. Transfer the steaks to a roasting pan and roast them in the oven for 12 to 14 minutes for a medium-rare center (the internal temperature should register 128°F on a meat thermometer).

Let the steaks rest for 10 minutes before slicing. Heat the veal stock in a small saucepan over medium-high heat. Keep warm until ready to serve.

**Cook the mushrooms and brussels sprouts:** Prepare an ice bath (see the User Manual, page xxv). Bring a pot of water to a boil and blanch the brussels sprout leaves for 1 minute. With a slotted spoon, drain the leaves and plunge them into the ice bath. Drain the leaves and pat them dry.

Heat the butter in a medium sauté pan over medium heat until it foams. Add the chanterelles and cook for 5 minutes, shaking the pan often to prevent the mushrooms from burning. Season the mushrooms with salt and pepper. Transfer the chanterelles to a plate lined with a paper towel to drain.

Return the pan to the stove over medium heat. Add the brussels sprout leaves and stir them occasionally until slightly charred, about 1 minute.

Toss the brussels sprout leaves, mushrooms, and pecans with ¼ cup of the butter-mustard sauce.

**To serve:** At the restaurant, we serve the steaks sliced. But you can certainly serve the steaks whole if you like. Either way, divide the meat, mushrooms, and brussels sprouts among 4 plates. Drizzle some veal stock over each steak. Serve immediately.

# brussels sprouts

To pluck brussels sprouts, cut off the tough, bottom quarter of the brussels sprouts (the thick stem) and discard it. Pull off all of the leaves and discard the hard core in the middle. You may need to cut off some of the larger leaves with a paring knife.

# paradise locker meats

When I was growing up in the late 1970s and early '80s, fear of meat gripped Americans. We were scared into believing that it was uniformly dangerous. Indeed, like many things, meat can be dangerous when it's not handled properly (as we have witnessed in recent factory farm mishaps). But with good provenance and the right care, there's very little reason to worry. That's why you should get to know your butcher or meat purveyor.

In the sleepy town of Trimble, Missouri, about an hour's drive north of Kansas City, is Paradise Locker Meats. Owned and operated by Mario Fantasma and his family, this small, USDA-inspected operation offers custom meat processing.

Discriminate sourcing—mostly from local farmers dedicated to sustainable practices—and unimpeachable standards make Paradise Locker Meats a reliable and trustworthy supplier of quality products for Bluestem. From them, we get information about the origin of our meat, the methods of animal husbandry involved, and how the meat has been handled from slaughter to service. They're also a great resource for all kinds of information related to meat and butchery; it's a relationship that is vital to Bluestem.

# capriole goat's milk sofia cheese, **quince** jam

**Makes one 13 by 9-inch pan**

1 cup water

½ cup white wine

½ cup brandy

3 quinces, peeled

1¾ cups sugar

Juice of 1 lemon

Capriole Farms' Sofia cheese, for serving

When it seems like everything else is preparing for hibernation, you have the quince—a fuzz-covered knot that defies the quickly bronzing world with a happy splash of neon yellow. When they arrive at the restaurant, I can't resist opening the box and sticking my face inside for a good smell of the wonderfully fragrant fruit.

To many, quinces are a mystery. It's usually the one fruit that my new pastry assistants know the least about. Quinces can't be eaten raw; they must be cooked. In Spain, quinces are reduced to a paste called *membrillo*. It's commonly served with cheese, which is what we do with it at Bluestem.

This version is a bit more jam-like and is extremely versatile. Keep a jar of it around as a condiment for cheese or turkey sandwiches or spread it over a prebaked tart shell, top it with sliced apples, and bake until the apples are tender.

---

Line a shallow 13 by 9-inch pan with a nonstick baking liner.

In a medium saucepan with a tight-fitting lid, combine the water, wine, brandy, and quinces. Cover and cook over medium-high heat, poaching the fruit until it is tender, 30 to 45 minutes.

Remove the fruit from the pan and cut the flesh off the fruit and discard the stems and core. Put the fruit into a blender and add just enough of the cooking liquid to puree (no more than 3 cups of liquid should be needed).

Transfer the puree back to the saucepan, add the sugar, and simmer over medium-low heat until the puree thickens and turns translucent, about 1 hour. Stir in the lemon juice and pour the hot quince paste into the prepared pan to cool completely. Wrap the pan with plastic wrap and refrigerate until ready to serve. Kept covered and chilled, it should keep up to 1 month.

Serve the cheese, one to two ounces per person, with a spoonful of the quince paste.

# oatmeal-ale cake, beer foam, caramel, salted pumpkin ice cream

**Serves 4**

½ cup (1 stick) unsalted butter, softened

1 cup packed light brown sugar

1 cup granulated sugar

2 large eggs

½ teaspoon vanilla extract

¼ teaspoon finely grated orange zest

1 cup all-purpose flour

1 teaspoon baking soda

½ tablespoon malt powder

⅛ teaspoon ground allspice

Pinch of freshly grated nutmeg

Pinch of ground cinnamon

½ cup whole-wheat flour

½ teaspoon salt

1¼ cups Boulevard Pale Ale

1¼ cups rolled oats

Caramel Sauce (recipe follows)

Beer Foam (optional; recipe follows)

Salted Pumpkin Ice Cream (page 266)

I'm not a beer drinker. But my husband makes up for it. I do, however, love baking and cooking with beer, which lends a wonderful yeasty fragrance to everything it touches.

This oatmeal-ale cake, accompanied by a scoop of Salted Pumpkin Ice Cream, has all the textures and flavors of fall. With a frothy head of beer foam spooned over it all, it reminds me of Oktoberfest.

You can use any kind of beer, but I find that ale gives the cake the right balance. The batter can be refrigerated, covered with plastic wrap, for up to 3 days before baking. Make sure to put the batter in an extra-large container, as the beer will ferment and release gas over time.

---

Preheat the oven to 325°F. Butter an 8-inch square baking pan.

In the bowl of a stand mixer fitted with a paddle attachment, cream the butter, brown sugar, and granulated sugar together on medium speed for 3 minutes. Scrape down the bowl with a rubber spatula and continue to cream the butter on high speed until fluffy, about 2 minutes more.

In a small bowl, lightly beat the eggs, vanilla, and orange zest together. Add to the creamed butter and mix until incorporated, scraping the bowl as needed.

Sift together the all-purpose flour, baking soda, malt powder, allspice, nutmeg, and cinnamon in a medium bowl. Add the whole-wheat flour and salt to the sifted ingredients.

With the stand mixer on low speed, mix in half of the dry ingredients until incorporated. Scrape down the bowl and add half of the ale. Again, mix until incorporated and scrape down the bowl. Repeat the process with the remaining half of the dry ingredients and the remaining half of the ale.

Using a spatula, fold in the oats. The batter will be loose and runny.

Transfer the batter to the cake pan and bake for 40 minutes, or until a toothpick inserted in the center comes out clean. While the cake is still warm, brush the top with some of the reserved syrup from the beer foam.

Let the cake cool completely on a wire rack. Cut into squares and serve with caramel sauce and a spoonful each of beer foam, and the salted pumpkin ice cream.

## *caramel sauce*  Makes 2 cups

2 cups plus 2 tablespoons sugar

¾ cup water

1 tablespoon light corn syrup

1 cup heavy cream

1 teaspoon freshly squeezed lemon juice

1 tablespoon unsalted butter

1 teaspoon vanilla extract

Pinch of salt

Combine the sugar, water, and corn syrup in a large saucepan. Using a wet pastry brush, brush down the sides of the inside of the pot. Cook the mixture over high heat until the sugar dissolves and turns dark amber. Watch the caramel closely when it starts to yellow, as it will turn dark very quickly thereafter.

Standing slightly back from the pot, whisk in the cream (the caramel will sputter and bubble vigorously for a while) and bring the caramel to a boil. Remove from the heat.

Whisk in the lemon juice, butter, vanilla, and salt. Carefully strain the hot caramel through a fine-mesh sieve and transfer it to a heatproof airtight container. Set aside to let cool completely. Cover and refrigerate until ready to use, or for up to 1 month.

To reheat, zap the caramel in the microwave for 30 seconds, or reheat on the stovetop over medium-low heat. Whisk until the sauce becomes fluid.

## beer foam

1 cup water

1 cup sugar

2 tablespoons honey

1 cup ale

Bring the water, sugar, and honey to a boil in a small saucepan over high heat. Let it cook for 30 seconds and then remove it from the heat. Transfer the syrup to a heatproof container and let it cool completely. Reserve 3 tablespoons for brushing the top of the baked cake.

Gently heat the ale, 2 tablespoons of the syrup, and the soy lecithin in a small saucepan over low heat. Transfer the liquid to a canister or a tall 4-cup container. Tip the container at an angle and, using a handheld blender or handheld milk frother, froth the liquid near the surface to make bubbles. As you plate the dessert, you may need to froth the beer foam repeatedly. Covered and chilled, the beer foam should keep for up to 1 week.

# poached **braeburn apples,** hot buttered cider rum, brown butter–pecan ice cream

**Serves 4**

8 cups apple cider

1 cup light rum (we use 10 Cane rum)

½ cup sugar

6 cloves

3 cinnamon sticks

2 teaspoons freshly grated nutmeg

Zest of 1 orange, peeled with a Y-peeler

1 large piece crystallized ginger, chopped into small pieces

4 Braeburn apples, peeled, halved, and cored

4 tablespoons (½ stick) unsalted butter

Brown Butter–Pecan Ice Cream (page 266)

Pecans, toasted and chopped, for garnish

As a kid, I loved going apple picking in the fall. There was always the promise of cider to be drunk and pies and fritters to be made and eaten afterward. I have distilled my childhood orchard memories into this comforting dessert, which is best served the day it is made.

The spices in the cider can and should be adjusted to your taste. The cider will perfume your house with a warm scent as your guests arrive for dinner.

---

Bring the cider, rum, sugar, cloves, cinnamon sticks, nutmeg, zest, and ginger to a boil in a large saucepan over high heat. Turn the heat down to low and add the apples. Bring the liquid to a low simmer and poach the apples for 20 minutes, or until the apples become tender but not soft or mushy.

Remove the apples with a slotted spoon and set them on a plate to drain. Cover and keep the apples warm while you let the cider steep for 10 minutes.

Strain the cider through a fine-mesh sieve. Discard the cinnamon sticks, orange peel, ginger, and cloves. Cover the cider and keep warm until ready to serve.

Divide the apple halves among 4 bowls. Vigorously whisk the butter into the cider. Pour the warm buttered cider over the apples and top each with a scoop of the ice cream. Garnish each bowl with chopped pecans and serve immediately. Extra cider can be refrigerated in an airtight container for up to 2 days.

# peanut cream fritters, **concord grape** sauce

**Serves 4 to 6**

### peanut filling

7 ounces cream cheese, softened

1½ cups creamy peanut butter

3 tablespoons confectioners' sugar

2 tablespoons heavy cream

1 tablespoon vanilla extract

½ teaspoon ground cinnamon

½ cup roasted unsalted peanuts, toasted and finely chopped

### concord grape sauce

2 cups unsweetened Concord grape puree (see Note)

1 cup granulated sugar

4 tablespoons (½ stick) unsalted butter

Juice of 1 lemon

### beignet sugar

2 cups granulated sugar

2 tablespoons ground cinnamon

1 teaspoon salt

### beignet dough

1 tablespoon plus 1½ teaspoons active dry yeast

¾ cup water

3 tablespoons whole milk

⅔ cup packed brown sugar

2 tablespoons unsalted butter

1 tablespoon creamy peanut butter

2 large eggs

1 teaspoon vanilla extract

3 cups all-purpose flour, plus more as needed

¾ teaspoon salt

Vegetable oil, for deep frying

**Autumn always** reminds me of going back to school. And school always reminds me of peanut butter and jelly. In this recipe, I reunite that childhood couple by incorporating peanut butter into beignet dough, stuffing the fried rounds with more peanut butter, and serving them alongside Concord grape sauce for dipping. It's sophisticated enough for adults but aimed right at the kid inside all of us.

**Make the peanut filling:** In the bowl of a stand mixer fitted with a paddle attachment, beat together the cream cheese, peanut butter, sugar, cream, vanilla extract, and cinnamon until smooth, scraping the bowl a couple of times during the mixing process. Using a spatula, fold in the chopped peanuts. Covered and chilled, it will keep for up to 1 week. Let the filling come to room temperature before using.

**Make the Concord grape sauce:** Bring all of the ingredients to a simmer in saucepan over medium heat. Let the sauce reduce by half, 10 to 12 minutes. Strain the sauce through a fine-mesh sieve and let to cool. Covered and chilled, it will keep for up to 1 week. When you are ready to serve, warm the sauce in small saucepan over low heat.

**Make the beignet sugar:** Combine the sugar, cinnamon, and salt in a small bowl. Set aside.

**Make the beignets:** Put the yeast in a large bowl. Heat the water, milk, brown sugar, butter, and peanut butter in a small saucepan over medium heat just enough to melt the butter and dissolve the sugar. Take the mixture off the heat and let it cool slightly—you want it to be no more than 110°F or else it will kill the yeast. Pour the warm mixture over the yeast and whisk to combine. Whisk in the eggs and vanilla.

In a separate large bowl, combine the flour and salt. Make a well in the center and pour the wet ingredients into the center. Mix the ingredients with your hands until they come together into a wet, sticky dough. Turn the dough out onto a lightly floured surface and knead until it doesn't stick to your hands, about 3 minutes. Add up to 4 more tablespoons of flour if needed.

Roll the dough into a ball and place it in a large, lightly oiled bowl. Cover with a damp towel and let it rest in a warm place for 1 hour to double in size.

Roll the dough out on a floured surface to a ½-inch thickness. Using a 1½-inch ring mold, cut out as many beignets as you can.

Heat 3 inches of vegetable oil in a heavy stockpot (or a countertop deep fryer) to 350°F. Line a baking sheet with paper towels. Working in batches of three or four, fry the beignets until golden brown, turning them to brown them evenly. Using tongs, transfer the beignets to the prepared baking sheet. Roll the beignets in the cinnamon sugar while they are still hot.

Fill a pastry bag fitted with a plain tip with the peanut filling. Stick the plain tip into the side of each beignet and pipe the peanut filling in, making sure not to overstuff the beignets. Serve the warm filled beignets with the Concord grape sauce on the side.

**NOTE:** The Concord grape is the grape of our childhood memories, quintessential and singular. Its ripening season in the Midwest is extremely short, usually a two-week window in the early fall. We get ours from Linda Hezel, who grows them at Prairie Birthday Farm in Kearney, Missouri. Her Concord grape vines are from cuttings taken from her uncle's farm near St. Louis.

**Here is Linda's recipe for Concord grape puree, which we use in our Peanut Cream Fritters recipe:**

Gently wash 8 cups of ripe Concord grapes (they should be dark purple and give off a heady grape scent). Put the wet grapes into a stockpot and set it over low heat. Gently mash the grapes, stirring, and cook the grapes for 8 to 10 minutes, until they start to break down into pulp. Do not boil the mixture. Press the pulp through a food mill or a fine-mesh sieve, extracting as much juice as possible. Discard the skins and seeds. If you are not using the puree immediately, you can freeze it for up to 1 month. Thaw and gently reheat the puree on the stove over low heat before using.

# cranberry floats

**Serves 4 to 6**

1 vanilla bean, halved lengthwise

2 cups sugar

4 cups water

2 cups cranberries

Juice and peel (pith removed) of 1 orange

1 teaspoon vanilla extract

2 cinnamon sticks

4 star anise

2 teaspoons freshly squeezed lemon juice

Champagne or dry sparkling wine, for serving

I love the color of cranberries. They provide a cheery blush to the otherwise rusty fall landscape. In this recipe, I round out the tartness of cranberries with orange and spices (and sugar). With a splash of sparkling wine, it becomes a lively, crisp end to an autumn meal. You can also serve the sorbet by itself.

Using the tip of a small knife, scrape the vanilla seeds out of the pod halves into a medium saucepan. Add the vanilla bean pod halves, sugar, 2 cups of the water, the cranberries, orange peel and juice, vanilla, cinnamon sticks, and star anise and bring the mixture to a boil over high heat. When the cranberries begin to pop, lower the heat to medium-high and continue to cook for another 5 minutes. Remove from the heat and let the mixture cool slightly. Remove and discard the vanilla pod halves, orange peel, cinnamon sticks, and star anise.

Pour the remaining contents into a blender. Holding the lid firmly with one hand wrapped in a kitchen towel, blend the mixture on high speed until liquefied. Strain the sorbet base through a fine-mesh sieve. Stir in the remaining 2 cups of water and the lemon juice. Cool to room temperature. Churn the chilled base in an ice cream maker according to the manufacturer's instructions. (This may require chilling the base before churning.) Freeze the sorbet for at least 2 hours before serving.

Using a small melon baller or a ½-teaspoon measuring spoon, scoop 3 balls of sorbet into a tall shot glass. Top the glass with Champagne and serve immediately with small straws or demitasse spoons.

# sarsaparilla marshmallows

**Makes one 13 by 9-inch pan**

½ cup plus 2 tablespoons cornstarch, for dusting

½ cup plus 2 tablespoons cold water

3½ teaspoons powdered gelatin

1½ cups plus 1 tablespoon sugar

¾ cup light corn syrup

¾ cup honey

½ teaspoon vanilla extract

2 teaspoons sarsaparilla powder

It seems almost wrong to demystify the magic of marshmallows by making them at home. But once you see how easy they are to make, the possibilities are endless. In this recipe, I use sarsaparilla, the ingredient that I describe as the "adult side of root beer," to evoke that fizzy, frothy childhood drink in marshmallow form. The spiciness of it goes well with many of the fall flavors you'll find on your table.

Both a rubber spatula and an offset spatula (most commonly used for frosting cakes) will be your best friends in this recipe. Spray them religiously with nonstick cooking spray as you use them to transfer the fluffy mixture to the pan to prevent sticking.

---

Line a 13 by 9-inch shallow baking pan with a nonstick baking mat. Spray the mat with nonstick cooking spray and dust with 1 tablespoon of the cornstarch. Use your hands to spread the cornstarch evenly over the surface of the mat. If you do not have a nonstick mat, spray and dust the pan with cornstarch. Set aside.

Put the cold water in a medium-size heatproof bowl. Sprinkle the powdered gelatin over the water and let it sit for 5 minutes to bloom.

In a medium-size saucepan, heat the sugar, corn syrup, and honey over high heat and cook until the sugar registers 252°F on a candy thermometer. Remove the syrup from the heat and allow the mixture to cool to 210°F.

While the syrup is cooling, gently heat the bloomed gelatin by setting the bowl over a double boiler. Once the gelatin has turned fluid, stir it into the cooked syrup.

Pour the mixture into the bowl of a stand mixer fitted with a whip attachment. Begin whipping the sugar syrup on medium-low speed (be careful; if you begin whipping too quickly, the hot sugar syrup will splatter out of the bowl). Once the syrup begins to foam, slowly increase the speed to high. Continue to whip on high speed for 8 to 10 minutes. The fluffy marshmallow should form and take on a glossy sheen. You will know that that mixture is nearly finished when the sound of the whipping drops an octave. Add the vanilla and sarsaparilla and continue to whip for another 1 to 2 minutes. You can't overwhip the marshmallow mixture. The danger, however, is that if you let the mixture cool too much, it will become stiff and impossible to work with.

Spray both sides of a rubber spatula with nonstick cooking spray. Working quickly, scrape the mixture out of the bowl into the prepared pan. You may need to spray the spatula between scrapes if the mixture begins to stick. Spray both sides of an offset spatula. With a pushing motion, use the offset spatula to spread the mixture out evenly in the pan. Do your best to get a smooth, even surface. Again, you will need to spray the offset spatula often to prevent the mixture from sticking.

Dust the marshmallow evenly with 1 tablespoon of the cornstarch; use more if needed. Gently run your hand over the surface to make sure that all of it is well coated. Wrap the sheet pan with two layers of plastic wrap. Set aside to cool at room temperature for at least 4 hours, or overnight if possible.

Put the remaining ½ cup of cornstarch in a bowl. Turn the "sheet" of marshmallows out onto a work surface lightly dusted with cornstarch. Spray both sides of a sharp knife with nonstick cooking spray and cut the marshmallows into cubes (you will have to spray the knife repeatedly to cut the entire sheet). Dust the marshmallows lightly with cornstarch to coat and store them in an airtight container wrapped in multiple layers of plastic wrap. Stored this way, the marshmallows should keep for up to 1 week.

## variations

This recipe makes a fantastic honey marshmallow if you omit the sarsaparilla. You may also use the base recipe and add other spices and flavorings in place of the sarsaparilla. Here are just a couple of ideas:

*vanilla marshmallows:*
Scrape the seeds from 2 vanilla beans and add them to the mixture along with the vanilla extract.

*cinnamon marshmallows:*
Add 2 teaspoons ground cinnamon to the mixture along with the vanilla extract.

# spicy **fig** cake

**Makes one 9-inch loaf**

10 ounces dried figs

1 cup ginger liqueur or brandy

½ cup (1 stick) unsalted butter, softened

¼ cup packed light brown sugar

¼ cup granulated sugar

4 large eggs

1 vanilla bean

¼ cup sour cream

3 tablespoons orange marmalade or
    apricot jam

2 tablespoons honey

1 teaspoon vanilla extract

Finely grated zest of 1 orange

2 teaspoons peeled and grated fresh
    ginger

1 teaspoon ground ginger

½ teaspoon ground allspice

¼ teaspoon ground cloves

1⅛ cups cake flour

½ teaspoon salt

Confectioners' sugar, for dusting

**I'm convinced** that people who bristle at fruitcake have never had a good one. This recipe will change their minds. Moist and soft, this is the antithesis of those dense bricks that modern mythology has us passing annually from family to family like a hot potato. I particularly love the meaty pieces of dried figs, the seeds of which give this cake a bit of crunch.

Soak the dried figs in the ginger liqueur overnight, covered.

Preheat the oven to 350°F. Butter the loaf pan.

Drain the figs, reserving the liqueur, and dice the figs.

In the bowl of a stand mixer fitted with a paddle attachment, cream the butter and the sugars together on medium-high speed until fluffy, about 3 minutes. Scrape down the bowl with a spatula. With the mixer on medium speed, add the eggs one at a time until incorporated. Scrape down the bowl once more.

Slice the vanilla bean in half lengthwise. Using a small knife, scrape the seeds from the vanilla bean into the batter. Add the sour cream, marmalade, honey, vanilla, zest, fresh and ground ginger, allspice, and cloves and mix well. Scrape down the bowl.

With the mixer on low speed, mix in the cake flour and salt until just incorporated. Scrape down the bowl and fold in the drained figs.

Pour the batter into the prepared loaf pan. Rap the pan firmly against the counter to remove any air bubbles. Bake the loaf for 40 to 45 minutes, until the surface

**Left to right: sarsaparilla marshmallows, spicy fig cake, cranberry floats**

cracks and a toothpick inserted into the center comes out clean.

Using the tines of a fork, prick the top of the cake all over. Pour the reserved liqueur from the dried figs over the top, letting it seep into the cake.

Allow the cake to cool completely. Flip the pan over to release the cake. Trim the cake with a serrated knife, removing the domed top and shaving the sides and bottom to create a block with squared edges. Slice the block into ½-inch-thick slices and cut each slice into thirds for petit-four–size pieces. Dust them with confectioners' sugar and serve.

This cake can also be served simply cut into slices. It needs nothing more than a dollop of fresh whipped cream and a cup of tea.

Wrapped tightly in plastic wrap, this cake will keep for up to 3 days. Wrapped in multiple layers of plastic wrap and stored in the freezer, it will keep for up to 3 months.

900

b

bluestem

reservations 816-561-1101

winter

# Winters in the Midwest can be brutal.

Temperatures plummet, and the occasional glaze of freezing rain can bring life quickly to a halt. It's the perfect time to stay home and cook.

Thankfully, the holidays buoy restaurants through the cold months. The weeks leading up to New Year's are often the busiest for us at Bluestem, sometimes insanely so. Christmas is a blur of lights, food, and cheer, as family and friends gather around our tables to reflect on another year mysteriously fading, seemingly before it has begun. Ringing in the New Year is always a popular occasion, followed by a much-needed lull in January, before we look toward Valentine's Day and the start of another season.

In the kitchen, winter is a time for creativity and comfort, as the chef's palette becomes dauntingly stark. In especially harsh winters, you won't find anything living springing from the ground. Traditionally, root vegetables and fall fruits that have been cellared in the autumn are the only produce available.

Although we try to keep the menu at Bluestem seasonally relevant, we also try to maintain a balance in flavor. Even in the coldest weeks of the year, you will find light and bright dishes like the nairagi (page 200) and the sole with five lilies (page 219)—both of which could be equally appropriate served in summer—alongside heartier dishes like a duo of ravioli with warm *brodo* (page 210) and braised lamb shanks (page 226).

In the pastry kitchen, Megan revels in the dry winter air, which keeps meringues stiff, caramel-glazed popcorn crunchy, and sugar glass brittle. Gingerbread, hot chocolate, and butterscotch appear at the end of meals, conjuring memories of childhood expeditions with mittens and sleds. Citrus also becomes abundant, bringing a splash of sunshine from abroad.

# winter

# menu

# wine

Once in a decade, Kansas City wins a shockingly mild winter (golf in January—yes, it happens!). But brutal and bone chilling is par for the course. Most years, the sun evacuates the city for months, making it the perfect season to break into your cellar and open those wines you've been waiting to drink.

If you've got an Amarone sitting around, now is the time to pull it out. Its rich, chewy body will stand up nicely to the braised short ribs on page 228, its high alcohol content an antidote to the fattiness of the meat and the creaminess of the grits.

For the braised lamb shanks on page 226, you'll also want something full-bodied, though you'll also want a bit of earthiness to match the bitter mustard greens served on the side. A Côtes du Rhône would be an excellent choice. It's an incredibly approachable wine—low in acidity with a moderate level of tannins. Côtes du Rhône wines also have a brightness that will pick up the glint from the preserved lemons in the stew.

White-fleshed fish, such as sole (page 219) and cod (page 220), will love the buttery popcorn flavors of a white Burgundy, like a Chassagne-Montrachet or Puligny-Montrachet.

# notes

The crab pasta (page 214) is one of the most popular dishes in the restaurant; it's been known to convert vegetarians. It's the perfect combination of sweet (crab), salt (panko, prosciutto), creamy (garlic cream sauce), and spicy (red pepper flakes). The spice is the last thing that lingers in your mouth, so I love to pair this dish with a good off-dry Riesling, with just slight amounts of sweetness to reset your palate between bites.

I haven't met many blue cheeses that don't get along with an elegant tawny port, and the Great Hill Blue (page 230) is no exception. The tart, creamy flavor of the blue cheese and the sweet, subtle viscosity of tawny port is always a good pairing.

With Megan's gingerbread ice cream sandwich (page 241), I recommend a cocktail. Have you ever had Bärenjäger? It's a stiff honey liqueur. You can serve it straight, or thinned with some water. But I like it in milk. If you are able to get Shatto Milk Company products (see page 232), try spiking a glass of their root beer or banana milk with Bärenjäger—it's dessert in itself.

# celery root soup

**Serves 8 to 10 as an amuse-bouche,**
**4 to 6 as a first course**

2 tablespoons unsalted butter

4 cups peeled and diced celery root

1 small onion, diced

6 cloves garlic, chopped

1¼ cups dry white wine

1 bay leaf

1 cup heavy cream

½ cup whole milk

2½ cups Vegetable Stock (page 255)

Salt and freshly ground white pepper

We serve this comforting soup at the restaurant on occasion as an amuse-bouche. If you find the soup a bit thick for your taste, you can always thin it out with some extra vegetable stock.

Heat the butter in a large saucepan over medium-high heat. Add the celery root, onion, and garlic and stir to sweat, about 5 minutes; you don't want the vegetables to develop any color. Add the wine and bay leaf and bring the mixture to a simmer. Reduce the mixture until the liquid has almost evaporated, about 10 minutes. Discard the bay leaf and add the cream, milk, and 2 cups of the stock. Return the soup to a simmer and let it reduce and thicken, about 8 minutes.

Carefully transfer the soup to a blender. With one towel-wrapped hand firmly held over the lid, blend the soup until it has completely liquefied. If the soup is too thick, thin it out, 1 tablespoon at a time, with the remaining ½ cup stock. Season with salt and pepper to taste. Strain the soup through a fine-mesh sieve.

Pour the soup into small cups and serve warm.

# cauliflower fritters, sauce gribiche

**Serves 6**

**sauce gribiche**

½ cup Aïoli (page 252)

½ teaspoon Dijon mustard

1 teaspoon Champagne vinegar

1 hard-boiled egg, chopped

1½ teaspoons chopped cornichons

1 teaspoon chopped capers

½ teaspoon chopped fresh chervil

½ teaspoon chopped fresh tarragon

½ teaspoon chopped fresh flat-leaf parsley

Salt and freshly ground white pepper

**cauliflower fritters**

Vegetable oil, for deep frying

¾ cup all-purpose flour

½ cup plus ½ teaspoon cornstarch

1 large egg

½ cup ice cubes

½ cup plus 2 tablespoons Champagne

6 large cauliflower florets

Salt and freshly ground white pepper

This is a simple but delicious way to use up stray pieces of cauliflower. Although this recipe calls for six cauliflower florets, the amount of batter in this recipe will be enough for double the amount of cauliflower. If you don't have Champagne, any sparkling wine will do.

---

**Make the sauce gribiche:** Combine the aïoli, mustard, vinegar, egg, cornichons, and capers in a small bowl. Stir in the chervil, tarragon, and parsley and season with salt and pepper to taste. Cover the sauce gribiche and let it chill in the refrigerator for at least 4 hours, or overnight if possible.

**Make the fritters:** Heat 2 inches of vegetable oil in a countertop fryer or deep skillet to 350°F. Line a plate with paper towels.

Combine the flour, cornstarch, egg, ice cubes, and Champagne in a large bowl. Mix until there are no more lumps of flour.

Dip the cauliflower florets in the batter to coat. Drop the battered florets into the hot oil and fry until the batter becomes puffy and golden brown, 2 to 3 minutes. Drain the cauliflower fritters on the prepared plate. Season with salt and pepper and serve immediately with the sauce gribiche.

# **prosciutto**, hot and sweet cipollini

**Serves 4**

1 tablespoon olive oil

1 small fennel bulb, trimmed and sliced
    into ¼-inch-thick slices

8 cipollini onions, peeled

2 cloves garlic, smashed and chopped

1 cup white wine

Juice of 2 oranges

2 tablespoons sherry vinegar

2 tablespoons sugar

12 drops mustard essence

Salt and freshly ground black pepper

2 tablespoons extra-virgin olive oil

4 thick slices rustic bread

4 ounces sliced prosciutto

This is a fork-and-knife crostini dish that could double as a simple lunch for two. If you can't find mustard essence (also called mustard oil), you can substitute ¼ teaspoon of dried red pepper flakes, adding them to the fennel and onions as they cook to give the mixture a spicy kick.

Heat the olive oil in a large sauté pan over medium-high heat. Add the fennel and onions and sauté until browned, stirring to get an even coloring, about 5 minutes. Add the garlic, wine, juice, vinegar, and sugar. Simmer and reduce for 5 minutes, just to soften the onions. Take the pan off the heat and stir in the mustard essence. Season with salt and pepper to taste. Set aside.

Brush the extra-virgin olive oil over both sides of each slice of bread. Toast the bread in a skillet over medium-high heat until just golden brown. Season with a bit of salt.

To serve, put a slice of toasted bread on each of 4 plates. Top each slice with some prosciutto and the fennel and cipollini mixture. Serve immediately.

# nairagi, blood orange, ginger

**Serves 4**

**ginger vinaigrette**

1 teaspoon peeled and grated fresh ginger

Juice of 1 orange

6 tablespoons ponzu

½ teaspoon sugar

½ teaspoon kosher salt

Freshly ground white pepper

½ cup extra-virgin olive oil

**salad**

2 heads baby bok choy

1 small red onion

1 small English cucumber

6 ounces sushi-grade nairagi, cut into ½-ounce slices

2 blood oranges, cut into supremes (see Note, page 155)

Pickled Blood Orange Zest (recipe follows)

Seasoning Mix (recipe follows)

Bright blood orange meets warm ginger vinaigrette and floral pink peppercorns in this play on fire and ice. If you can't find nairagi, a peach-colored fish, you can substitute sushi-grade tuna, hamachi (yellowtail), or salmon.

---

**Make the vinaigrette:** Combine all of the ingredients for the vinaigrette in a nonreactive bowl. Whisk to combine. Reserve the vinaigrette.

**Make the salad:** Julienne the bok choy, onion, and cucumber using a sharp knife or mandoline. Set aside in a medium bowl.

**To serve:** Divide the fish slices among 4 plates. Dress the fish on each plate with 1 tablespoon of the reserved vinaigrette. Toss the reserved salad together with the remaining vinaigrette. Divide the salad on top of the dressed fish followed by the orange supremes and pickled zest. Finish by garnishing each plate with a sprinkle of the seasoning mix to taste. Serve immediately.

**NOTE:** Pressing gently on the fruit, roll your citrus fruits before juicing; it makes it easier to squeeze and yields a higher volume of juice.

## pickled blood orange zest

¾ cup water

¾ cup seasoned rice vinegar

½ cup honey

½ tablespoon kosher salt

¼ teaspoon dried red pepper flakes

1 teaspoon coriander seeds, toasted

Zest of 2 blood oranges, thinly sliced

Heat the water, vinegar, honey, salt, red pepper flakes, and coriander seeds in a small saucepan over medium heat until thoroughly blended.

Simmer for 2 minutes, remove from the heat, and pour into a medium bowl over the blood orange zest. Let it cool, then cover and refrigerate until ready to use.


## seasoning mix  Makes approximately ⅛ cup

2 tablespoons pink peppercorns, crushed

½ teaspoon fleur de sel

1 tablespoon fresh cilantro leaves, chopped

½ teaspoon fresh tarragon leaves, chopped

1 teaspoon extra-virgin olive oil

Mix all of the ingredients together in a small bowl.

# chawanmushi, hon shimeji, scallion, **dashi**

**Serves 4**

**dashi**

2 ounces kombu

8 cups water

35 grams bonito flakes (usually sold in 5-gram packs)

*chawanmushi* **broth**

2½ cups Dashi

2 tablespoons soy sauce

2 tablespoons rice vinegar

1 tablespoon plus 1 teaspoon mirin

**mushrooms**

1 tablespoon dark sesame oil

4 ounces hon shimeji mushrooms

2 tablespoons water

1 tablespoon mirin

*chawanmushi* **base**

2½ cups Dashi

1 tablespoon soy sauce

1 tablespoon mirin

½ teaspoon unseasoned rice vinegar

3 large eggs

Thinly sliced scallions, for garnish

My chef de cuisine, Bill Espiricueta, is perhaps more Asian than he is Mexican. This recipe for *chawanmushi*—an impossibly delicate Japanese egg custard—is his. Make sure to serve it warm.

**Make the dashi:** Rinse the kombu under cold water. In a medium saucepan, bring the kombu and water to a boil over high heat. Turn off the heat. Remove the kombu and add the bonito flakes. Set aside to steep. The bonito will become pulpy and slowly sink. When all of the bonito has settled below the water line, strain the dashi broth through a fine-mesh sieve, discarding the bonito.

**Make the *chawanmushi* broth:** Combine the dashi with the soy sauce, vinegar, and mirin in a medium saucepan.

Bring it to a low simmer over medium heat. Turn off the heat and keep the broth warm.

**Sauté the mushrooms:** Heat the sesame oil in a small sauté pan over medium heat. Add the mushrooms, water, and mirin and sauté lightly for about 30 seconds to slightly soften the mushrooms. Remove the mushrooms from the pan.

**Make the *chawanmushi* base:** Preheat the oven to 275°F. In a blender, mix the dashi, soy sauce, mirin, vinegar, and eggs on low speed. Strain the base through a fine-mesh sieve. Divide the *chawanmushi* base evenly among 4 small bowls. Cover the bowls tightly with plastic wrap. Place the bowls in a casserole dish with 1 inch of water. Put the casserole dish with the bowls of *chawanmushi* in the oven and bake the bowls for about 40 minutes, until the *chawanmushi* is just set but still a little jiggly in the middle. Let the bowls cool slightly and carefully unwrap them, being careful of the escaping steam.

**To serve:** Pour ⅛ cup of the chawanmushi broth over each custard. Top with some sautéed mushrooms and sliced scallions as a garnish. Serve immediately.

# "green **eggs** and ham"

**Serves 4**

### green sauce

2 tablespoons vegetable oil

1 medium yellow onion, diced

4 cloves garlic, smashed and chopped

1 cup dry vermouth

4 cups tightly packed fresh baby spinach

1 cup fresh flat-leaf parsley leaves

Salt and freshly ground white pepper

6 Potatoes Confit, halved lengthwise (page 260)

4 large scallions, green parts removed and halved

1 tablespoon extra-virgin olive oil

Salt and freshly ground white pepper

6 large eggs

1 cup whole milk

2 cups all-purpose flour

2 cups Herb Crumbs (page 262)

Peanut oil, for deep frying

Salt and freshly ground white pepper

2 ounces prosciutto, thinly sliced

This is my ode to Dr. Seuss, who has brought much joy to my daughter, Madi. Poaching, breading, and frying the egg takes a bit of finesse, as the barely cooked eggs are very delicate. But with a little patience, you'll have a magical little package—a golden, crispy outside and a creamy, runny yolk inside—that will be as wonderful as Seuss's creatures.

**Make the sauce:** Heat the oil in a large saucepan over medium-high heat. Add the onion and garlic and cook until the onion begins to turn translucent, about 2 minutes. Deglaze the pan with the vermouth, scraping up any browned bits, and reduce by half, about 4 minutes. Add the spinach and parsley and stir just to wilt the greens. You don't want the greens to cook, or they will brown. Remove from the heat.

Transfer the contents of the saucepan to a blender, season with salt and pepper, and puree until smooth. Strain the sauce through a fine-mesh sieve. Set aside.

**Cook the vegetables:** Preheat a grill to 400°F. Toss the potatoes and scallions with the oil and season with salt and pepper. Grill the potatoes and scallions for about 2 minutes, or until heated through.

**Poach and fry the eggs:** Set a small wire rack in the bottom of a large stockpot or crumple aluminum foil in the bottom to make a nest. Fill the pot with water and heat it to between 144°F and 146°F. (Use an instant-read thermometer to test the water temperature.) Nest 4 of the eggs on the rack and cook for at least 40 minutes, but for no more than 50 minutes.

While the eggs are poaching, prepare on ice bath (see the User Manual, page xxv). When the eggs are done poaching, plunge them in the ice bath to cool.

Lightly beat the remaining 2 eggs and the milk together in a small bowl. Put the flour and herb crumbs in two separate, shallow dishes.

Gently crack the poached eggs and peel away the shell. Work carefully as the eggs will be very soft.

Carefully roll the poached eggs around in the flour to coat lightly, then in the eggs, and finally in the herb crumbs to make a crust.

Heat 2 inches of peanut oil in a medium skillet to 350°F. Carefully fry the eggs one at a time for about 1 minute, or until they are golden brown, rolling them around in the oil for an even crust. Season with salt and pepper.

**To serve:** Smear a generous spoonful of the green sauce across 4 plates. Top each plate with an egg, some prosciutto, and grilled vegetables. Serve immediately.

# roasted **radicchio**, crispy sweetbreads, sherry vinegar

**Serves 4**

4 tablespoons extra-virgin olive oil, plus more for drizzling

1 large head radicchio, quartered

Salt and freshly ground black pepper

Fried sweetbreads (page 162)

2 tablespoons sherry vinegar

Finely shaved Parmesan cheese, for serving

Bitter is a flavor that's rarely explored. In this recipe, it is the focus, showcased with wedges of charred radicchio that are spiked with a dash of sherry vinegar. Together, the bitterness and tartness of the radicchio and vinegar counterbalance the creamy richness of the crispy sweetbreads.

Gently rub 3 tablespoons of the olive oil over the quartered radicchio. Heat the remaining 1 tablespoon of olive oil in a large sauté pan over medium-high heat. Sear the cut sides of the radicchio wedges until slightly charred, about 2 minutes per side. Season with salt and pepper to taste.

To serve, divide the sweetbreads and charred radicchio among 4 plates. Drizzle a little olive oil and sherry vinegar over the radicchio followed by shaved parmesan. Serve immediately.

# chicken **livers,** corn bread sauce

**Serves 4**

### vegetables

1 medium carrot, peeled and shaved into ribbons with a Y-peeler

1 small daikon radish, peeled and shaved into ribbons with a Y-peeler

2 tablespoons Sherry Vinaigrette (page 254)

### corn bread sauce

1 tablespoon vegetable oil

2 shallots, chopped

3 cloves garlic, chopped

¾ cup whiskey

1 batch Corn Bread, crumbled (recipe follows)

3⅓ cups Chicken Stock (page 256)

2 tablespoons Dijon mustard

1 tablespoon sherry vinegar

½ teaspoon salt

### chicken livers

Vegetable oil, for deep frying

4 cups all-purpose flour

2 tablespoons onion powder

1½ tablespoons garlic powder

1 tablespoon salt

2 large eggs

1½ cups whole milk

1 pound chicken livers

This recipe recognizes that there's a touch of the South in the Midwest. It's also a reminder that there's nothing about a chicken you can't fry.

You'll find these fried chicken livers on our Sunday brunch menu, served over cheesy grits. It's a hearty plate. For a more refined version, suitable as a first course at dinner, I've replaced the grits with my version of a corn bread sauce, inspired by one that Sean Brock, the executive chef of McCrady's and Husk in Charleston, made at a cooking event that we both attended. Brock's is a purist version, with nothing more than cornmeal, buttermilk, eggs, and bacon. As you can see, mine is more Midwestern.

**Dress the vegetables:** Toss the carrot and radish with the vinaigrette. Set aside.

**Make the corn bread sauce:** Heat the oil in a medium skillet over medium heat. Add the shallots and garlic and sweat for 1 minute. Deglaze the pan with the whiskey, scraping up any browned bits, and simmer for a couple of minutes, just to soften the onions. Transfer the mixture to a blender and add the corn bread, stock, mustard, vinegar, and salt. Blend on high speed until smooth.

**Fry the livers:** Heat 2 inches of vegetable oil in a deep skillet over high heat until the oil reaches 350°F.

Combine the flour, onion powder, garlic powder, and salt in a shallow bowl. In a separate, shallow bowl, beat together the eggs and milk.

Pat the livers dry with a paper towel. Toss the livers in the egg and milk mixture to coat. Transfer the livers to the flour mixture and toss to coat. Drop the livers into the hot oil, in batches if necessary, and fry until the outside is golden brown and the inside is creamy and hot, about 3 minutes.

**To serve:** Divide the chicken livers among 4 plates. Top with some of the vegetables and serve with a side of the corn bread sauce.

## corn bread  Makes one 9-inch square cake

½ cup unsalted butter (1 stick) melted,
   plus more for greasing the pan

1 cup yellow cornmeal

1 cup all-purpose flour

¼ teaspoon salt

1 tablespoon baking powder

1 cup buttermilk

1 egg, slightly beaten

Preheat the oven to 425°F.

Grease a 9-inch square baking pan generously with butter.

Combine the cornmeal, flour, salt, and baking powder in a large bowl. Stir in the buttermilk, egg, and melted butter just until a thick batter forms. Transfer the batter to the greased baking pan and bake for 25 minutes, or until a toothpick inserted into the middle comes out clean.

# roasted **escargots**, butter, oregano, parsley

**Serves 4**

¼ cup dry white wine, such as a Pinot Gris

5 cloves garlic, finely minced

2 shallots, minced

1 cup (2 sticks) unsalted butter, slightly chilled and cut into 1-tablespoon pieces

4 teaspoons chopped fresh oregano

4 teaspoons chopped fresh flat-leaf parsley

4 teaspoons finely chopped fresh chives

Salt and freshly ground white pepper

1 pound snails (see Sources, page 272)

Juice of 2 lemons

Toasted bread, for serving

Snails go well with copious amounts of butter and garlic, and I won't be the one to change that formula. At Bluestem, we serve the tender morsels of meat in a little cocotte under an avalanche of frothy butter that has been whipped with lots of garlic and a splash of white wine. Diners love diving into the cloud with their forks to fish out the snails one at a time.

---

In a medium saucepan over medium-high heat, bring the wine, garlic, and shallots to a simmer. Whisk in the butter, 1 tablespoon at a time, until thick. Stir in the oregano, parsley, and chives and season with salt and pepper to taste.

Preheat the oven to 325°F. Line four 8-ounce ramekins with a single layer of snails. Pour enough whipped butter over each to cover the snails (about ¼ cup per ramekin).

Set the ramekins on a baking sheet and bake in the oven for 8 to 10 minutes, until the snails are warmed through and the butter is bubbling. Squeeze the juice of ½ lemon into each ramekin. Serve hot with toast.

# **ravioli** duo, campo lindo egg, braised hen, parmesan brodo, oregano, pancetta, watercress

**Serves 4**

*brodo*

4 cups Chicken Stock (page 256)

1 head garlic, oven roasted (see box on
  page 141)

4 ounces Parmesan cheese rind

1 ounce prosciutto

**chicken marinade**

2 cloves garlic, peeled

⅛ cup fresh flat-leaf parsley leaves

⅛ cup fresh lemon thyme leaves

2 shallots

¾ cup extra-virgin olive oil

2 tablespoons sherry vinegar

½ teaspoon salt

Freshly cracked black pepper

2 chicken thighs, boned and skinless

2 tablespoons canola oil

1 cup white wine

1 cup Chicken Stock (page 256)

**pasta dough**

2½ cups "00" flour (see headnote on
  page 23)

4 egg yolks

2 large eggs

1½ teaspoons extra-virgin olive oil

½ teaspoon of salt and freshly ground
  black pepper

2 large eggs (to seal the ravioli)

4 egg yolks, cold

**salad**

4 sprigs fresh oregano

4 sprigs fresh flat-leaf parsley

4 sprigs fresh watercress

¼ cup shaved or thinly sliced shallots

6 paper-thin slices coppa (Italian
  dry-cured ham)

2 tablespoons olive oil

2 tablespoons freshly squeezed lemon
  juice

Pinch of salt and freshly ground black
  pepper

Freshly grated Parmesan cheese,
  for garnish

**I don't know** which came first, but the chicken and the egg make a fantastic pair. At Bluestem, we serve them together in a duo of ravioli bathed in a warm chicken broth, or *brodo*, enriched with Parmesan. The *brodo* is a fantastic way of using up old Parmesan rinds that are otherwise too hard to eat.

---

**Make the *brodo*:** Put all of the ingredients in a small saucepan over medium heat, bring simmer, and let it simmer for 30 minutes. Set aside until ready to use, keeping it warm.

**Make the marinade:** Coarsely chop the garlic, parsley, thyme, and shallots in a food processor. Add the oil, vinegar, salt, and pepper to taste through the top feeder and continue to process the ingredients until a thick sauce forms.

**Marinate and cook the chicken:** Pour the marinade over the chicken thighs in a shallow baking dish and toss to coat. Let the chicken marinate, covered in the refrigerator, overnight, or for at least 6 hours.

Preheat the oven to 300°F. Heat the oil in a skillet over medium heat. Wipe the marinade off the chicken and add it to the hot pan. Be careful not to burn any garlic left on the chicken. Let the chicken cook for 1 minute. Deglaze the pan with the white wine, scraping up any browned bits, and add the stock. Cover the skillet and remove from the heat. Put the skillet in the oven and let the chicken braise in the skillet for 40 minutes.

Let the chicken cool. Shred the chicken into small pieces with your hands. Season with salt and pepper to taste. Moisten the meat with ¼ cup of the *brodo*.

**Make the pasta dough:** Put the flour in a large bowl. Form a well in the flour and crack the egg yolks and whole eggs into the well. Add the olive oil, and salt and pepper. Using your hands, bring the mixture together to form a dough. Knead the dough for 5 minutes. Wrap the dough tightly in plastic wrap and let it rest in the refrigerator for 1 hour.

**Make the ravioli:** Using a pasta machine, roll the pasta dough down to the fifth setting, or the next to the last stop on your pasta machine. You should have a long sheet of pasta.

Beat together the 2 eggs to make an egg wash.

Using a pastry brush, brush half the length of the sheet of pasta with the egg wash. Carefully put the four egg yolks on the brushed pasta, leaving 2 inches between yolks. Then put 8 generous tablespoons of chicken meat in 8 different mounds on the brushed pasta, leaving 2 inches between mounds.

Carefully pull the other half of the sheet of pasta over the half with the fillings. Gently press the pasta down around the fillings to seal the ravioli, trying to press out any air pockets that form.

Using a knife, cut out individual ravioli, leaving at least a 1/8-inch-wide pasta "skirt" around the filling. Alternatively, you can use a ring mold that is slightly larger than the diameter of the filling to stamp out the individual ravioli.

**Make the salad:** Toss all of the ingredients together in a large bowl.

**Cook the ravioli:** Bring a large saucepan filled with generously salted water to a rolling boil. Cooking the chicken ravioli first, and the egg yolk ravioli second together in one batch, carefully slip the ravioli into the water, making sure they don't stick to each other. Cook the ravioli for exactly 2 minutes and not a second more. Working quickly, remove the ravioli and divide them evenly among 4 bowls—1 egg yolk ravioli and 2 chicken ravioli per person. Top with salad and pour 1 cup of hot *brodo* around the ravioli in each bowl. Garnish with Parmesan and serve immediately.

# campo lindo farms

Head 40 minutes outside of Kansas City in any direction and you'll find yourself in a patchwork of farmland. About an hour north of the city is Jay and Carol Maddick's Campo Lindo Farms, a small square of land on which they raise chickens in a sustainable and natural way. Here the chicks that arrive at the Maddicks' farm are given space to roam and forage, to grow and develop the way delicious chickens should. It's the closest thing to a chicken spa.

The quality of care and benefits of natural animal husbandry are evident in the finished product. The poultry we get from Campo Lindo Farms is nonpareil.

The meat and bones are full of flavor, a reminder of what chicken is really supposed to taste like. People who normally won't order chicken in fine-dining restaurants will order it at Bluestem.

The eggs from the Maddicks' chickens are equally wonderful, bearing creamy yolks the color of traffic cones. We use them raw in our beef tartare (page 16) and cook them slightly for a warm, runny filling for ravioli that are made with pasta using the eggs (page 210). Megan loves using Campo Lindo Farms eggs in her pastries. They give everything a more golden hue, from cakes to custards, from ice cream to panna cotta.

# crab, **trofie**, garlic, prosciutto, chile

**Serves 4**

1 tablespoon vegetable oil

2 large shallots, diced

½ fennel bulb, trimmed and diced

4 cloves garlic, chopped

2 tablespoons Pernod (optional)

1 cup white wine

1 sprig fresh tarragon

2 cups heavy cream

½ cup whole milk

14 ounces trofie

6 ounces fresh crabmeat, picked over for shells and cartilage

¼ cup finely diced prosciutto

1 teaspoon dried red pepper flakes

½ cup freshly grated Parmesan cheese, plus more for garnish

Salt and freshly ground white pepper

¼ cup Herb Crumbs (page 262)

I whipped up this simple, creamy pasta dish on a whim on a busy winter night at the restaurant a few years ago. Since, it has become one of the restaurant's most popular dishes. Even when it's not on the menu, people ask for it. This dish combines the sweetness of crabmeat with the savory flavors of garlic and Parmesan. A pinch of red pepper flakes gives it just a little heat. Trofie pasta is somewhat similar to fusilli in shape, but it is more tightly rolled into a squiggle.

Heat the oil in a medium saucepan over medium-high heat. Add the shallots, fennel, and garlic and cook until the shallots begin to soften, about 2 minutes. Add the Pernod, wine, and tarragon. Continue cooking until the liquid has reduced by half, about 5 minutes. Add the cream and milk and turn the heat down to medium-low. Continue to cook until the cream sauce is reduced by half, 10 to 12 minutes. Strain the cream sauce through a fine-mesh sieve and discard the aromatics. Return the cream sauce to the stove in a small saucepan and bring it back to a simmer over medium heat. Reduce the sauce to 1½ cups, about 15 minutes.

Meanwhile, bring a large stockpot of heavily salted water to a boil over high heat. Add the pasta and cook until just tender. Drain the pasta well.

Add the pasta, crab, prosciutto, red pepper flakes, and Parmesan to the cream sauce, stirring until the cheese has melted evenly. Season the sauce with salt and pepper to taste. Divide the pasta among 4 bowls. Top each portion with 1 tablespoon of herb crumbs and more grated Parmesan.

# **bouillabaisse**, mussels, clams, shrimp, calamari, edamame

**Serves 4**

2 tablespoons freshly squeezed orange juice

2 large pinches of saffron

2 tablespoons olive oil

1 large knob fresh ginger, peeled and cut into large pieces

1 large stalk lemongrass, cut into 2-inch-long pieces and smashed

2 cloves garlic, smashed and chopped

1 large onion, sliced

1 small fennel bulb, trimmed and thinly sliced

2 cups sake

4 cups Fish Stock (page 255) or clam juice

½ (13-ounce) can coconut milk

¼ cup soy sauce

1 (24-ounce) can whole peeled tomatoes, in juice (San Marzano if you can't get good organic canned tomatoes)

3 strips orange zest

1 teaspoon five-spice powder

8 ounces medium-size shrimp, peeled and deveined

4 ounces cleaned whole squid

12 littleneck clams

12 mussels, debearded and scrubbed

⅓ cup edamame beans, steamed according to the package directions and shucked

1 bunch flat-leaf parsley, chopped

This isn't really a bouillabaisse, but it shares the same concept—an assortment of seafood stewed together in a broth. For this stew, I've drawn inspiration from the East, adding Asian aromatics including saffron, ginger, and lemongrass. A touch of coconut milk gives the stew some body and a tropical fragrance. While fresh is always preferable, you will also find edamame beans in the freezer case at your grocery store. Serve this with crusty bread.

In a small saucepan, heat the orange juice and saffron over medium heat until warm. Remove from the heat and set aside to let the saffron steep.

Heat the olive oil in a large Dutch oven over medium-high heat. Add the ginger, lemongrass, garlic, onion, and fennel and sauté until just brown, 5 to 10 minutes. Deglaze the pot with 1 cup of the sake, stirring to scrape up any browned bits, and slightly reduce. Remove and discard the large pieces of ginger and lemongrass. Add the saffron and orange juice, stock, coconut milk, soy sauce, tomatoes, and orange zest. Bring to a boil and simmer until the liquid is reduced by half, about 40 minutes. Add the five-spice powder and reduce the heat to medium. Add the shrimp and simmer for 3 minutes. Remove the shrimp with a slotted spoon and set aside.

Add the squid to the stew and simmer for 3 minutes. Remove the squid with a slotted spoon and set aside with the shrimp.

Heat the remaining 1 cup sake in a shallow saucepan over medium-high heat. Add the clams, cover, and cook them until the shells open, about 3 minutes. Remove the clams and discard any unopened ones. Add the mussels

to the pot, cover, and steam until the shells open, about 3 minutes. Remove the mussels and discard any unopened ones.

To serve, divide the shrimp, squid, clams, mussels, and edamame among 4 shallow bowls. Pour the stew around each bowl, sprinkle with fresh parsley, and serve.

# dover sole, five lilies

**Serves 4**

### sauce

1 cup Fish Stock (page 255)

1 cup Champagne

3 strips lemon zest

2 tablespoons Crème Fraîche (page 251)

### five lilies

4 cipollini onions

1 tablespoon unsalted butter

4 large shallots, halved

8 pearl onions

2 large scallions, halved

1 cup leeks sliced ½ inch thick

Salt and freshly ground white pepper

### fish

Fillets from 4 (1-pound) Dover soles or comparably sized flat fish

Salt and freshly ground white pepper

4 cups Whipped Butter (with Fish Stock instead of water, pages 251 and 255)

This dish showcases a collection of five members of the lily family—onions, shallots, pearl onions, leeks, and scallions—which have been paired simply with some delicate rosettes of flaky white sole. At Bluestem, we serve this with a simple sauce brightened with Champagne and crème fraîche.

---

**Make the sauce:** Bring the stock, Champagne, and zest to a simmer in a medium saucepan over medium heat. Reduce the liquid by one-third, about 30 minutes. Remove and discard the zest. Remove the stock from the heat and whisk in the crème fraîche.

**Cook the five lilies:** Blanch the cipollini for 3 minutes (for blanching instructions, see the User Manual, page xxiv).

Melt the butter in a large sauté pan over medium heat. When the butter starts to foam, add the shallots, pearl onions, scallions, cipollini, and leeks and cook, stirring

them occasionally, until slightly softened, about 4 minutes. Season with salt and pepper to taste.

**Prepare and poach the fish:** Season the fish fillets with salt and pepper. Starting from the widest end of the fillet, roll each fillet tightly. Melt the whipped butter in the top of a double boiler over medium-high heat and poach the fish rosettes in the butter for 15 minutes.

**To serve:** Froth the sauce with a handheld blender. Divide the five lilies mixture and sole rosettes among 4 plates. Spoon some of the frothed sauce over the fish and vegetables. Serve immediately.

# cod, parsnips, carrots, brodo, pancetta vinaigrette

**Serves 4**

### pancetta vinaigrette

6 ounces pancetta, diced

1 tablespoon minced shallots

2 cloves garlic, thinly sliced

2 tablespoons Banyuls vinegar or sherry vinegar

¼ teaspoon sugar

3 tablespoons extra-virgin olive oil

Salt and freshly ground white pepper

### vegetables

8 ounces carrots, peeled and cut into ½-inch-thick slices

8 ounces parsnips, peeled and cut into ½-inch-thick slices

1½ cups *Brodo* (see Ravioli Duo, page 210)

1 cup Glazed Cipollini (page 259)

### fish

2 tablespoons vegetable oil

4 (6-ounce) cod fillets

1 tablespoon unsalted butter

Cod is one of my favorite fishes. Its white flesh works well with both delicate and strong flavors. In this recipe, I match the cod with an assortment of root vegetables that are tossed with a pancetta vinaigrette. Try to get a variety of carrots; it will give this dish a splash of color.

---

**Make the vinaigrette:** Preheat the oven to 375°F.

Put the pancetta in a medium skillet. Roast the pancetta in the oven for 20 minutes to render the fat, turning the pieces over once or twice so they don't burn. Transfer the skillet to the stovetop over medium heat. Add the minced shallots and garlic and cook until the shallots turn translucent, about 1 minute. Stir in the vinegar, sugar, and oil. Season with salt and pepper to taste. Remove the skillet from the heat and set aside.

**Make the vegetables:** Set up an ice bath (see the User Manual, page xxv). Bring a pot of water to a boil and blanch the carrots and parsnips separately for 3 minutes each (see the blanching instructions in the User Manual, page xxiv). Cool the vegetables in the ice bath, then drain them.

Put the brodo, carrots, parsnips, and cipollini in a medium saucepan and bring to a low simmer over medium-low heat. Cook the vegetables until they are tender and warmed through, about 10 minutes. Keep warm.

**Cook the fish:** Lower the oven temperature to 350°F.

Heat the vegetable oil in a large, ovenproof sauté pan over medium-high heat. Add the fish fillets and cook for 3 minutes. Turn the fillets over and transfer the sauté pan to the oven. Roast the fish for 5 minutes.

**To serve:** Using a slotted spoon, remove the vegetables from the brodo. Stir the butter into the brodo to melt. Toss the vegetables with 2 tablespoons of the vinaigrette and divide them among 4 bowls. Place a fish fillet over the vegetables in each bowl. Pour a little of the brodo around the fish at the table.

# monkfish, red wine, mustard greens, **potato-horseradish** puree

**Serves 4**

### red wine vinaigrette

3 tablespoons olive oil

1 clove garlic, thinly sliced

1 tablespoon minced shallot

1 cup dry red wine, preferably
    Tempranillo

1 tablespoon Veal Jus (page 257)

¼ teaspoon sugar

Juice of ½ lemon

Salt and freshly ground black pepper

### mushrooms

2 tablespoons olive oil

5 ounces royal trumpet mushrooms,
    trimmed and sliced ¼ inch thick

Salt and freshly ground white pepper

### potato-horseradish puree

1 pound russet potatoes, peeled and
    coarsely chopped

2 tablespoons unsalted butter

1⅛ cups heavy cream

2 tablespoons prepared horseradish

Salt and freshly ground white pepper

### fish

½ cup roasted unsalted cashews

4 (6-ounce) monkfish slices

2 tablespoons vegetable oil

### mustard greens

2 ounces thick-cut bacon, diced

2 cloves garlic, thinly sliced

1 bunch mustard greens, stalks removed
    (about 4 cups packed)

1 tablespoon white wine

Salt and freshly ground white pepper

Juice of 1 lemon

At Bluestem, we usually serve our potato-horseradish puree with beef. However, in this recipe I pair it with monkfish—one of the few meaty fishes that stands up well to traditional meat accompaniments. Be sure to wash the mustard greens thoroughly, as they are often sandy.

**Make the vinaigrette:** Heat 1 tablespoon of the olive oil in a medium saucepan over medium-high heat. Add the garlic and shallots and sauté them just enough to sweat them a bit, about 30 seconds. Turn the heat down to medium and add the wine, veal jus, and sugar. Bring the sauce to a simmer and reduce by half, 4 to 5 minutes. Transfer the mixture to a bowl and let it cool slightly. Whisk in the remaining 2 tablespoons olive oil and the lemon juice. Season with salt and black pepper to taste. Set aside.

**Cook the mushrooms:** Heat the olive oil in a sauté pan over medium heat. Add the mushrooms and sauté until golden brown, about 2 minutes. Season with salt and white pepper to taste. Remove the mushrooms from the heat and set aside.

**Make the potato-horseradish puree:** Bring the potatoes to a boil in a pot of salted cold water over medium-high heat and cook for 20 minutes, or until they are fork-tender. Drain the potatoes and return them to the empty pot. Add the butter, cream, and horseradish and mash it all together with a wooden spoon until you have a thick slurry. Don't worry if there are still some chunks of potato bobbing about. Push all of it through a fine-mesh sieve. The puree should be loose and form a light ribbon when drizzled over itself. If it's a little thick, just add a splash of milk. Season with salt and white pepper to taste. Keep the puree warm in a covered saucepan until you are ready to serve.

**Cook the fish:** Preheat the oven to 350°F.

Spread the nuts on a small baking sheet and toast them in the oven, shaking the pan once or twice during the toasting process to prevent them from burning, for 5 minutes, or just until they start to release a nutty aroma. Let the nuts cool. Transfer the nuts to a food processor and chop them.

Truss the fish by tying kitchen twine around the monkfish slices them to make them round.

Heat the vegetable oil in a large ovenproof skillet over medium heat. Crust one end of each fillet with the chopped cashews. Sear the fillets on the uncrusted end until golden brown and delicious, about 1 minute. Transfer the skillet to the oven and roast the fish for 10 minutes.

**Cook the mustard greens:** Heat a large skillet over medium heat. Add the bacon and cook, shaking the pan every few seconds, until the bacon takes on a golden crust and some of the fat has rendered, about 3 minutes. Add the garlic and cook until the garlic starts to turn translucent. Add the mustard greens and cook, stirring the greens so they get evenly coated with fat. Add the wine, season with salt and white pepper to taste, and cook until the greens have wilted, about 2 minutes. Add the lemon juice and toss to coat. Remove from the heat.

**To serve:** Spoon some of the potato puree onto each dish. Top with some wilted greens, mushrooms, and a monkfish fillet. Drizzle a bit of the vinaigrette around the fish and serve immediately.

# rack of **venison**, pickled lady apples

**Serves 4**

**pickled lady apples**

12 Lady apples or 6 Gala apples

1 lemon (for acidulating water)

2 cups water

2 cups sugar

2 cups cider vinegar

½ cup gin

1 bay leaf

Leaves from 1 bunch sage, plus ¼ cup chopped

3 tablespoons black peppercorns

3 tablespoons coriander seeds

2 tablespoons juniper berries

Zest and juice of 1 lemon

Zest and juice of 1 orange

¾ cup extra-virgin olive oil

Salt and freshly ground black pepper

¼ cup chopped fresh flat-leaf parsley

**venison**

2 tablespoons olive oil

1 (8-bone) venison rack

Salt and freshly ground black pepper

Megan gets wonderful Lady apples in the winter for her desserts, and I steal them for a light pickled accompaniment for game meats. If you can't find Lady apples, you can substitute small Gala or Jonathan apples. This is a very simple dish that can be assembled in less than an hour if you have all of the ingredients in place and ready to go.

---

**Make the pickled apples:** Peel and core the apples. If you are using large Gala or Jonathan apples, halve or quarter them as necessary. They should be around 3 inches around. Soak them in cold water acidulated with the juice of 1 lemon.

Put the water, sugar, vinegar, gin, bay leaf, sage leaves, black peppercorns, coriander seeds, juniper berries, lemon zest and juice, and orange zest and juice in a large saucepan. Heat the mixture over medium heat to dissolve the sugar. When the mixture has come to a simmer, add the apples and cook until tender, about 5 minutes.

Drain the apples and save 1 cup of the pickling liquid. Whisk the extra-virgin olive oil into the reserved pickling liquid to make a vinaigrette. Season with salt and black pepper to taste.

**Cook the venison:** Preheat the oven to 375°F. Heat the vegetable oil in a large ovenproof skillet. Season the venison rack with salt and black pepper. Brown the venison rack on all sides, about 1 minute per side. Transfer the skillet to the oven and roast for 12 minutes for a medium-rare interior (the internal temperature should read 138°F on a meat thermometer). Let the meat rest for 10 minutes before cutting the meat into 1-inch-thick slices.

**To serve:** Gently toss the apples in the vinaigrette and sprinkle with the chopped sage and parsley. Cut the rack of venison, one bone per slice. Serve immediately with the pickled apples.

# braised **lamb shank**, mustard greens, preserved lemon, vermouth, saffron

**Serves 4 to 6**

### lamb shanks

4 (8- to 10-ounce) small lamb shanks, cut into 2-inch slices (like osso buco)

Salt and freshly ground black pepper

2 tablespoons vegetable oil

1 small yellow onion, coarsely chopped

2 celery stalks, coarsely chopped

1 large carrot, coarsely chopped

6 cloves garlic, chopped

2 bay leaves

2 cups dry red wine

4 sprigs fresh thyme

4 sprigs fresh oregano

1 tablespoon black peppercorns

1½ cups Veal Stock (page 257)

### vegetable stew

2 tablespoons olive oil

8 cipollini onions, peeled

1 small fennel bulb, trimmed and coarsely chopped

2 cloves garlic, chopped

1 bay leaf

3¼ cups vermouth

1 cup Chicken Stock (page 256)

2 tablespoons champagne vinegar

1 large pinch of saffron

Salt and freshly ground black pepper

1 large leek, trimmed of all greens and coarsely chopped

½ Preserved Lemon, cleaned and diced (page 263)

4 cups coarsely chopped napa cabbage

2 cups stemmed and coarsely chopped mustard greens

Juice of 2 lemons

I wanted to give this rather hearty braised dish some pep, so I added preserved lemons, lemon juice, and a touch of Champagne vinegar to the braising liquid to help brighten and lighten the flavor a bit. This recipe will make more than you need for four servings. But having leftovers of this stew is a fantastic boon on a day when you don't want to cook. Just seal the leftovers in a heavy-duty freezer bag and store in the freezer for up to 2 weeks.

**Sear the shanks:** Preheat the oven to 325°F. Season the shanks with salt and pepper.

Heat the oil in a Dutch oven over high heat. Add the lamb shanks and sear them on all sides until brown, about 4 minutes per side. Do not crowd the pot, so sear them in batches if necessary. Transfer the seared shanks to a plate.

**Braise the shanks:** Add the onion, celery, carrot, garlic, and bay leaves to the Dutch oven and cook for 4 to 5 minutes to soften the vegetables. Return the seared shanks to the Dutch oven. Deglaze the Dutch oven with the wine, scraping up any browned bits from the bottom. Wrap the thyme, oregano, and black peppercorns in cheesecloth to make a sachet, tying it closed with kitchen twine, and drop it into the pot. Turn the heat down to medium-low and reduce the wine by one-quarter, about 10 minutes. Add the veal stock and bring the mixture back to a simmer.

Cover the Dutch oven with a heavy lid and braise in the oven for 2½ hours.

**Cook the vegetables:** Heat the oil in a large saucepan over medium-high heat. Sauté the cipollini, fennel, garlic, and bay leaf to soften, about 4 minutes. Add the vermouth and stock, cover with a tight-fitting lid, and simmer until the cipollini are cooked through, about 7 minutes. Add the Champagne vinegar and saffron. Cover with the parchment lid and continue to cook for 8 minutes. Season with salt and pepper to taste.

Add the leek and preserved lemon. Simmer for 3 minutes.

Add the cabbage, mustard greens, and lemon juice. Simmer until the cabbage and greens are softened, about 5 minutes. Season the vegetables again with salt and pepper to taste.

**To serve:** Divide the lamb shanks among 4 shallow bowls. Spoon some of the braising liquid into each bowl over the shanks and serve with the stewed vegetables on the side.

# braised **short ribs**, grits

**Serves 4**

**short ribs**

5 pounds beef short ribs, boned (bones reserved)

Salt and freshly ground black pepper

6 tablespoons vegetable oil

1 medium onion, coarsely chopped

2 celery stalks, coarsely chopped

1 medium carrot, coarsely chopped

4 cloves garlic, smashed and chopped

4 cups stout

6 cups Chicken Stock (page 256)

**grits**

1 cup stone-ground white corn grits

3 cups whole milk

1 cup heavy cream

½ cup water

Salt

2 ounces Parmesan cheese, thinly sliced

You won't find a more honest plate of comfort food at Bluestem than braised short ribs and grits. This is just about as slow as food can get: The short ribs braise for 3 hours, the grits for 4 hours.

For braising heavy meats such as short ribs, I like to use a light chicken stock or veal stock. I enrich the stew with a little stout but rely mostly on the flavor and fat of the beef to create the flavor and body of the stew.

---

**Brown the short ribs:** Season the short ribs with salt and pepper.

Heat 4 tablespoons of the vegetable oil in a large skillet over medium-high heat. Brown the meat on each side, about 3 minutes per side.

**Braise the short ribs:** Preheat the oven to 325°F.

In a 4-quart stockpot, heat the remaining 2 tablespoons oil over medium-high heat. Add the onion, celery, carrot, and garlic and stir to soften, about 2 minutes. Season the vegetables with salt and pepper to taste. Add the stout

and short rib bones (but not any trimmings, as they'll just add extra grease) and reduce by one-third, about 20 minutes. Season again with salt and pepper to taste.

Put the short rib chops into the stout reduction and add just enough of the stock to barely cover the meat. If you don't have enough stock, top it off with water. Cover the saucepan with foil, securing it around the pot with kitchen twine to seal the sides. Cut a slit in the top.

Braise the short ribs in the oven for 3 hours, or until the short rib meat is extremely tender and the fat is meltingly soft.

Remove the short ribs from the liquid and keep warm. Strain the braising liquid through a fine-mesh sieve and return the liquid to the stovetop over medium-high heat. Bring to a simmer and reduce by half to make a sauce, about 10 to 12 minutes. Season with salt and pepper to taste.

**Make the grits:** Bring a large saucepan about half full of water to a simmer over medium-high heat. Set a large heatproof bowl over the simmering water to make a double boiler (make sure the bottom of the bowl does not touch the water). Stir together the grits, milk, cream, and water in the bowl. Seal the bowl with plastic wrap

and let the grits cook for 4 hours, lifting the plastic wrap every 45 minutes to give it a stir. Be careful when you open the plastic wrap, as the steam that escapes is very hot. Season the cooked grits with salt to taste.

**To serve:** Spoon a generous ½ cup of grits into each of 4 shallow bowls and top with Parmesan. Divide the braised short rib meat among the bowls and drizzle each with some of the braising sauce. Serve immediately.

# great hill blue cheese, spiced **nutty corn**

**Serves 18 to 20**

### spiced nutty corn

½ cup almonds, coarsely chopped

½ cup roasted unsalted peanuts, coarsely chopped

3 tablespoons vegetable oil

¾ cup popcorn kernels

¼ cup water

2 cups sugar

2 tablespoons heavy cream

Seeds scraped from 1 split vanilla bean

Finely grated zest of ½ orange

¾ teaspoon ground cinnamon

1½ teaspoons freshly grated nutmeg

⅛ teaspoon ground cloves

¼ teaspoon ground cardamom

½ tablespoon kosher salt

1 teaspoon freshly ground black pepper

Great Hill Blue cheese, for serving

---

Creamy, pungent, and salty, blue cheese begs for a sweet, crispy counterpart. At Bluestem, we serve a raw-milk blue cheese from Great Hill Dairy in Massachusetts with a nutty caramel popcorn. Warm with wintry spices, the popcorn also makes a fun snack on its own. Make sure you keep the popcorn stored in an airtight container, as any bit of moisture will make the caramel tacky and the popcorn limp.

---

Preheat the oven to 325°F. Spread the almonds and peanuts on a baking sheet and lightly toast them in the oven, stirring them at least once to prevent them from burning, about 6 minutes. Remove the nuts from the oven and set aside to cool.

In a large stockpot with a tight-fitting lid, heat the oil over high heat. Add the popcorn kernels and cover the pot. Once the kernels begin to pop, shake the pot constantly until all the corn stops popping. Uncover and remove from the heat.

Heat the water and sugar in a large stockpot over high heat until the sugar dissolves and the syrup comes to a boil. Let the syrup cook until it reaches a golden amber color; you'll notice the bubbles getting bigger and forming more slowly. Watch it carefully, as once the sugar starts to turn yellow it can burn very quickly. Swirl in the cream—the caramel will sputter. Remove from the heat and stir in the vanilla, zest, cinnamon, nutmeg, cloves, cardamom, salt, and pepper.

Using a wooden spoon, stir the popcorn and nuts into the hot caramel until all of it is well coated. It helps to vigorously shake the stockpot up and down and rap it against a sturdy work surface between stirs to get the popcorn at the bottom to move to the top. You'll want to work as quickly as possible since the caramel will stiffen as it cools, making it harder to work with.

Spread the caramel-coated popcorn on a large baking
sheet lined with a nonstick baking mat (or parchment
paper sprayed with nonstick cooking spray). Allow the
popcorn to cool completely before breaking it into bite-
size pieces. Store the popcorn in an airtight container. It
will keep for up to 1 week. Serve with wedges of the blue
cheese, 1 to 2 ounces per person.

# shatto milk company

"Milk at its finest." That's the motto of Shatto Milk Company, a family-run operation just north of Kansas City. Although the farm has been in the Shatto family for more than a century, Barb and Leroy Shatto didn't start bottling and selling their own milk until 2003. But true to their motto, in seven short years, the Shattos have become the best source of dairy in our region.

All of their products come from their own cows, none of which have been treated with growth hormones (recombinant bovine somatotropin, or rbST). The Shattos go to great lengths to ensure that their milk is handled as little as possible—it can go from cow to store in less than 12 hours.

The milk is sealed in glass bottles, which are not only recycled (you put a deposit on the bottle, which is refunded when you return it), but also keep the milk especially cold and odor-free.

At the restaurant, we use Shatto's dairy products almost exclusively. The milk fat in their dairy products is of such high quality and percentage that a little goes a long way. For the pastry kitchen, their cream is a dream, making ice creams and custards especially luscious and rich.

# meyer lemon tart, candied fennel, pomegranate caramel

**Makes one 9-inch tart or eight 4-inch tartlets**

2 teaspoons powdered gelatin

2 tablespoons cold water

½ cup freshly squeezed Meyer lemon juice (about 3 lemons)

¾ cup granulated sugar

¼ cup packed light brown sugar

½ vanilla bean, split and scraped

½ teaspoon ground star anise

1 large egg

5 egg yolks

½ cup (1 stick) unsalted butter, softened and cut into 1-inch cubes

¾ cup heavy cream, cold

1 tablespoon Crème Fraîche (page 251)

1 Graham Cracker Tart Shell (recipe follows)

Pomegranate Caramel (recipe follows)

Candied Fennel and Citrus Salad, for garnish (recipe follows)

**Bright and sunny,** citrus fruits seem so anachronistic in winter, when they're actually at their peak. But we're thankful for them. I especially enjoy working with Meyer lemons, which are immensely fragrant and sweeter than regular lemons. At Bluestem, we use them to create a twist on Key lime pie. This tart is not only refreshing but colorful as well and will enliven any winter meal.

---

Sprinkle the gelatin over the cold water in a small bowl. Let it set for 5 minutes until it blooms.

In the top of a double boiler or in a heat-resistant bowl set over an inch of simmering water in a saucepan, whisk together the lemon juice, both sugars, the vanilla, star anise, egg, and egg yolks until the mixture thickens, 6 to 8 minutes. Make sure that the bottom of the bowl doesn't touch the simmering water and that the water doesn't get too hot, as it will cook the curd too quickly.

When the curd has thickened, remove it from the heat and whisk in the butter, one piece at a time, making sure that each piece is fully incorporated before dropping in the next. Continue whisking until smooth.

Strain the curd through a fine-mesh sieve into a large bowl.

Set the bowl with the bloomed gelatin over a double boiler. Warm the gelatin over medium-low heat, just to melt it slightly. Fold the melted gelatin into the warm lemon curd with a spatula until fully incorporated. Let cool to room temperature.

Whip the heavy cream and crème fraîche together until soft peaks form. Fold the whipped mixture into the lemon curd.

Pour the curd into the prebaked tart shell or shells and chill in the refrigerator for at least 2 hours. Drizzle 2 teaspoons of caramel on each plate followed by each small tart. For one large tart, serve the caramel sauce on the side. Top the tart(s) with the candied fennel and citrus salad right before serving or serve a little salad with each slice as a garnish.

## graham cracker tart shell

½ cup graham cracker crumbs

1 cup all-purpose flour

½ cup cake flour

¼ cup granulated sugar

1 tablespoon brown sugar

⅛ teaspoon salt

½ cup (1 stick) unsalted butter, cut into several pieces and chilled

1 egg, lightly beaten

½ teaspoon vanilla extract

3 tablespoons ice water

Combine the graham cracker crumbs, both flours, both sugars, and the salt in a medium bowl. Using a food processor (pulse) or a pastry cutter, work the butter into the dry ingredients until a sandy mix with pea-size rounds forms. Add the egg and vanilla and knead until the dough is dry and crumbly. Add the ice water, 1 tablespoon at a time, until the dough comes together but is not sticky. Form the dough into a ball and pat it into a 1-inch-thick patty. Wrap it tightly with plastic wrap and refrigerate for at least 30 minutes.

Roll the dough out to ⅛-inch thickness. Line a 9-inch tart shell or eight 4-inch tart shells with the dough and refrigerate for 1 hour.

Preheat the oven to 325°F. Bake the tart shell for 15 minutes, or until lightly golden brown. Let the shell cool completely before filling it.

## pomegranate caramel  Makes about 3 cups

2 cups sugar

6 tablespoons water

2 tablespoons light corn syrup

1 cup pomegranate juice

Bring the sugar, water, and corn syrup to a boil in a large saucepan over high heat. Cook until the caramel turns a medium blond color. Carefully whisk in the pomegranate juice—the caramel will bubble vigorously and sputter. Allow the caramel to come to a boil. Remove from heat and strain through a fine-mesh sieve. Transfer the caramel to a heatproof container and let cool. Refrigerated in an airtight container, the caramel will keep for up to 1 month.

## candied fennel and citrus salad

Makes approximately 2 cups

¾ cup packed light brown sugar

1½ cups freshly squeezed orange juice

Juice of 1 lemon

½ vanilla bean, split and scraped

½ fennel bulb, trimmed and thinly sliced

1 blood orange or clementine, cut into supremes
    or wedges (see Note, page 155)

1 lime, cut into supremes or wedges

½ cup pomegranate seeds

Leaves from 1 sprig fresh tarragon

Heat the brown sugar, orange juice, lemon juice, and
vanilla in a small saucepan over high heat. Stir to
combine and cook until reduced by a third, about 8 to 10
minutes. Remove from the heat, remove the pod, and let
the mixture cool completely.

Toss the fennel, citrus supremes, and pomegranate seeds
with the cooked syrup. Add the fresh tarragon to the
salad right before serving.

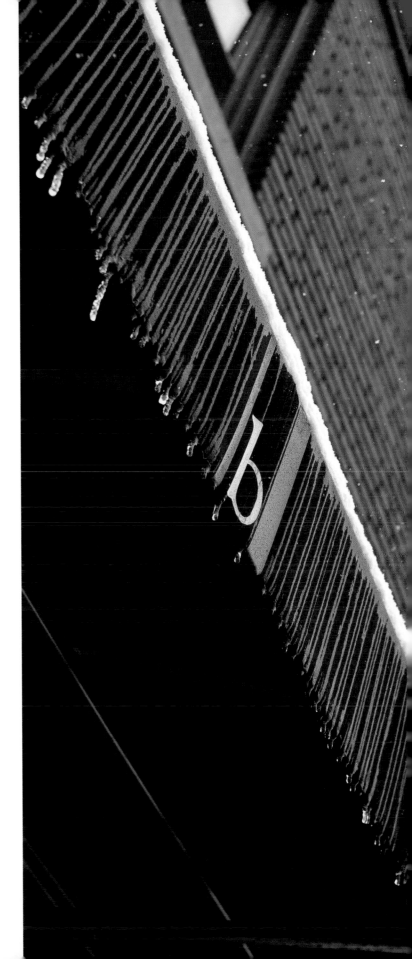

# graham cracker pound cake, hot chocolate–poached pears, tangerine sherbet

**Makes one 8 by 4 by 2½-inch cake**

1 cup (2 sticks) unsalted butter, softened

¾ cup sugar

¼ cup plus 1 tablespoon half-and-half

3 large eggs

2 teaspoons vanilla extract

¾ cup graham cracker crumbs

1 cup all-purpose flour

1 teaspoon baking powder

¼ teaspoon salt

Hot Chocolate–Poached Pears (recipe follows)

Tangerine Sherbet (recipe follows)

The core idea for this recipe began with chocolate, even though it plays a subtle role in the finished dessert. Although the components of this dessert work wonderfully in concert, the cake, the poached pears, and the tangerine sherbet stand very well on their own.

Preheat the oven to 350°F. Generously butter an 8 by 4-inch loaf pan.

In the bowl of a stand mixer fitted with the paddle attachment, cream the butter and sugar together on medium-high speed until fluffy and light, scraping the bowl with a spatula as needed, about 15 minutes.

In a small bowl, whisk the half-and-half, eggs, and vanilla together. In a separate bowl, combine the graham cracker crumbs, flour, baking powder, and salt.

With the stand mixer on medium speed, add one-third of the wet ingredients to the creamed butter and mix until incorporated. Scrape down the bowl. With the

stand mixer on low speed, repeat the process with half of the dry ingredients. Repeat the process, alternating the wet and dry ingredients until everything is incorporated.

Transfer the batter to the loaf pan and bake for 60 to 65 minutes, or until a toothpick inserted in the middle of the loaf comes out clean. Let the cake cool completely on a wire rack.

To serve, slice the cake into 1-inch-thick slices. Place one slice of pound cake on each plate. Nest half of a warm poached pear next to each slice and top each slice with a small scoop of tangerine sherbet. Serve immediately.

# hot chocolate–poached pears   Serves 4

This is a comforting and lovely alternative to wine-poached pears. Letting the cooked pears steep in the chocolate poaching liquid overnight helps intensify the chocolate flavor. These pears are best served warm. This recipe can be doubled.

---

3¼ cups water

1¼ cups sugar

2 cinnamon sticks

½ teaspoon allspice berries

3 cloves

2 ounces bittersweet chocolate, chopped

1 ounce unsweetened chocolate, chopped

1 tablespoon plus 1 teaspoon unsweetened cocoa powder

2 tablespoons dark rum

Pinch of salt

2 semifirm ripe pears, peeled, halved, and cored

In a large saucepan, bring the water, sugar, cinnamon sticks, allspice, and cloves to a simmer over medium-high heat to dissolve the sugar. Add the chocolates, cocoa powder, rum, and salt and whisk until the chocolate is melted and smooth. Add the pears and poach them for 45 minutes over low heat. Turn them over once halfway through the cooking process so they cook more evenly. They should be tender enough that a knife inserted in the thickest part will easily slip in and out.

Keep the pears warm until ready to serve. If you're not using them right away, you may refrigerate the pears in their poaching liquid in an airtight container for up to 2 days. To reheat, warm the pears in their poaching liquid in a saucepan over medium-low heat.

## sanding fruit

Do you ever wonder how restaurants get such smooth and shapely fruit after they peel them? After peeling apples and pears, we buff them smooth and round with a clean, heavy-duty scouring pad (make sure to use one made of fibers; do not use a wire or steel wool pad).

# tangerine sherbet *Makes about 1½ quarts*

2 cups freshly squeezed tangerine juice

1¼ cups Simple Syrup (page 265)

¾ cup cold water

Pinch of salt

¾ cup buttermilk

Whisk together the tangerine juice, simple syrup, water, and salt in a large bowl. Freeze the sherbet base in an ice cream maker according to the manufacturer's instructions (this may require chilling the base before churning). While the sherbet is churning, add the buttermilk.

Transfer the churned sherbet to a freezer-safe container and freeze for at least 2 hours before serving.

# gingerbread ice cream sandwich, milk chocolate–walnut ice cream, butterscotch

**Makes 1 dozen**

1½ cups all-purpose flour

1 teaspoon baking soda

½ teaspoon ground cinnamon

⅛ teaspoon ground allspice

¼ teaspoon ground cardamom

¼ teaspoon salt

½ cup packed light brown sugar

½ cup dark or blackstrap molasses

3 large eggs

½ cup vegetable oil

¼ cup porter or stout beer (try Boulevard Bully! Porter if you can find it)

¼ cup peeled and grated fresh ginger

1 batch Milk Chocolate–Walnut Ice Cream, softened (recipe follows)

Butterscotch Sauce (recipe follows)

Who says ice cream sandwiches only appear in the summer? At Bluestem, we adapt this fun dessert to winter by layering a spicy gingerbread cake with a milky chocolate ice cream studded with nuts. A drizzle of warm butterscotch laced with citrus gives it a perky edge.

With the center rack in place, preheat the oven to 325°F. Butter an 18 by 13-inch baking sheet and line it with parchment paper.

Sift together the flour, baking soda, cinnamon, allspice, cardamom, and salt in a bowl.

In the bowl of a stand mixer fitted with a whisk attachment, beat the brown sugar and molasses until combined. Add the eggs one at a time, scraping down the bowl as necessary. Add the oil and beat until combined.

With the mixer on low speed, beat in the dry ingredients until just combined. Add the porter and ginger, beating just enough to make the batter smooth. Pour the batter into the prepared baking sheet. Bake the cake for 9 to 10 minutes, or until a wooden toothpick inserted into the center comes out clean. Let the cake cool completely on a wire rack.

Turn the cake out of the pan onto a large work surface. Carefully remove the parchment paper. Cut the cake in half, yielding two 13 by 9-inch pieces. Line a clean large baking sheet with plastic wrap, leaving at least a 6-inch overhang on all sides. Put one of the cake pieces on the baking sheet and top it with the softened ice cream, spreading it over the cake evenly with an offset spatula. Top the ice cream with the second piece of cake to create one giant ice cream cake sandwich. Wrap the pan and cake tightly with multiple layers of plastic wrap and freeze for at least 6 hours.

To serve, cut the cake into 12 equal pieces. Serve each sandwich on a plate with a drizzle of warm butterscotch sauce. Wrap the remaining ice cream sandwiches separately in multiple layers of plastic wrap and freeze for up to 1 week.

# milk chocolate–walnut ice cream   Makes about 1 quart

3 egg yolks

1½ cups heavy cream

1½ cups whole milk

1 cup sugar

⅛ cup unsweetened cocoa powder

6 ounces milk chocolate, chopped, or pastilles

½ cup walnuts, toasted and chopped

Whisk the egg yolks together in a medium-size bowl.

In a large saucepan, bring the cream, milk, and sugar to a low simmer over medium-high heat. Simmer the mixture until the sugar has fully dissolved, about 2 minutes. Watch the pot closely, as it may boil over quickly.

In a large bowl, sift the cocoa powder over the milk chocolate. Add the chocolate and cocoa to the hot cream and whisk until the chocolate has fully melted.

Temper the egg yolks by whisking 1 cup of the hot cream mixture in a thin, steady stream into the yolks. You want to add the hot cream slowly to gradually increase the temperature of the egg yolks without scrambling them. Once the egg yolks are tempered, add them to the rest of the hot ice cream base.

Strain the ice cream base through a fine-mesh sieve into a large bowl. Set the bowl over ice and stir with a whisk until it has cooled.

Churn the ice cream base in an ice cream maker according to the manufacturer's instructions. (This may require chilling the base before churning.) While the ice cream is churning, set a large bowl over a larger bowl filled with ice. When the ice cream has thickened, but not yet hardened, scoop the ice cream into the bowl set over ice. Working quickly, fold in the nuts.

At this point, you can fill your ice cream sandwiches with the softened ice cream or transfer the ice cream to a freezer-safe container and freeze for up to 1 month. Thaw the ice cream until softened before using.

## butterscotch sauce  Makes about 1¾ cups

I love butterscotch (in fact, our wedding cake was chocolate devil's food with butterscotch). It's basically a caramel made with brown sugar instead of granulated sugar—a wonderful meeting of creamy, buttery, sweet, and salty.

The secret to this sauce is the addition of salt and lemon juice. The salty acidity cuts the richness of the butterscotch and makes an amazingly delicious sauce.

1 cup lightly packed brown sugar

10 tablespoons unsalted butter

½ cup heavy cream

1 teaspoon vanilla extract

1 teaspoon butterscotch liqueur

½ teaspoon salt

1 teaspoon freshly squeezed lemon juice

In a small saucepan, combine the brown sugar, butter, cream, vanilla, liqueur, and salt. Whisking constantly, bring the mixture to a rapid boil over high heat. Remove from the heat and continue to whisk for a few seconds more.

Strain the hot butterscotch through a fine-mesh sieve into a bowl. Stir in the lemon juice. Keep warm until ready to serve. If you are not using the butterscotch immediately, transfer the butterscotch to an airtight container and let it cool. Refrigerated in an airtight container, it will keep for up to 1 month. Over time, the fat will separate from the sugar. To bring the butterscotch back to its proper consistency, soften the butterscotch slightly by heating it on the stovetop over low heat or zapping it in a microwave for about 30 seconds. Whisk the butterscotch vigorously until it re-emulsifies (a handheld blender is particularly useful for this).

# white coffee, passion fruit parfait

**Serves 8 to 12**

**white coffee mousse**

1 cup heavy cream

⅔ cup whole coffee beans

2½ ounces white chocolate, chopped

2 egg whites

2 tablespoons plus 1 teaspoon sugar

Pinch of salt

**passion fruit froth**

½ cup passion fruit puree

¼ cup Simple Syrup (page 265)

2 tablespoons water

1 tablespoon whole milk


Espresso powder, for garnish

Not only does the bracingly tart passion fruit froth counterbalance the rich, creamy coffee mousse in this parfait, but the color of the two together is quite pretty as well—a frothy orange hat on a milky white body. Make sure to serve these in clear glasses for the full visual effect. You can find the passion fruit puree at specialty food markets.

**Make the mousse:** In a small saucepan, scald the heavy cream and coffee beans over high heat. Remove the pot from the heat and let the mixture steep for 2 hours.

Strain the cream and discard the coffee beans. Let cool to room temperature. In the bowl of a stand mixer fitted with a whisk attachment, whip the cream to soft peaks, about 4 minutes on high speed. Cover and chill.

In the top of a double boiler or in a heat-resistant bowl set over simmering water, melt the white chocolate. Do not let the water touch the bottom of the double boiler or bowl.

In a separate double boiler or heat-resistant bowl set over simmering water, whisk together the egg whites and sugar until slightly foamy. Let the mixture heat for a couple of minutes, until the sugar has fully dissolved (you can check by sticking your index finger into the egg whites and rubbing it against your thumb for sugar granules). When the sugar has fully dissolved, remove the top of the double boiler from the heat and whip the egg whites—either with a handheld mixer or by

transferring them to the clean bowl of a stand mixer fitted with a whisk attachment—until stiff peaks form, about 5 minutes on high speed. Whisk one-third of the white chocolate into the meringue. Fold the meringue into the remaining white chocolate. Add a pinch of salt and fold in the whipped cream. Transfer the mousse to a piping bag and pipe the mousse into 8 to 12 individual 2-ounce cups or ramekins. Chill the piped mousse in the refrigerator, uncovered, for 1 hour.

**Make the passion fruit froth:** Combine the passion fruit puree, simple syrup, water, and milk in a small bowl. Using a handheld blender or a milk frother, blend or froth the mixture until a layer of bubbles forms on top (it is most effective if you blend or froth the liquid just under the surface).

**To serve:** Spoon a large dollop of froth onto each parfait. Refroth the passion fruit mixture as necessary. Garnish each with a small sprinkle of espresso powder. Serve immediately.

Front: chocolate-grapefruit tartlets, white coffee, passion fruit parfaits.
Back: hot chocolates, bourbon meringue.

# hot chocolate, bourbon **meringue**

**Makes 4 cups; serves 8**

### hot chocolate

2 cups water

1½ cups heavy cream

¼ cup packed light brown sugar

1 cinnamon stick

2 star anise

1 teaspoon ground allspice

¼ teaspoon ground cloves

5 ounces milk chocolate, chopped

5 ounces bittersweet chocolate, chopped

Pinch of salt

### meringue

1 cup granulated sugar

3 egg whites

2 tablespoons bourbon

While working as interns in New York, my roommate and I once devoted a whole weekend to eating desserts. It was one of those unmonitored, indulgent episodes of adolescence one never forgets and, sadly, never repeats.

One of our stops during that sugar binge was at Balthazar, a brasserie in SoHo. Whereas most restaurants offer hot chocolate by the cup, Balthazar offers it by both the cup and the bowl. Of course, I ordered the bowl and spent the better half of the afternoon lapping it up like a carefree kid on a snow day.

Hot chocolate coats everything on the inside with rich and luscious warmth. This hot chocolate is perfumed with winter spices and topped with a toasty meringue doubling as a marshmallow. Although the hot chocolate can be made a day ahead, the meringue must be used immediately after you make it.

**Make the hot chocolate:** Bring the water, cream, brown sugar, cinnamon stick, star anise, allspice, and cloves to a boil in a medium saucepan. Remove the mixture from the heat and stir in the chocolates and salt. Keep stirring until the chocolate has fully melted. Let the hot chocolate stand for 5 to 10 minutes to steep. Strain the hot chocolate through a fine-mesh sieve and discard the spices. Keep warm until ready to serve or let the mixture cool completely, transfer it to an airtight container, and refrigerate up to 2 days. Bring the hot chocolate to a simmer in a saucepan over medium-low heat. Using a handheld immersion blender, zap it to reincorporate the ingredients.

**Make the meringue.** Whisk together the sugar and egg whites in the top of a double boiler or a heat-resistant bowl set over a pot of water. Cook at a low simmer until the sugar has dissolved and the mixture becomes frothy, about 3 minutes. Using a handheld electric mixer, whip the egg whites on high speed until stiff peaks form, about 5 minutes. Add the bourbon and whisk for 1 minute. Transfer the meringue to a piping bag and use immediately.

**To serve:** Divide the hot chocolate among small shot glasses or demitasse cups. Top each with a dollop of bourbon meringue. If you like, toast the meringue with a crème brûlée torch. Serve immediately.

## the angels of bluestem

When Colby and I took over Bluestem, there was a decorative, faux plaster bas-relief of angels above the front door on the inside of the restaurant. It didn't fit the look we wanted, so we removed it and stashed it in our storage area.

Shortly after we expanded the restaurant to include a lounge in the adjacent space, one of our servers took the angels home. That night, inexplicably, the ceiling of the restaurant collapsed—thankfully after service, when no one was around. In a temporary bout of superstition, the server brought the angels back to Bluestem, out of fear that their removal from the restaurant had caused the accident. We now keep the bas-relief tucked away in a little space right above the kitchen.

# chocolate-**grapefruit** tartlets

**Makes about twenty
2-inch tartlets**

### candied grapefruit zest

Zest of ½ grapefruit, peeled with
a Y-peeler

1 cup Simple Syrup (page 265)

Granulated sugar, for coating

### *sablé* **dough**

¾ cup all-purpose flour

⅛ cup unsweetened natural cocoa
powder

Pinch of salt

4 tablespoons (½ stick) unsalted butter,
softened

¼ cup plus 2 teaspoons granulated sugar

1 large egg

2 tablespoons natural cocoa nibs, finely
ground (optional)

### ganache

4½ ounces unsweetened chocolate

1½ ounces bittersweet chocolate (such as
Valrhona 55% Equatoriale)

½ cup heavy cream

⅛ cup granulated sugar

1 tablespoon unsalted butter

1 tablespoon finely grated grapefruit
zest

½ teaspoon vanilla extract

1 tablespoon freshly squeezed grapefruit
juice

### whipped cream

1 cup heavy cream

2 teaspoons confectioners' sugar

I think that grapefruit is an underused and underappreciated fruit. Its zest is immensely fragrant, and its flavor blossoms particularly well in chocolate.

---

**Make the candied zest:** Bring a small pot of water to a boil and blanch the zest for 2 to 3 minutes to remove the bitterness. Drain and transfer the zest to a small saucepan. Add the simple syrup and simmer over medium heat until the zest turns translucent, about 15 minutes. Drain the zest (reserve the syrup for flavoring teas or cocktails, as it will have taken on a fragrant grapefruit scent). Let the zest cool slightly. Pat the zest with a damp towel, toss with granulated sugar to coat it, and spread it out on a large plate or baking sheet to dry for a few hours. Store the zest in an airtight container for up to 2 weeks.

**Make the *sablé* dough:** Sift together the flour, cocoa powder, and salt in a medium bowl.

In the bowl of a stand mixer fitted with a paddle attachment, cream the butter and sugar together, stopping to scrape the sides of the bowl with a spatula at least once, until soft and fluffy, about 5 minutes. Add the egg and cocoa nibs and mix until incorporated. Scrape down the bowl. Add the dry ingredients and mix until a dough forms.

Turn the dough out onto a clean surface and shape it into a flat disk. Wrap the dough tightly with plastic wrap and chill for at least 1 hour.

Preheat the oven to 325°F.

Roll out the *sablé* dough on a lightly floured surface to ⅛-inch thickness. Line twenty 2-inch tartlet shells with the dough.

Bake the shells for 6 to 8 minutes.

**Make the ganache:** Combine the chocolates in a bowl.

In a small saucepan, bring the cream, sugar, grapefruit zest, and butter to a boil, stirring to dissolve the sugar. Pour the hot cream over the chocolate and let it sit for a minute. Add the vanilla extract and grapefruit juice and stir until the chocolate has fully melted and becomes smooth. Strain the hot ganache through a fine-mesh sieve.

Divide the warm ganache among the tartlet shells. You can either spoon the warm ganache into the prebaked shells or let the ganache cool, transfer it to a pastry bag, and pipe it into the shells for a neater look.

**Whip the cream:** In the bowl of a stand mixer fitted with a whisk attachment (or with a whisk in hand), whip the cream until it begins to froth. Slowly add the confectioners' sugar and continue to beat until soft peaks form. Use it immediately.

**To serve:** Top the filled tartlets with a dollop of whipped cream and garnish with some candied grapefruit zest.

essentials

## whipped butter  Makes about 1 cup

Anyone familiar with classical French cuisine will know that this is essentially a *beurre monté*, or mounted butter—an emulsification of butter, water, and a touch of white wine. Kept warm, this whipped butter will keep for up to 2 hours. Once it cools, it will solidify and you can't reheat it without the emulsion "breaking" (that is, the liquids and butter will separate).

¼ cup water

1 tablespoon white wine

1 cup unsalted butter (2 sticks), chilled and cut into ½-inch cubes

1 teaspoon freshly squeezed lemon juice

In a small saucepan, bring the water and wine to a simmer over medium heat. Reduce the liquid by half, about 4 minutes. Turn the heat down to low and, while whisking vigorously, add the butter one piece at a time, letting each piece melt before adding the next. Whisk until the butter has melted and the sauce has emulsified and taken on a pale yellow color. Stir in the lemon juice to taste.

## crème fraîche  Makes 1½ cups

Crème fraîche is readily available in specialty markets. But given how inexpensive and simple it is to make, at Bluestem we make our own.

1 cup heavy cream

¼ cup buttermilk

2 tablespoons freshly squeezed lemon juice

In a stainless steel bowl, combine the cream, buttermilk, and lemon juice. Cover and let it sit at room temperature for at least 24 hours but not more than 48 hours. (The crème fraîche will be ready to serve after it has fermented for 1 day.) Cover and chill.

To whip, transfer the crème fraîche to the bowl of a stand mixer fitted with a whisk attachment. Whip the crème fraîche on medium speed until it becomes soft and fluffy, about 3 minutes. Cover and chill. Once whipped, it will keep for up to 3 days.

*mayonnaise* Makes about 4 cups

Mayonnaise tastes better when freshly made. Making mayonnaise is also a cheap and easy way for the home cook to practice emulsifying—the process in which fat is dispersed and suspended in liquid, resulting in a creamy substance. Using fresh eggs is especially important in this recipe, since they are not cooked.

1 cup olive oil

1½ cups grapeseed oil

3 egg yolks

1 teaspoon salt

¼ cup water

Combine the olive oil and grapeseed oil in a large measuring cup (you want to make sure that you'll be able to pour the oil out in a thin stream without dripping or spilling).

Put the egg yolks and salt in a blender. With the blender running, drizzle in the oil in a thin stream until all of the oil is added. The contents should emulsify to a thick, mayonnaise-like consistency. If it is too thick, you can thin it out by drizzling up to ¼ cup of water into the blender with the machine running.

Covered and refrigerated, the mayonnaise will keep for up to 1 week.

## aïoli

Aïoli is an emulsified sauce resembling mayonnaise that is spiked with garlic. Traditionally made with just garlic and olive oil, at Bluestem we add egg yolks, cayenne pepper, and mustard to give it some flavor and help stabilize the emulsion. If you would like to make aïoli, add 1 tablespoon Dijon mustard, 3 cloves garlic, and ½ teaspoon cayenne pepper to the egg yolks and salt in the blender.

## garlic butter  Makes about 4¾ cups

This garlic butter is a delicious way to add flavor to any dish. At the restaurant, we keep a pot of it warm throughout service, using it for everything from escargots (see page 209) to the French fries that we serve in our lounge.

Cloves from 2 heads garlic, chopped

2 cups clarified butter (see Note)

Pulse the garlic cloves in a food processor until chunky.

In a medium stockpot, melt the clarified butter over medium heat. Turn the heat down to low and add the garlic. Let the garlic steep in the butter for 30 minutes. Remove the pot from the heat and let it sit for 10 minutes more. Use warm or transfer to an airtight container and refrigerate for up to 1 week.

**NOTE:** Clarified butter (or "drawn butter") is simply butter with the milk solids and water removed. What is left is pure butterfat. Without the milk solids, clarified butter has a higher smoking point, making it possible to cook with butter at higher temperatures. To make clarified butter, gently melt butter in a saucepan over medium-low heat (to make 2 cups of clarified butter, you'll need about 2½ cups of butter, or 5 sticks). The butter will separate into three layers: a foamy layer on top; a clear, golden layer of butterfat in the middle; and a milky layer of the solids and water at the bottom. Skim off the foamy top and discard. Carefully pour or ladle out the golden layer of clarified butterfat into a container. Discard the milk solids left behind at the bottom. Kept covered and chilled, the clarified butter will keep for up to 3 weeks.

## champagne vinaigrette  Makes about 1¾ cups

With a nice balance of sweet and sour, this is an extremely versatile vinaigrette. At Bluestem, we find a place for it in every season.

1 cup Champagne vinegar

⅓ cup olive oil

1 tablespoon freshly squeezed lemon juice

⅓ cup honey

Combine all of the ingredients in a nonreactive bowl, adding the honey last to prevent it from sticking to the bottom of the bowl. Whisk vigorously until combined. Tightly sealed, the vinaigrette will keep in the refrigerator for up to 1 month. Before using the vinaigrette in a recipe, bring the vinaigrette back to room temperature and rewhisk to combine.

## sherry vinaigrette   Makes 2 cups

This vinaigrette has a touch of sweetness to help balance out the tartness of the sherry vinegar. It's great for salads, vegetables, fish, and even meats.

---

1¼ cups olive oil

3 shallots, minced

1¼ cups sherry vinegar

¾ cup sugar

Salt and freshly ground black pepper

Heat 1 tablespoon of the olive oil in a small sauté pan over medium-high heat. Add the shallots and cook until soft and translucent, about 1 minute. Remove from the heat and let the shallots cool completely.

In a bowl, whisk together the vinegar and sugar until the sugar has dissolved. Vigorously whisk in the remaining olive oil and the shallots until combined. Season with salt and pepper to taste.

Kept chilled in an airtight container, the vinaigrette will keep for 1 week. Let the vinaigrette come to room temperature before using.

## candied pecans   Makes about 1 cup

We always have candied nuts on hand to use as a garnish for everything from salads to desserts. This recipe calls for pecans, but you may substitute any unsalted nut, though the wrinkly ones (like walnuts) give the candied glaze something to cling to. Just make sure that you adjust the baking time according to the size of the nut so that you don't burn them.

---

1 cup pecans (about 3½ ounces)

2 tablespoons light corn syrup

1 tablespoon sugar

½ teaspoon salt

¼ teaspoon freshly ground black pepper

Pinch of cayenne pepper

Preheat the oven to 325°F.

Spray a baking sheet or pan with nonstick cooking spray. Combine all of the ingredients in a bowl, tossing to coat the nuts with the seasonings and corn syrup (use your hands or a wooden spoon to get everything evenly mixed). Spread the nuts on the sheet evenly so that they don't touch (clusters will be hard to break up after baking).

Stirring or shaking the pan occasionally to break up clumps, bake the nuts until they turn a deep golden brown and the sugar mixture is bubbling (about 15 minutes). Let the nuts cool completely on the baking sheet. Gently break the nuts apart if necessary and store them in an airtight container for up to 1 month.

Vegetable stock is simple to make and very useful. At the restaurant, we always have an extra pot of it on hand so that we can broaden the range of dishes that can be made vegetarian-friendly.

---

3 quarts plus 2 cups water

2 cups white wine

¼ cup Champagne vinegar

1 large yellow onion, coarsely chopped

1 fennel bulb, including fronds, trimmed and coarsely chopped

½ celery stalk, coarsely chopped

1 head garlic, top third sliced off

1 leek, coarsely chopped

6 sprigs fresh tarragon

6 sprigs fresh lemon thyme or regular thyme

1 bay leaf

1 tablespoon black peppercorns

Combine all of the ingredients in an 8-quart stockpot. Bring the stock to a simmer over medium-high heat and then turn the heat to low. Allow the stock to simmer, uncovered, for 45 minutes.

Remove the pot from the heat and strain the stock through a fine-mesh sieve into a heatproof container set in an ice bath (see the User Manual, page xxv). Discard the solids. Cool the vegetable stock in the ice bath. Transfer the chilled stock to an airtight container. Refrigerate the stock until you are ready to serve it. The stock can also be frozen for up to 2 months.

## fish stock

For fish stock, add 2 pounds of fish bones and trimmings (fish heads and scrap pieces of fish, for example) to the vegetable stock at the very beginning, along with all the other ingredients. Proceed with the recipe.

## *chicken stock*  Makes 1 quart

Chicken stock is the water of the professional kitchen. Serving as the base for soups, braises, and sauces, it adds a layer of flavor that you wouldn't get if you used just water. It can also be used as a poaching liquid.

Making chicken stock is a great way to use up chicken carcasses left over from deboned chicken. At home, I freeze carcasses until I have enough to make a batch of stock.

---

6 quarts cold water

2 cups white wine

6 pounds chicken bones

1 large carrot, chopped

½ celery stalk, chopped

1 large onion, chopped

1 bay leaf

1 tablespoon white peppercorns

Put all of the ingredients in a 12-quart stockpot. Bring the stock to a simmer over medium-high heat. Turn the heat down to medium-low and simmer the stock uncovered for 2½ hours, or until reduced to 4 cups. Skim the top of the stock often to get rid of the scum that gathers.

Remove the pot from the heat and strain the stock through a fine-mesh sieve into a heatproof container set in an ice bath (see the User Manual, page xxv). Discard the solids. Cool the chicken stock in the ice bath. Transfer the chilled stock to an airtight container. Refrigerate the stock until you are ready to use it. The stock can also be frozen for up to 2 months.

*veal stock or jus*   Makes 3 quarts stock; 1 quart jus

"Jus" is my shorthand for a sauce made from reduced meat stock. The richness and complexity of flavors achieved through hours of simmering and reducing meat stock cannot be matched. We always have it on hand. In addition, you can make "jus" from the bones of any other animal, such as lamb.

3 pounds veal knuckle bones

12 quarts water

1 large carrot, chopped

½ celery stalk, chopped

1 large onion, chopped

4 cloves garlic, smashed and chopped

1 tablespoon tomato paste

3 cups dry red wine

1 bay leaf

1 small bunch fresh thyme

## lamb jus

For lamb jus, substitute 3 pounds lamb bones for the veal knuckle bones. Proceed with the recipe.

Rinse the veal bones under running water, scraping away any blood spots you see.

Prepare a large ice bath (see the User Manual, page xxv).

Put the veal bones in a 12-quart stockpot and cover with 8 quarts of the water. Bring the water to a boil over high heat. Turn the heat down to medium-low and simmer the bones for 15 minutes, skimming the top periodically to get rid of the frothy scum that gathers.

Drain the bones and plunge them into the ice bath. Rinse out the stockpot. Return the bones to the clean stockpot and add the remaining 4 quarts water. Bring to a boil over high heat. Turn the heat to low and simmer for 2 hours, uncovered, skimming the top periodically.

Strain the stock and let it cool. Kept covered and chilled, it will keep up to 3 days, or frozen for up to 2 months.

**To make veal jus:** Set the prepared veal stock in a large stockpot over medium-high heat. Bring to a simmer and cook, uncovered, for 6 hours, skimming periodically, or until reduced to 4 cups jus.

Remove the pot from the heat and strain the jus through a fine-mesh sieve into a heatproof container set in an ice bath. Discard any solids. Cool the jus in the ice bath. Transfer the chilled jus to an airtight container. Refrigerate the jus until you are ready to use it. The jus can also be frozen for up to 2 months.

# *duck jus*  Makes 1 quart

Because duck can be gamey, in this recipe we used port wine instead of dry red wine to enhance the flavor.

---

3 pounds duck bones

3 cups tawny port

1 large carrot, chopped

½ celery stalk, chopped

1 large yellow onion, chopped

4 cloves garlic, smashed and chopped

1 bay leaf

1 tablespoon tomato paste

1 tablespoon juniper berries

4 cups water

Preheat the oven to 400°F.

Spread the bones on a large baking sheet and roast them for 40 minutes, or until golden brown, rotating the baking sheet halfway through the cooking time.

In a 12-quart stockpot, combine the duck bones, port, carrot, celery, onion, garlic, bay leaf, tomato paste, and juniper berries. Bring to a simmer over medium-high heat. Turn the heat to medium-low and reduce by half, about 25 minutes, skimming the top periodically to get rid of the scum that gathers.

Add the water and continue to simmer, uncovered, until reduced to 4 cups (about 4 hours), skimming the top regularly.

Remove the pot from the heat and strain the stock through a fine-mesh sieve into a heatproof container set in an ice bath (see the User Manual, page xxv). Discard the solids. Cool the jus in the ice bath. Transfer the chilled stock to an airtight container. Refrigerate the stock until you are ready to use it. The stock can also be frozen for up to 2 months.

## *glazed cipollini*  Makes about 20

At the restaurant, we use these glazed onions on fish and meat dishes. They're great as a garnish for charcuterie as well, or sliced into a salad. At home, I'll pop them right out of a jar, like olives. Make more than you'll need; they won't last long.

3 cups dry white wine

2½ cups Vegetable Stock (page 255)

1 pound cipollini (about 20 onions)

2 tablespoons sugar

¼ teaspoon salt

Freshly ground white pepper

Bring 2½ cups of the wine and the stock to a boil in a large saucepan over high heat. Add the onions and blanch for 2 minutes, covered. Cool in an ice bath (see the User Manual, page xxv).

Peel and trim the tails off the onions. Combine the onions with the sugar and the remaining ½ cup wine in a sauté pan. Set the pan over medium heat and bring it to a simmer. Cook for about 8 minutes, or until the wine has evaporated, leaving a light syrupy glaze on the onions. Add the salt and season with pepper to taste.

Covered and chilled, the glazed cipollini will keep for up to 1 week.

*potatoes confit*  Makes 6

Cooking potatoes gently in olive oil makes them particularly soft and silky. In this recipe, we use fingerling potatoes, but you can substitute any similar-size waxy potato, such as red-skinned, purple Peruvian, yellow Finn, white round, or huckleberry potatoes. If you use a potato that is significantly larger than the fingerling, cut the potato into pieces approximately the size of a fingerling potato.

---

6 fingerling potatoes

2½ cups extra-virgin olive oil

4 garlic cloves, smashed and chopped

4 sprigs fresh thyme

1 tablespoon sea salt

Heat the potatoes, olive oil, garlic, thyme, and salt in a medium saucepan over low heat until the oil registers 180°F on an instant-read thermometer. Lower the heat slightly and continue to cook the potatoes for 50 minutes more, maintaining the oil temperature as steady as possible at 180°F.

Remove the pan from the heat and allow the potatoes to cool to room temperature in the oil. Drain the potatoes (reserve the oil, if you like; see below) and store them in an airtight container. Refrigerated, they will keep for up to 1 week.

**NOTE:** Cooled and strained, the poaching oil, which is infused with garlic and thyme, can be used to make salad dressings.

If you do not want to poach the potatoes, we recommend roasting them for recipes in this book that call for Potatoes Confit. To do this, preheat the oven to 450°F. Toss the potatoes with 2 tablespoons extra-virgin olive oil, ½ teaspoon sea salt, ½ teaspoon freshly ground black pepper, 4 cloves garlic (smashed), and 4 sprigs fresh thyme. Spread the potatoes on a baking sheet and roast for 10 to 12 minutes. Let them cool completely before slicing them.

*white beans*  Makes 2 cups cooked beans

If you can master the bean, you will always eat well. That's not a proverb; it's the truth. A nicely cooked bowl of beans hardly needs dressing; maybe some good olive oil, salt, and a little bit of pepper, but not much more. This recipe will work for any bean, though you may have to adjust the soaking and cooking times slightly based on the size, type, and age of the bean (the longer it has been on the shelf, the longer it will need to be soaked before cooking). At Bluestem, we like to use Rancho Gordo's beans (see Sources, page 272), which tend to be fresher. You can't go wrong with soaking dried beans overnight, so that's what we recommend here.

---

½ cup dried white beans

6 cups Chicken Stock (page 256)

4 ounces bone-in ham hock

1 clove garlic, smashed and chopped

1 leek, white part only, coarsely chopped

1 shallot, halved

½ cup fennel bulb, trimmed and chopped

1 bay leaf

1 sprig fresh oregano

Soak the beans in about 2 cups of water overnight. Drain.

Tightly wrap the beans in cheesecloth and secure the bundle with kitchen twine. Combine the stock, ham hock, garlic, leek, shallot, fennel, bay leaf, and oregano in a large stockpot. Add the wrapped beans to the stockpot and heat over medium-high heat until it comes to a simmer. Cover and cook for 1 hour. Check the beans. If they are not cooked, continue to simmer and check for doneness every 20 minutes. It should not take more than 2 hours. Store refrigerated in an air-tight container for up to 1 week.

## *herb crumbs*  Makes about 3½ cups

This is one of the most versatile garnishes around. You can use it to top macaroni and cheese, gratins of any kind, pastas, or just about anything savory.

2 cups bread crumbs or panko

½ cup toasted pine nuts

Leaves from 1 bunch flat-leaf parsley

⅓ cup Garlic Butter (page 253)

In a food processor, pulse together the bread crumbs, nuts, and parsley until the parsley has become evenly incorporated into the bread crumbs. Slowly drizzle in the garlic butter and continue to pulse until the mixture turns to the consistency of damp sand. Transfer the crumbs to an airtight container. Refrigerated, they will keep for up to 1 week.

## *orange powder*   Makes 2 tablespoons

If you're lucky enough to have access to a dehydrator, this is an easy recipe that produces an amazing product. If you don't, you can substitute finely grated orange zest (using a Microplane zester) where orange powder is called for in this cookbook.

---

6 medium oranges

Peel the zest from the oranges with a Y-peeler. Using a sharp knife, remove any pith that has come off with the zest. Dehydrate the zest in a dehydrator for 48 hours, or until completely dry and brittle.

Grind the zest in a spice grinder or coffee mill until finely ground. Sift the zest power through a fine-mesh sieve. Return any large pieces of zest to the grinder and repeat the sifting and grinding process until all of it is finely ground to a powder. Stored in an airtight container, the orange powder will keep for up to 1 week.

## *preserved lemons*   Makes 6

Preserved lemons aren't hard to make; they just take patience. They are used sparingly because their flavor is so strong, but luckily they keep for quite a long time (tightly sealed in the refrigerator, up to 1 year). At the restaurant, we always have them on hand, because they're an easy way to brighten dishes at any time of year. This recipe involves a lot of salt and acid, so if you have any cuts on your hands, it's probably best to wait until they heal before making these.

---

6 lemons

2½ cups kosher salt

Freshly squeezed lemon juice, if needed

Wash and thoroughly dry the lemons. Starting from the end opposite the stem, cut each lemon into quarters, stopping ¼ inch short of the stem. (The 4 wedges should hold together at the stem end.)

Generously pack salt into the center of the quartered lemons. Pack the salted lemons snugly into a sterilized container with a tight-fitting lid. Cover the lemons with a generous layer of salt and tightly seal the container. Store the lemons at room temperature for 2 days, or

until the lemons have released enough juice to submerge them. If the lemons do not excrete enough of their own juice, add some freshly squeezed lemon juice to cover the citrus. Refrigerate the container for at least 3 weeks before using. Unopened, preserved lemons will keep in the refrigerator for up to 1 year. After opening, they will keep refrigerated for up to 1 month.

To use the preserved lemon, cut through the stem so that the lemon is fully quartered. Trim the flesh and pith from the rind according to how much you need for your recipe, saving the rind and discarding the rest. Rinse the lemon rind with water and then soak in water for at least 30 minutes to remove the excess salt.

*lavosh*  Makes approximately 3 18 by 13-inch sheets

Baking, slicing, and toasting bread takes a considerable amount of time. Making flatbread doesn't. This recipe is an easy shortcut for making a crisp and delicious accompaniment for a plate of charcuterie or cheese.

Also, you can scatter a variety of toppings onto the rolled-out dough, after brushing it with olive oil, to make a flatbread "pizza." Some of our favorite toppings include chopped olives, fresh figs, herbs, prosciutto, and grated Parmesan.

---

1 tablespoon plus 1 teaspoon active dry yeast

1⅛ cups warm water

3¼ cups all-purpose flour

2 teaspoons salt, plus more for sprinkling (optional)

2 teaspoons honey

2 tablespoons extra-virgin olive oil

¼ cup chopped fresh herbs (we use 1 tablespoon each of thyme, flat-leaf parsley, chives, and basil or sage, depending on the season)

Freshly ground black pepper (optional)

Freshly shaved Parmesan cheese (optional)

Combine the yeast and water in a bowl and let it sit until the yeast fully dissolves, about 5 minutes.

Meanwhile, in a stand mixer fitted with a dough hook, combine the flour, salt, honey, 1 tablespoon of the olive oil, and the herbs. Mix on low speed until the ingredients are incorporated. Add the yeast and water mixture and continue to mix until a smooth dough ball forms.

Turn the dough out onto a smooth surface and knead it a few times, just enough to bring the dough together. It should be smooth and elastic. At this point, you can either roll and bake the dough immediately or flatten it into a thick disk, tightly wrap it in plastic wrap. Refrigerate it for 2 days or freeze it for later use, for up to 6 months.

When you are ready to bake the lavosh, preheat the oven to 400°F. Lightly grease a baking sheet with olive oil.

Using a rolling pin, roll the dough out to about ⅛-inch thickness. The dough will shrink as you roll it. The shape doesn't really matter, as long as it fits on your baking sheet. Transfer the dough to the prepared baking sheet.

Using a pastry brush or your hand, coat the dough with the remaining 1 tablespoon olive oil. Prick the dough all over with a fork. Sprinkle salt, pepper, and Parmesan over the dough as desired.

Bake until golden and crispy, about 12 minutes. Serve warm.

## cinnamon sugar   Makes about 2 tablespoons

Cinnamon sugar is to my pastry kitchen what salt and pepper are to Colby's side of the world. I use it to "season" my cookies, cobblers, and just about anything else that needs a little sweetening. You can make cinnamon sugar in any quantity you want and use any ratio of sugar to cinnamon that you like. This recipe is simply a guideline.

---

2 tablespoons sugar

¼ teaspoon ground cinnamon

Combine the sugar and cinnamon in a small airtight container and shake to blend well. It will keep in an airtight container for up to 3 months.

## simple syrup   Makes about 1 quart

Simple syrup is to the pastry station what chicken and vegetable stocks are to the other side of the kitchen. We use it to sweeten, thicken, thin, smooth, poach, and glaze. It goes into sorbet bases, onto cakes, and is essentially the starting point of all caramels. Our bartenders use it to flavor cocktails. This recipe makes quite a lot of simple syrup, but it goes quickly and keeps well.

---

3 cups sugar

3 cups water

In a large saucepan, whisk together the sugar and water. Bring the sugar water to a rapid boil over high heat. Turn the heat to medium and simmer for 5 to 7 minutes, until the sugar is completely dissolved. Remove the syrup from the heat and let it cool to room temperature. Store the syrup in an airtight container in the refrigerator for up to 1 month.

*vanilla ice cream*  Split and scrape the seeds of 1 vanilla pod. Add the scraped seeds, vanilla pod, and 2 teaspoons of vanilla extract to the cream mixture in step 2. Proceed with the recipe, straining out and discarding the vanilla pod in step 4.

*honey ice cream*  Substitute ⅓ cup honey for ⅓ cup of the sugar in step 2 and proceed with the rest of the recipe.

*brown butter–pecan ice cream*
Substitute ⅓ cup granulated sugar and ⅓ cup packed light brown sugar for the ¾ cup sugar. Melt ½ cup (1 stick) unsalted butter in a sauté pan over medium heat. Watch the butter carefully while cooking as it can burn easily. Once the foam subsides the butter should have a nutty aroma and a golden brown color with dark specks. Remove the browned butter from the heat and let it cool to room temperature. Stir the browned butter into the base along with a pinch of salt at the end of step 2. Proceed with steps 3 and 4. Churn the ice cream as directed in step 5. Place the churned ice cream in a chilled bowl and fold ½ cup chopped toasted pecans into the ice cream and freeze.

*salted pumpkin ice cream*  Add 2 teaspoons of vanilla extract, ¼ teaspoon of ground cinnamon, ¼ teaspoon of freshly grated nutmeg, and ¼ teaspoon of allspice to the Ice Cream Base in step 1. Continue with the recipe, stirring 1½ cups pumpkin puree and ¼ teaspoon salt into the base after straining in step 4.

*ice cream base*  Makes about 1 quart

This recipe serves as a base for most of the ice creams in this cookbook. It's essentially a sweet cream ice cream to which flavors are added to make a variety of ice creams.

---

6 egg yolks

2 cups heavy cream

1 cup whole milk

¾ cup sugar

1.  In a medium bowl, whisk the egg yolks together.

2.  In a large saucepan, bring the cream, milk, and sugar to a low simmer over medium-high heat for 2 minutes, or until the sugar has fully dissolved. Watch the pot closely, as it may boil over quickly.

3.  Temper the eggs by whisking 1 cup of the hot cream mixture into the yolks in a slow, steady stream. You want to add the hot cream slowly to gradually increase the temperature of the egg yolks without scrambling them.

4.  Strain the ice cream base through a fine-mesh sieve into a large bowl. Set the bowl over ice and stir the ice cream base with a whisk until it has cooled.

5.  Churn the base in an ice cream maker according to the manufacturer's instructions (this may require chilling the base before churning). Transfer the ice cream to a freezer-safe container. Freeze for at least 2 hours before serving.

## *chocolate sauce*  Makes 3 cups

This is a variation of Richard Leach's chocolate sauce. His inclusion of vegetable oil makes it easier to reheat and gives the sauce a particularly silky and shiny texture.

---

8 ounces bittersweet chocolate, finely chopped

2 tablespoons salted butter, cubed and softened

¾ cup light corn syrup

¾ cup heavy cream

¼ cup whole milk

⅛ cup vegetable oil

¼ cup unsweetened natural cocoa powder, preferably Valrhona

In a medium heatproof bowl, combine the bittersweet chocolate and butter.

In a medium saucepan, bring the corn syrup, cream, milk, and vegetable oil to a boil over medium-high heat. Remove from the heat and pour the hot mixture over the chocolate and butter. Stir the ingredients in a slow, circular motion until the chocolate has melted. Whisk in the cocoa powder.

Strain the chocolate sauce through a fine-mesh sieve and pour it into a squeeze bottle or an airtight container.

**NOTE:** Extra chocolate sauce can be stored in an airtight container in the refrigerator for up to 3 months or in the freezer for up to 6 months. To achieve the best consistency, the chocolate sauce should be slightly warmed before serving. Reheat the sauce in a double boiler set over simmering water. Whisk the sauce as it warms until it is smooth. Or you can microwave it for approximately 30 seconds.

**Top, left to right: Megan Garrelts and Dawn Gregory**
**Bottom, left to right: Bill Espiricueta, Colby Garrelts, and John Brogan at Arthur Bryant's**

# acknowledgments

**We thank:**

Our families, whose unwavering support for Megan and me in our pursuit of a "nontraditional" career stands stronger today than when we both began behind the line. For this, we are immensely grateful. Our mothers, Kristie and Kaye, for their love, patience, and home-cooked meals that still inspire. Our fathers, Greg and Robert, for their strength and will. And to Greg, especially, for his early negotiations at the table, his elbow grease, and his know-how in building Bluestem board by nail. Our sister Amy and brother Jason, for having a constant sense of pride, not only in what we do but also in our family. To our children, Madilyn and Colin, for their patience during our many hours at Bluestem, either working or enjoying time as a family.

Our entire staff at Bluestem, past and present, who have helped us create and sustain our dream: Jeremy Lamb, our general manager, who keeps the front of our house on track and reminds our guests why we appreciate them so much. Jeremy started as our manager and is now a longtime friend to our family. Bill Espiricueta, the first cook we hired, our right-hand man and chef de cuisine. He is a tireless cook with an amazing drive. Dave Crum, our first chef de cuisine, who helped us breathe life into Bluestem and helped shape the restaurant in its early years. Justin Pera, the last original Bluestem server standing. Justin is the only one who knows our dining room from our first day of service onward. John Brogan, Dawn Gregory, and Van Zarr, the newest members of our management team. They take pride in the restaurant we have created. With their help, loyalty, and dedication, our restaurant becomes better each day we work together.

John Fitzgerald, Deana Molloy, Andrew Holmes, and Jessica Shoop, former service employees who have made an enormous impact on the consistently high level of service we are able to provide at Bluestem. Joe West, Kate Graver, Quillan Glenn, and Nate Nichols, former cooks and pastry assistants who have embraced our way of cooking and contributed to our menus.

Bonjwing Lee, who began as our harshest critic, became a friend and now has collaborated with us to write this book and capture our food and restaurant with his amazing images. We could not have dreamed of a more knowledgeable and passionate person with whom to work on this project.

Our editor, Jean Lucas, publisher Andrews McMeel, and our agent, Jane Dystel, for believing in our book and helping us make it a reality. Our publicists, Jamie Estes and Tammie Franck.

Chip Schmelzer, the best landlord we could hope for!

The farmers and food producers who supply us with the bounty of each season. You are our life source. Thank you for your dedication.

Our colleagues in the restaurant and hospitality community in Kansas City, with whom we work and share our great city. Together we must continue to believe that we make a difference!

Megan also thanks chefs Richard Leach, Gale Gand, and Megan Romano for teaching her their methods and secrets for creating great desserts. The impressions they made on her are evident in our pastry kitchen every day. Megan also dedicates this book to the memory of her grandmother Mary: I will forever cherish our teatimes together, and thank you for always having sprinkles for ice cream. And to my grandma Frances, thank you for adding brown sugar to everything!

Colby also thanks chefs Patrick Webber, Kevin Donavan, Rick Tramonto, Hans Röckenwagner, Graham Elliot Bowles, Michael Smith, and Debbie Gold for their mentorship. They have helped instill a passion and drive to strive for the best.

Last, we could not end these acknowledgments without thanking the many, many people who have walked through Bluestem's door over the years. You are the reason that Bluestem stands today and tomorrow. Thank you for your support.

*—Colby and Megan Garrelts*

A sincere debt of gratitude:

To my Lord and savior, Jesus Christ, through whom all things are truly possible.

To my family, for ignoring my shortcomings, forgiving my selfishness, celebrating my successes, and loving me every day.

To my grandparents, who always made sure that life was delicious.

To my dad, Hsiang Lin, for lending me your Canon AE-1 and letting me try to stand on your shoulders.

To my mom, Kwang-Ting, for giving me the world as a classroom.

To my brother, Bonyee, and my sister, Bonyen, for your patience and for bringing color into my otherwise dull life.

To Colby, Megan, Madi and Colin Garrelts, for feeding me in countless ways. Thank you for Bluestem. Thank you for your friendship. Thank you for the salads.

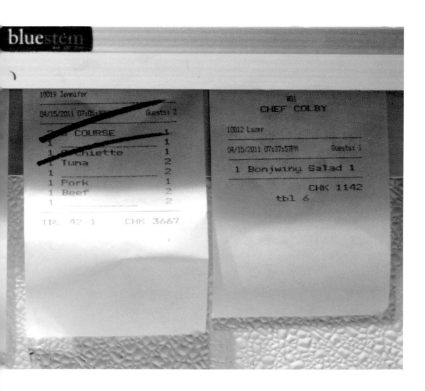

To Jeremy Lamb, Bill Espiricueta, John Brogan, and the staff at Bluestem for including me in your fold without smelling me twice. Thank you for making room for me. Thank you for the laughs. Thank you for the salads.

To Dave Crum, my twin, and Jim and Debbie Crum, my ever-smiling farmer friends, thank you for always setting a lovely table full of lovely things from your lovely garden.

To Charley Huebner and Corby Ewing, for showing me how to breathe life into an image.

To Michael Tetelman, Michael Elyanow, and L. S. Kim, for teaching me that there is more to writing than a pen and keyboard.

To my varsity cheerleading squad, thank you for your jazz hands, your shoulders, your constant encouragement, and, above all else, your honesty: Harriet Bell, Monica Bhambhani, Scott and Tanya Boswell, Lisa Callaghan, Mike and Teresa Castillo, J. J. and Suzanne Greenwood, Ashley Hutcheson, Gavin Kaysen, Michelle Keller, Phyllis Leach, Kathryn Lewis, Jennifer Rappaport, Michael and Rosalind Rappaport, Dean and Danielle Rodenbough, Joe and Judy Roethli, and Ingrid and Rob VanBiber.

To our publisher, Andrews McMeel, and editor, Jean Lucas, thank you for helping us tell Bluestem's story.

To my agent, Jane Dystel, thanks for not hanging up on me. You are a gem.

And finally, to all the writers, photographers, artists, and chefs who have made my journey meaningful and beautiful, thank you.

—*Bonjwing Lee*

# sources

Although we have tried to make the recipes in this cookbook accessible and doable for the home cook, depending on where you live, you might have a hard time finding some of the required ingredients in your local, mainstream supermarket. While the following list of sources is certainly not comprehensive, it includes purveyors that we trust. Needless to say, the Internet is an invaluable directory of sources.

## ingredients

**Arrowhead Specialty Meats**
Meat, game meat, and specialty cuts
www.gamemeat.com

**Blis**
Maple syrups, vinegars, caviar, and other specialty ingredients
www.blisgourmet.com

**Campo Lindo Farms**
Organic poultry and eggs
www.campolindofarms.com

**Cooking Enthusiast**
Bottarga
www.cookingenthusiast.com

**D'Artagnan**
Specialty and game meats, foie gras, and duck fat
www.dartagnan.com

**Dean & Deluca**
Specialty ingredients, including foie gras, cheese, pasta, saba, oils, baking ingredients, caviar, snails, and fiddlehead ferns, passion fruit puree
www.deandeluca.com
(800) 221-7714

**Green Dirt Farm**
Sheep's cheese and lamb meat
www.greendirtfarm.com
(816) 386-2156

**King Arthur Flour**
00 flour
www.kingarthurflour.com

**L'Epicerie**
Specialty foods, including oils, salts, *sel rose* (pink salt), Banyuls vinegar, and caviar
www.lepicerie.com

**La Tienda**
Arrope
www.latienda.com

**Manicaretti**
Pastas
www.manicaretti.com

**Mid America Gourmet**
A comprehensive inventory of pastry ingredients
www.midamericagourmet.com
(866) 517-8645

**Paradise Locker Meats**
Specialty meats, including slab bacon, cured meats, pork, beef, lamb, and offal (organ meats)
www.paradisemeats.com

**Penzeys Spices**
Spices, including togarashi
www.penzeys.com
(800) 741-7787

**Rancho Gordo**
Beans and posole
www.ranchogordo.com

**Shatto Milk Company**
Dairy products, including milk, cream, and butter
www.shattomilk.com
(816) 930-3862

**Sur La Table**
Specialty ingredients, including burrata,
Banyuls vinegar, saba, arrope, and oils
www.surlatable.com
(800) 243-0852

**Tekla**
Cheese
(312) 915-5914

**Tsar Nicoulai Caviar**
Salmon and trout roe and other caviar products
www.tsarnicoulai.com

**The Better Cheddar**
Cheese, chocolate, and specialty ingredients, including
oils, Banyuls vinegar, saba, arrope, and salts
www.thebettercheddar.com
(816) 561-8204

**Williams-Sonoma**
Specialty ingredients, including vinegars, oils, sugars, and
some spices
www.williams-sonoma.com
(877) 812-6235

**A note on Asian ingredients:** While ingredients such as mirin, miso, togarashi, and shiitake mushrooms are becoming more readily available in mainstream supermarkets, the Asian ingredients in this cookbook, including bonito flakes, can best be found in your local Asian market. If you don't have one near you, the Internet will be your best resource.

**A note on fresh produce:** There is no better source for produce than your local farmers. Buying from them means that you're buying in season and ensures that you're probably getting fresher produce than you would in a mainstream supermarket.

**A note on meat and seafood:** Getting to know your local butcher and fishmonger is the best way to get the best meats and fishes. Good butchers and fishmongers should be knowledgeable and honest about their products. They can also order special cuts that you might not normally find in their cases. If you need help finding a dependable butcher or fishmonger, ask a local chef or inquire at a restaurant that you trust.

## equipment

**JB Prince**
A comprehensive inventory of both professional and
home kitchen equipment, including service ware, dishes,
and utensils
www.jbprince.com
(800) 473-0577

**Pryde's Old Westport**
A gourmet housewares and kitchen and home
accessories store, Pryde's specializes in hard-to-find
kitchen items
www.prydeskitchen.com
(800) 531-5588

**Sur La Table**
www.surlatable.com
(800) 243-0852

**Williams-Sonoma**
www.williams-sonoma.com
(877) 812-6235

# metric conversions and equivalents

**Metric Conversion Formulas**

| To Convert | Multiply |
|---|---|
| Ounces to grams | Ounces by 28.35 |
| Pounds to kilograms | Pounds by .454 |
| Teaspoons to milliliters | Teaspoons by 4.93 |
| Tablespoons to milliliters | Tablespoons by 14.79 |
| Fluid ounces to milliliters | Fluid ounces by 29.57 |
| Cups to milliliters | Cups by 236.59 |
| Cups to liters | Cups by .236 |
| Pints to liters | Pints by .473 |
| Quarts to liters | Quarts by .946 |
| Gallons to liters | Gallons by 3.785 |
| Inches to centimeters | Inches by 2.54 |

**Approximate Metric Equivalents**

**Volume**

| | |
|---|---|
| ¼ teaspoon | 1 milliliter |
| ½ teaspoon | 2.5 milliliters |
| ¾ teaspoon | 4 milliliters |
| 1 teaspoon | 5 milliliters |
| 1¼ teaspoons | 6 milliliters |
| 1½ teaspoons | 7.5 milliliters |
| 1¾ teaspoons | 8.5 milliliters |
| 2 teaspoons | 10 milliliters |
| 1 tablespoon (½ fluid ounce) | 15 milliliters |
| 2 tablespoons (1 fluid ounce) | 30 milliliters |
| ¼ cup | 60 milliliters |
| ⅓ cup | 80 milliliters |
| ½ cup (4 fluid ounces) | 120 milliliters |
| ⅔ cup | 160 milliliters |
| ¾ cup | 180 milliliters |
| 1 cup (8 fluid ounces) | 240 milliliters |
| 1¼ cups | 300 milliliters |
| 1½ cups (12 fluid ounces) | 360 milliliters |
| 1⅔ cups | 400 milliliters |
| 2 cups (1 pint) | 460 milliliters |
| 3 cups | 700 milliliters |
| 4 cups (1 quart) | 0.95 liter |
| 1 quart plus ¼ cup | 1 liter |
| 4 quarts (1 gallon) | 3.8 liters |

**Weight**

| | |
|---|---|
| ¼ ounce | 7 grams |
| ½ ounce | 14 grams |
| ¾ ounce | 21 grams |
| 1 ounce | 28 grams |
| 1 ¼ ounces | 35 grams |
| 1 ½ ounces | 42.5 grams |
| 1⅔ ounces | 45 grams |
| 2 ounces | 57 grams |
| 3 ounces | 85 grams |
| 4 ounces ( ¼ pound) | 113 grams |
| 5 ounces | 142 grams |
| 6 ounces | 170 grams |
| 7 ounces | 198 grams |
| 8 ounces (½ pound) | 227 grams |
| 16 ounces (1 pound) | 454 grams |
| 35.25 ounces (2.2 pounds) | 1 kilogram |

**Length**

| | |
|---|---|
| ⅛ inch | 3 millimeters |
| ¼ inch | 6 millimeters |
| ½ inch | 1¼ centimeters |
| 1 inch | 2½ centimeters |
| 2 inches | 5 centimeters |
| 2½ inches | 6 centimeters |
| 4 inches | 10 centimeters |
| 5 inches | 13 centimeters |
| 6 inches | 15¼ centimeters |
| 12 inches (1 foot) | 30 centimeters |

## Oven Temperatures

To convert Fahrenheit to Celsius, subtract 32 from Fahrenheit, multiply the result by 5, then divide by 9.

| Description | Fahrenheit | Celsius | British Gas Mark |
|---|---|---|---|
| Very cool | 200° | 95° | 0 |
| Very cool | 225° | 110° | ¼ |
| Very cool | 250° | 120° | ½ |
| Cool | 275° | 135° | 1 |
| Cool | 300° | 150° | 2 |
| Warm | 325° | 165° | 3 |
| Moderate | 350° | 175° | 4 |
| Moderately hot | 375° | 190° | 5 |
| Fairly hot | 400° | 200° | 6 |
| Hot | 425° | 220° | 7 |
| Very hot | 450° | 230° | 8 |
| Very hot | 475° | 245° | 9 |

## Common Ingredients and Their Approximate Equivalents

1 cup uncooked white rice = 185 grams

1 cup all purpose flour = 140 grams

1 stick butter (4 ounces • ½ cup • 8 tablespoons) = 110 grams

1 cup butter (8 ounces • 2 sticks • 16 tablespoons) = 220 grams

1 cup brown sugar, firmly packed = 225 grams

1 cup granulated sugar = 200 grams

Information compiled from a variety of sources, including *Recipes into Type* by Joan Whitman and Dolores Simon (Newton, MA: Biscuit Books, 2000); *The New Food Lover's Companion* by Sharon Tyler Herbst (Hauppauge, NY: Barron's, 1995); and *Rosemary Brown's Big Kitchen Instruction Book* (Kansas City, MO: Andrews McMeel, 1998).

# index